ALL
YOU NEED
TO KNOW
ABOUT
THE IRS

ALL YOU NEED TO KNOW ABOUT THE IRS

A Taxpayer's Guide
1981 Edition

Paul N. Strassels

and Robert Wool

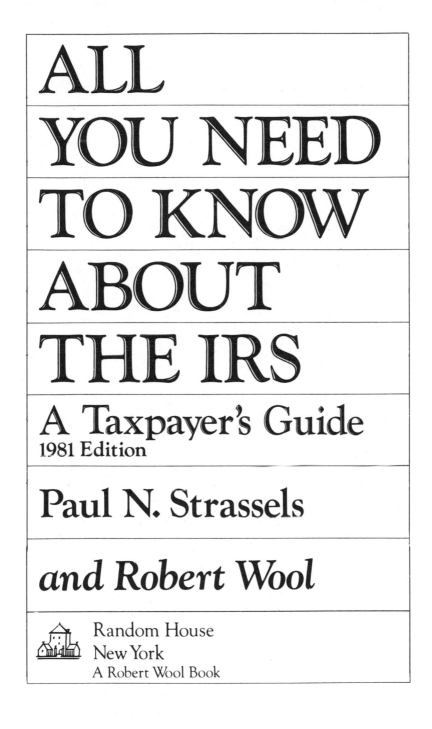

Random House
New York
A Robert Wool Book

A Robert Wool Book

Library of Congress Cataloging in Publication Data

Strassels, Paul N.
All you need to know about the IRS.

1. Tax auditing—United States. 2. United States. Internal Revenue Service. 3. Income tax—United States—Deductions. I. Wool, Robert, 1934– joint author. II. Title.
HL3252.S7   1981   343.7305'2   80–19868
ISBN 0-394-51675-3

Manufactured in the United States of America

9 8 7 6 5 4 3 2

FIRST EDITION

To Deborah
PS

For Bridget
RW

Acknowledgments

Our thanks to friends and former colleagues in the IRS, who were willing to answer a number of questions, clear up a few mysteries, and double-check us for accuracy.

Our special thanks to Grant Ujifusa, who had the toughness to keep this book on track, and the extraordinary editing skill to enable us, finally, to perceive its proper shape and tone.

Also to Jean McNutt, who did such a swift and able job of copy-editing.

And to Jason Epstein, Editorial Director of Random House, whose fine grasp of the larger issues and personal support meant so much to this book.

P.N.S. and R.W.

Contents

ALL
YOU NEED
TO KNOW
ABOUT
THE IRS

1 | What They Can Do
to You ... The Real and
the Imagined

Are you crazy? A total paranoid to think that *they* really do know everything about you? That given half a chance, the IRS will wipe you out and send you to jail?

No, I can assure you, there's nothing paranoid, even neurotic, about feeling that way. Mental instability in no way creates that state of fear and loathing. What you feel exists for good reason: the IRS has worked hard to put it there.

Nothing is more central to the IRS strategy of tax collection than scaring you, the taxpayer, and keeping you that way. Only then, they maintain, is there any chance that you, the t/p, as IRS calls the taxpayer, will be honest with them. Or, to see it the way they see it, even the slightest bit honest.

Their campaign to spread fear operates on several levels.

Take the relatively simple matter of public image. General Motors, Mobil, ITT, and other big corporations spend millions of dollars trying to get you to like them. It's as if it were not enough that you buy whatever they make and sell. They also want you to think of them as a friend, concerned about your First Amendment rights, the air you breathe, the water you drink—warm folks you can depend on and trust.

The IRS strives for just the opposite public image and response. The more they can get you to despise and hate them, to curse and dread them, the happier they are.

Like the large corporations, the IRS also uses the press in their public relations campaign. But they don't spend millions advertising on television. Neither do they take out those low-key ads, disguised as editorials, in newspapers around the country—those chatty observations on the shared American experience. The IRS doesn't spend a penny this way, but their message still comes over loud and clear.

Have you ever noticed, for example, that each year from January through April 15, most especially, there are stories in your local paper about people being sent to prison by the IRS?

During 1980, there were a couple of certified biggies.

There was the case of the once highly regarded attorney general of Illinois, the chief law enforcement officer of a major state, being nailed by the IRS. That's the solid, traditional variety of biggie.

There was also the Studio 54 case, an IRS dream come true.

The leading celebrity disco in the country, the place we read about in our favorite gossip columns, and they bust it. Not only do they send two of its owners to prison, the case reaches right into the White House. Page 1 everywhere, nightly news on all three networks, press agent's bliss.

And every time we read or hear yet another juicy morsel of the saga, there is, somewhere deep inside of us, a twinge, a current. Someone very, very big's been caught messing with those guys, the current warns us. The IRS knows about those currents, is connected right into their circuits, and that is precisely the message they have coded into it.

An attorney general, Studio 54, are obviously special. Still, you should know that it is the unstated policy of the Public Affairs Office of the IRS to issue stories of that sort at a time when they know you are doing your taxes and thinking about what you might be able to hide. Usually the people they nail that you read about are much smaller folk, but the effect on you is the same. A twinge.

That sort of thing is child's play for the IRS. They know that prison stories make good copy, and reporters love to write them. They also know that there are few editors in newspapers, magazines, TV, or any media who have the wit to realize, or care, that they are being manipulated by the IRS with these same stories. Indeed, if anything, the sad truth is just the opposite.

Ever notice, once again around tax time, how every newspaper, every radio and TV station, runs special features on taxes? Usually they're meant to be helpful hints: How to claim child care credit. What the average mileage deduction is for business trips with your car. How to document your charitable deductions properly. That sort of thing. Like a public service. Your local newspaper or radio station is making a special effort to help you.

In fact, each year the IRS puts together a neat and clever press package. It anticipates all of the normal needs of the media, and provides it all the information it can use on, say, child care credits, mileage allowances, charitable contributions, among others. Not only provides the information, but writes it out in such a way that all a reporter or an editor has to do is scribble some setting instructions across the top, along with a by-line, and print it. All a TV or radio newscaster has to do is turn on the mike and read it.

Just in case some reporter or editor might have a special little twitch of another sort, the always thoughtful IRS keeps this press material undated. That way, each item can be released whenever they want during tax season, and a date can be put on it when it goes out. That way, the charade of "news" is maintained.

Needless to say, each of these "news" stories is shaded to IRS interpretation, which, as we shall see, might be quite different from that of your accountant, or even that of a federal court. Still, it is the way they'd like you to think about the tax law. In fact, these "news" stories are so shaded that they really ought to say "By the Internal Revenue Service" right across the top. Though I suppose my friends at the IRS are far too modest to take such credit.

For those radio and TV stations with absolutely no shame,

the IRS sends IRS spokespeople to go on shows and answer questions. Another great public service from your local airwave info center. This one is also at no expense. As you might imagine, the IRS is willing to provide these helpful people free of charge.

Generally speaking, there isn't much of a contest between reporter and IRS, since there are only a few reporters covering the Service who understand tax law. For most people, the National Office in Washington, D.C., is a beat, like covering City Hall.

The IRS, of course, is only too happy to educate a confused reporter who is trying to sort his way through a press release on a complicated ruling. The reporter goes to a friendly IRS Public Affairs Officer and asks him to explain it. The PAO does, and the reporter writes it down. What he has written in his notebook is tax law as the IRS sees it, and wants everyone in America to interpret it. The reporter usually doesn't even know enough to ask the right questions. He just writes it down and perhaps pretends to be skeptical: "Yeah, but how important is all this, anyway?"

When the IRS officer assures him it's important, the reporter nods solemnly, goes off in ignorance and writes his story, which advertises the IRS's position at no cost.

So it is that, unlike any other government agency, the IRS sees itself at war with its constituency, with all of the citizen taxpayers of the United States. It believes, and not without reason, that you lie and cheat on your tax returns. So, for the purposes of tax strategy, it starts from the position that you, the enemy, are guilty until you prove yourself innocent.

Nothing personal of course, nothing is ever personal with the IRS. It's all just a matter of interpreting, applying the law, and collecting the money.

But it is also war. Us against them. When I was with the Service, that's how I used to look at the world: us against you.

In this war we were outnumbered. There are today only 89,000 IRS employees pitted against individuals filing some 86 million tax returns. Add to that the corporations, partnerships, estates, and the rest, and the IRS finds itself with 140 million tax returns to worry about.

What that means if you're inside the IRS is that you not only have to be smarter than the taxpayers, you also have to possess a sense of zeal and mission about your work. And we did, we really did. We were convinced that our work was enormously important, absolutely crucial. Because if we didn't keep you in line and collect the revenue, there wouldn't be any money for the federal government. Nothing would work. Chaos. Catastrophe.

That was the feeling we shared, and it's still there. Outnumbered, we can still do the job. We are, after all, the full-time savvy professionals, and you people out there are the part-time dumb, often crooked amateurs.

Beyond spirit and competence, the IRS has a sophisticated arsenal of weapons. Manipulating the press is easy. They have other, much more painful ways of hurting you, which you have never heard of, and will never hear about from the IRS. Their position is sensible: you don't tell the enemy your secrets. You also don't tell him how to fight back, or what his rights are, or who we really are, or what we can do and cannot do.

What they're really after when they audit you.

We've all heard about the audit, and dread it in a special way. The worry and anxiety produced by the audit is ever-present: the thing could strike at any time, zap you right out of the past.

Surely, they have hit a colleague or friend. And he or she has told you all about it—the agony, the fear lasting for weeks that he might be ruined.

Well, that conversation with your friend is worth more to the IRS than the money they may have actually retrieved. Most people assume that if they get audited, it's because the IRS wants to pull more money out of them. Perfectly reasonable assumption. But wrong.

The primary reason the IRS selects your return to audit is because they want to put the fear of the IRS into you. They will certainly take more tax dollars from you if they can, but what means much more to them is to frighten you so much that from then on you will never again lie and cheat on your returns. You will decide it just isn't worth the anxiety.

Also part of their strategy is the "ripple effect." They expect you to talk, just as your friend did to you. They expect you to cry and moan to all your friends and everyone at the office, "Jesus Christ, what they did to me."

The IRS figures you will also unnerve them. You will cause them, as well, to pause and take a very deep breath the next time they are tempted to write off half the vacation trip to London, or pretend that their kid's tuition was a contribution to the school's scholarship fund.

The policy of creating fear among the citizenry was never proclaimed at the Service. In fact, we never talked about it. It was assumed. One of our many shared secrets.

I was quite surprised, then, to hear a Commissioner admit it in a most public way, shortly after I left the Service. I was covering a hearing of a House committee for one of the Washington tax newsletters I had begun to write for, and Donald Alexander, who was then IRS Commissioner, was testifying.

At one point a congressman started in on him, saying in effect: Commissioner, how can you defend what we now know to be the established policies and regular practices of your agency, namely to wage a campaign of terror among the American people? How can you—the Commissioner of a major division of the U. S. government—defend the use of tactics that are carefully designed to threaten the American taxpayer, to keep him in a constant state of fear? This is a democracy we live in, Commissioner, need I remind you? And I would like to know how you can defend these tactics.

I squirmed and stared disdainfully at the politician. Fresh from the Service, I still suffered from the tunnel vision and the self-righteousness you develop there. How dare he accuse me and my friends of things like that. Okay, Commissioner, let him have it.

He did, but in a way that absolutely stunned me. "It is our

responsibility to make the tax system work," he told the congressman. "While I would like to think that voluntary compliance would be there, irrespective of the fact that the IRS policeman is at the corner, I think that we might have only a couple of years of continued voluntary compliance if we simply had neighbor A looking over what neighbor B was doing.

"We need not only have the direct effect, but also the ripple effect. We need to make sure that we do have an effective presence throughout our taxpayer population, both those who make their income from illegal sources and those who do it legally."

Quite honestly, I couldn't quite believe what I'd heard. I remember going home that evening practically babbling. " 'An effective presence throughout our taxpayer population,' " I said to my wife, Debbie. "Do you realize what that means? That means that the only way to keep people in line, the only way to keep them honest and paying their taxes, is to keep them afraid. That's what that means."

"Take it easy," she said. "How can you get so worked up?"

"Because that's scary, that's why."

Well, live and learn. Since then I've heard former Commissioner Sheldon S. Cohen put it even more gracefully. "The primary purpose of the audit is to keep honest people honest," he phrased it. And Commissioner Jerome Kurtz, who has just recently resigned, said, only a few months ago, that "the compliance activity of the IRS serves two functions: One is to pick up whatever revenue results from doing an audit. The other, and perhaps more important, aspect is to have a presence to encourage people to comply in the first place."

Let me quote from a memo, a thing called "Review of Theory and Practice of Internal Revenue Service Audit Efficiency." It's a study that was done in 1978 for the IRS Commissioner's Advisory Group to see if the audit program is as efficient and successful as it might be.

"If the IRS used only the maximization of yield approach," the report states, "it would meet its goals of using its resources most effectively to yield the most revenue. The purpose, how-

ever, of the audit program, is not to produce the greatest revenue but to produce the greatest level of voluntary compliance . . ."

"Voluntary compliance" means telling the truth on your
return voluntarily. In other words, they could use the "maximization of yield approach," i.e., audit only those returns where
the amounts they can recoup are substantial, and their chances
for taking it, high. The IRS spends about one-third percent of
its whole budget for the audit program, so being cost efficient
there is important.

Nevertheless, that is not their primary objective. It is instead
"to produce the greatest level of voluntary compliance." Which
means that more than a third of the IRS's entire budget goes
to trying to get people to tell the truth. The audit is the most
powerful weapon the IRS possesses in that effort, and the Service uses it carefully, skillfully, very deliberately.

If all they wanted was to rake in more money, the whole
process would be relatively simple, and very cost effective. The
computers could almost do that by themselves. As we'll see in
Chapter 3, they are programmed to kick out returns with the
"highest audit potential," which means, among other things,
returns with the most questionable deductions, write-offs, and
other soft areas. They could kick out only the fattest, most
likely candidates.

But since the IRS is balancing dollars with "voluntary compliance," they operate differently. They want "visibility."

This means the IRS carefully plans a statistical strategy that
allows them to reach all across America, across all income
levels and classes, and into as many pockets of society as they
can.

The strategy also means that they go after some kinds of
people who are more "visible," than others, hence more useful.
If they can cause problems for movie stars, sports heroes, and
celebrities in general, the IRS knows the media will play it up,
and their implicit warnings will spread wide. When I was in the
IRS, I remember writing several interpretive memos on cases
affecting Jack Benny and Groucho Marx, Olivia De Havilland,

and Sugar Ray Robinson, all very complicated cases. And I recall Skitch Henderson's being sent to jail, and all the headlines that went with it.

We joked about the best publicity the IRS could possibly receive. Put Johnny Carson through the wringer and have him tell a few scary, funny stories on late-night TV.

There are other occupational groups that are somewhat less in the public eye, but still furnish very popular audit candidates. Airline pilots, for example, are carefully checked. They're always traveling, have heavy deductions related to it, and lots of questions about primary and other residences. They earn good money, too, and tend to be fairly sophisticated when it comes to taxes. The IRS doesn't like the sophisticated t/p.

The IRS doesn't trust car dealers any more than most people, nor real estate developers. Both are high audit groups.

Doctors and dentists are heavily audited, not so much because they are distrusted as an occupational group, but because they tend to be careless and stupid when it comes to taxes. Agents are continually surprised that so many of them do not realize that they are one-man and one-woman businesses. We were always getting agents' stories from audits about how incredibly sloppy—or even nonexistent—records were for people earning $100,000 or more.

Also, doctors and dentists are prime targets for tax shelter promoters. And shelters, as we'll see, legitimate or otherwise, are at the top of the IRS most-wanted list.

In its quest for visibility, the IRS must plot strategy and tactics with its available and limited manpower. Commissioners are eternally parading before various House and Senate committees and pleading poverty. They don't have enough people to do the job. Depending, of course, on how you define "the job," they are right.

Presently, the IRS has about 28,500 examiners and auditors of various kinds. They are able to audit only a fraction more than 2 percent of all the returns filed by individual taxpayers, a surprisingly low number (the significance of which to you and your survival strategy we'll consider in Chapter 3).

Commissioner Kurtz said he'd really like to have another 20,000 auditors, and with them he could raise the percentage of audited returns to 5 or 6 percent. According to IRS studies, that would generate another $6 billion net in revenue.

Interestingly, however, all Kurtz and the IRS had the nerve to ask Congress for this year was an additional 170 auditors because, I do believe, Kurtz and his colleagues are realistic people. They know that Congress will not let them run rampant. Congress does not want to see that "effective presence" of the IRS truly become a police-state presence. And Congress can and does control the IRS in a way that no other body does. The IRS respects the power of Congress and cares about its relationship with the Hill as it cares about its relationship with no other governmental power. Presidents come and go, but Congress and congressmen not only, as a rule, linger, they also write the tax laws and the IRS's budget to implement those laws.

So there are only a finite number of auditor-soldiers to be deployed, and only a limited number of returns can therefore be audited. Which leads to an IRS strategy that recognizes those limitations and that means, among other things, surprise attacks.

That means that as part of its "visibility" strategy, the IRS will deliberately select a steelworker living in Pittsburgh, Pennsylvania. They know he has very few deductions and there's going to be scarcely any money to be squeezed out of him, especially these days. But they also know that he will tell everyone in his plant, in his neighborhood, and in half of Pittsburgh, just like you and your friend: bitch, moan, complain.

They also know something about human psychology: they expect that steelworker will actually feel a bit special, proud that he was selected. He will brag. They know that, whacky or not, there is something macho about being audited: you're such a big person, so important, make so much dough, the IRS must come after you.

Same strategy holds for the coal miner in Parkersburg, West Virginia, and the aerospace engineer in Burbank, California.

The truck driver, meanwhile, might actually have a number

of real deductions to claim, traveling as he does up and down the East Coast all year. What appeals to the IRS about the man with the CB, however, is a rolling, talking advertisement for the long arm of the Internal Revenue Service, spreading audit fear in every truck stop, diner, and roadside tavern for 1500 miles.

The dreaded TCMP . . . all your nightmares come true.

My friends and former colleagues at the IRS can be quite arbitrary and unfair about a lot of things, but when it comes to their attitude toward you as a cheater, they have real evidence to confirm their deep suspicions.

You might protest that "cheating" and "lying" are unduly harsh descriptions. That all you are trying to do is make "broad interpretations" or merely take a few chances on your return in the name of saving a few dollars for yourself and your family.

The IRS doesn't care what you call it. They know what you're doing, and the way they know is through the Taxpayer Compliance Measurement Program.

The TCMP is the single most valuable source of taxpayer information the IRS has, and not surprisingly, for years the IRS has refused to release information gathered by this program. A recent court challenge that has gone to the door of the Supreme Court could change this.

The TCMP shows the IRS exactly where people are cheating (and telling the truth) on their returns, and I mean on exactly which items. It also gives them the highest and lowest levels of "voluntary compliance," according to income levels and other categories, important in establishing their audit strategy.

Though you probably have never even heard of it, I have to tell you that if you are chosen to undergo a TCMP audit, it is the single worst thing the IRS can inflict on you, short of sending you to jail. The TCMP is every nightmare you have ever had about an IRS audit come true. And there is nothing you can do to stop one from happening.

TCMP returns are selected by a totally random statistical

sampling technique. You could be chosen and be the most honest person in the United States of America. Doesn't matter.

Every so often, the IRS selects returns for TCMP audits. This time it will be 55,000 returns filed for 1979. My friends in the Statistics Division decide how many returns will be needed from each income class to make the sample valid, then they pick them. They take the last digits from social security numbers or employee identification numbers and select returns.

This is not a garden variety audit experience by any means. In the TCMP, the agent checks every single line of your return. *Every single item.*

And he requires you to *prove* every single line, and every single deduction.

"You say you're married, Mr. Goodale? Could you prove that, please?"

"Prove I'm married?" Mr. Goodale replies incredulously. "I've been married for . . . 19 years."

The agent shakes his head.

"Well, here. I'm wearing a wedding ring."

"Sorry, Mr. Goodale, that might be evidence, but it is not really proof. How about a marriage license?"

"You've got to be kidding."

"No, I'm not, Mr. Goodale," he replies. "Why don't you bring that in tomorrow. Perhaps it would be a good idea if you started a little list of things to bring in."

"What about my kids? Should I bring them in tomorrow as well? Pull the kid out of Stanford and fly him in here so you can see for yourself he's alive?"

"That's really not necessary, Mr. Goodale. A birth certificate will do."

And so it goes, for days. Maybe even weeks or months.

Every single item questioned. Proof for all sources of income and every single deduction—major, minor, big and little, demanded, examined, and verified.

And, of course, while all this is happening, Mr. Goodale— or, heaven forbid, you—is not only suffering the extended torture of the auditor's grilling, he is also losing days and weeks of his valuable time. Think about that in terms of income lost.

To make matters worse and more costly, he might also have the meter running during all those days for his accountant.

Something of a rare situation. You are losing your time and the income you would be generating in your own work, perhaps running up an awesome accountant's bill as well—and for what? Because you have defrauded the government? Been greedy and sly, inflated all your so-called business expenses, and they caught you?

Nothing of the sort. As I told you, TCMP candidates are selected by a completely impersonal random process. You could be the most honest person in America and still be chosen.

All of which means that if you are selected, it is not because you have committed the slightest irregularity on your returns. It means, rather, that you have been chosen to subsidize IRS research. That's actually what you're doing, underwriting the cost of this elaborate, critical IRS research program.

Some extremely patriotic taxpayers might welcome such an opportunity. But I for one have never heard of any volunteering for a TCMP audit. In fact, I'm fairly certain that if any t/p stepped forward, the IRS would apply its own Catch-22 and certify the patriotic citizen as "suspicious and unstable . . . and not selected by the established random selection system."

In recent years there have been t/ps challenging the IRS in the courts to release TCMP data. The IRS lost the most serious challenge, temporarily at least, when the Supreme Court, in April 1980, refused to review a lower court ruling on the TCMP.

This case was brought by Phil and Sue Long of Bellevue, Washington, a couple that has fought the IRS on several issues for several years. They contended that they were entitled to TCMP research data under the Freedom of Information Act. Though at first their claim was rejected by the U.S. District Court in Seattle, the U.S. Court of Appeals for the Ninth Circuit in San Francisco held for them.

The IRS appealed, claiming that disclosure of its TCMP data would "destroy the efficacy" of one of its "most important investigative techniques in enforcing the tax laws," and that, further, it would "provide taxpayers with a statistical road map of tax avoidance."

The Longs and the rest of us might well be entitled to the TCMP info under Freedom of Information, but the IRS is nonetheless quite right in stating the impact of such a decision on them. In fact, my friends in the Service tell me they are extremely disturbed by the prospect, and are now making plans to go to Congress for a law that will block the court's decision and protect the data.

Look, for a moment, at what they are so frantically protecting.

Earlier, we considered the question of whether they really knew everything about you, and where and for how much you were lying to them.

The IRS is not, in fact, omniscient. But the TCMP data allows them to act as if they were, and with considerable confidence.

The TCMP reveals to the IRS where you are likely to be coming from, where your head is, as the expression has it. Imagine a scientific sampling of 55,000 taxpayers, grilled face to face for days. Gallup, Roper, and other pollsters claim they can tell us what to expect, who will win a national election through telephone interviews with a sample of only 1500 people. Predicting voter behavior, it's called. Paltry compared with the IRS effort.

From the TCMP data, the IRS can not only anticipate where you're likely to cheat, they can also decide how much to let you get away with. Relatively small amounts are not worth their time. The TCMP data shows them what is a "normal"—normal being the number that constitutes a verified statistical "truth"—and therefore an acceptable deduction for, say, business entertaining, according to various income levels, occupational groups, and geographic areas. If you violate your "norm" a bit, they'll let you steal a few dollars. All you get is some points against you from the computer, which has been programmed with all of the TCMP information. The computer, in other words, knows what is "normal" in the TCMP statistical category for your specific business entertainment item, and if you are too greedy, the computer might just spit out your return and recommend an audit. (We'll explore the mechanics of this in Chapter 3.)

It's not hard to see what the IRS ultimately fears about the Longs' case. If the TCMP data becomes regular reading with the morning paper, t/ps and/or their accountants will be able to figure out what the norms are and "fine-tune" their returns accordingly, and that would be the end of the system as we know it.

Further, it's worth noting that there are actually twelve different current TCMP projects, the monster audit program being the largest of them.

Among the others are some fairly interesting efforts. One they started in 1978, to determine how many people with income from dividends and interest pay proper taxes on it.

Another is a special study of tax-exempt organizations.

A new one started in 1980 is called "Individual Non-Filer Program." As a reflection of the times, the IRS is making a special study of tax protesters and others who, for ideological reasons or other, less lofty ones, simply aren't filing returns.

Of course, the largest and most important TCMP efforts are those monster audits. The odds of your being selected are only 1 in 1636, only .061 percent, which are better than the odds of your being hit by a bus, and about as comforting if it happens.

You can see that even if you don't have to suffer an actual TCMP audit, you are deeply affected by the program. All citizens are. It is a powerful IRS weapon. It can paralyze you and cost you real money if you have to go through one yourself. And the results of the TCMP survey, digested by the computer, will anticipate your tax behavior with so much precision that the IRS can almost read your mind. It is the closest thing to Orwellian *1984* market research our country has.

The Problem Preparer's Program: how they scare your accountant.

Believe it or not, the IRS for its own reasons prefers you to have a tax pro doing your return. This is partly because they think you are stupid and don't know tax law. Also, they realize that most of you have all kinds of problems when it comes to money matters, psychological and others. These can lead to errors and complications, which can be a waste of precious IRS time and manpower.

So they want you to have a professional who will know enough to protect you from yourself and avoid obvious mistakes.

But they don't want your professional to be too clever or devious, not to mention dishonest. To that end, the IRS has a "Problem Preparer's Program," or as we used to call it, "Unscrupulous Preparer's Program."

We also referred to a Problem Preparer's *List,* those names of tax preparers the IRS did not like. Some are people they've caught doing something illegal. Others, they haven't caught yet, but suspect are helping their clients to steal. Still others are preparers who they think quite simply are incompetent, people who don't know what they're doing and continually make mistakes on returns they prepare.

Every paid preparer must sign each return he does, and enter his IRS identification number, or his social security number.

The IRS then puts together a list of all the returns done by each preparer simply by running the preparer's I.D. through the computer and retrieving all the names of his clients.

As I said, we used to call it a "list." And that was the way I referred to the thing last year in the first edition of this book.

However, we seem to have a problem of semantics. The head of Public Information for the IRS now has protested that they have no "black list" of preparers, and Commissioner Kurtz himself told the American Institute of Certified Public Accountants Tax Division at its tax-deductible convention in Tarpon Springs, Florida, last May that they certainly have no "hit list."

What they do have, Kurtz informed *U.S. News & World Report,* is "the capacity, if we find a preparer who is particularly problem-prone, to identify all the returns that the preparer did. For example, if we find fraudulent returns prepared by the same preparer, we can get all the other returns the preparer handled and look for those items."

Auditors inform me that they know who the Problem Preparers are in their districts, who is identified under the Problem Preparer Program.

So whether there is an actual old-fashioned written list or whether its equivalent is produced by the magic of computers, if a preparer gets into the Problem Preparer's Program, the Service can quickly check every return he has prepared and signed. Sometimes the same error appears on each return, and it might not be as serious as fraud.

What is truly ominous about this program, with or without an actual written list, is what the IRS will do if they really want to get a preparer. They can and will hound him out of business. I have heard IRS people brag of several cases in which they took the list of a Problem Preparer's clients and audited every single one of them. Year after year. They figured that eventually the word would get around that if Mr. X does your return, expect to be audited. Not a very good recommendation for Mr. X, and before long he has no more clients.

Sadly, there is no way of knowing whether your preparer is on the invisible list or not. The IRS is not going to tell you. All you will know is you are called in for an audit.

Though the Problem Preparer's Program is the most ominous weapon the IRS holds in its intimidation game with your accountant, it has others, known as "penalties." We'll look at those in Chapter 2.

Your checking account and safe-deposit box are not secret and private.

You are the enemy, guilty until you prove yourself innocent, and you greatly outnumber them. Talk about paranoia, the IRS is paranoid about all taxpayers. We used to speculate on what would happen if only 10 percent of the t/ps didn't cough up. That would mean billions of dollars the federal government wouldn't have. We used to make up lists of who wouldn't be paid, and then imagine what the effect would be on the country.

As protectors of the national cash flow, we were most definitely the good guys, the white hats. It isn't a very great leap from there to a few tactics and procedures that are actually above the law. Of course we never looked at them as anything wrong. They were simply ways of letting us do the important job we had to do, efficiently.

For example, getting hold of your bank records.

You think of them as private and secret, but they are not. If the IRS is investigating you and has reason to believe that you are hiding income from them, or trying to defraud them in some other way, an IRS Agent will go to your bank. Like it or not, banks cooperate with the IRS.

Even without a court order, which would take time and a lot of paper work, the Agent can usually find out what he wants simply by showing his badge and having a brief, private conversation with the bank manager.

It was, and still is, standard practice to pull out the microfilm records of your checking and savings accounts. To an Agent, your checking account, especially, is a real economic biography of you. It not only reveals how you spend your money, and therefore how much money you really have to spend, but it can show how much you are hiding. I recall one Agent's telling me in my early years about such a search.

"The man had a balance of $135,000 in his checking account," he told me.

I was puzzled. "In his personal account?"

"Of course, personal. That's the point."

"But that's stupid," I said, this being in the days before banks paid any interest on checking accounts. "Look at the interest he's losing."

The Agent looked at me as if I were as dumb as a taxpayer. "Yeah. But if he put it in a savings account, the bank would be sending us a 1099 to let us know just how much interest it paid to that fellow. He may not be collecting any interest, but we're not collecting any 1099s and he's not paying any taxes on all that income."

The other thing the Agent can do at the bank is to go into your safe-deposit box, a notorious hiding place used by bookmakers, gamblers, illegal operators of all kinds, as well as less exotic citizens who work for cash: cab drivers, waiters, independent contractors of all sorts.

I hear you saying in a controlled tone that breaking open your safe-deposit box is a violation of your privacy and your contract with the bank.

A number of courts are beginning to agree with you. Several cases have been heard on the issue in recent years, and different states now have different laws and levels of protection for you.

The IRS currently says that they won't go into your bank box unless they have a court order to do so. And that if they get the order, you will be informed and have an opportunity to go to court to try to stop them.

I really don't know if Agents these days are following those procedures. I know they never used to. Their attitude is, as I said, "We are on the side of the law. You are the criminal."

I have been told by Agents recently that they still go after other records the way they always did, by showing the badge and talking with the bank manager.

This practice is particularly common in smaller towns. There, as you can imagine, the appearance of an IRS Agent is especially menacing.

Paid informers.

One of the darker IRS techniques is the use of paid informers. Though here, I think, more has been made than the facts warrant.

True, there are people whom the IRS pays for information. Bank employees, for example, who are able to tell them when your personal checking account does rise to $135,000. The IRS pays them very little, and our feeling in the Service was that they turned up very little.

There are special undercover informants feeding the IRS information mostly on narcotics operations and organized crime. It doesn't amount to all that much: in fiscal 1979, the IRS paid only $42,000 to those informants.

Much more common are those people who contact the IRS claiming to have information about a tax evader and asking for a percentage of what the IRS picks up from that information. The percentage is negotiable, never more than 10 percent of what's collected, with a ceiling of $50,000.

In 1977, more than 5200 people tried to make such deals. The IRS ended up actually paying 483 of them a total of $360,000. From those tips, the IRS swept up $15 million.

In 1979, over 7000 good citizens contacted the IRS, but only 439 of them had stuff that stood up. The IRS paid them a total of $281,367, or an average of $641 each. The leads yielded about $10.5 million in additional taxes.

All such IRS payments to informers are fully taxable.

A large number of the informers are angry people. An ex-wife or husband who knows where undeclared income is hidden. A partner who has been cut out of his firm. An employee who had access to some of the corporation's secret books and who got fired.

There are also crazies and semicrazies, neighbors who have had enough of your late parties and who have nothing more than suspicions about how you really earn your living and what you earn.

These leads are checked out, quickly and quietly. Only a handful stand up.

Frankly, this is one IRS weapon that I don't think is worth worrying over. You might say you simply don't like the idea of paid informers in a democracy, and you question the legal authority of the IRS to have them. To my knowledge, the courts have never ruled against the Service on this one.

When I've talked with friends about IRS informers, they have thrown the specter of Hitler's Germany at me. But that clouds the point, which quite simply is that if you have a nasty break with a loved one or a business associate, and you have some money to hide, don't be surprised if, in addition to hearing from the lawyers of the wounded parties, you also get a call from the IRS.

The IRS is, in fact, careful about the way it uses any informer's charges. It has to be. There are, after all, laws that even the IRS must respect.

Playing legal games.

The IRS loves to go to court to get the rulings it wants. And when it comes to court battles, once again, they have a strategy uniquely their own.

On items from the super-sensitive Prime Issues Appeals Coordinated List, which we'll discuss in Chapter 5, or any other major tax issue, IRS policy has long been to go from one court district to another, until they finally get the decision they think is the right one.

If they lose in New York over limited partnerships, they'll order agents in Atlanta to crack down and make very tough interpretations on that aspect of the law. Sooner or later, they figure, someone will say, "You have no right to disallow us our losses. We're going to take you to court." Which of course is just what the IRS wants.

If the judge in Atlanta says more or less the same thing as the judge in New York did, well, there're always Houston, Chicago, Denver, all kinds of fine places.

They won't stop until they get what they want, or until the Supreme Court speaks.

Providing, that is, the Supreme Court speaks clearly. Otherwise, the IRS can be quite hard of hearing.

One of my favorite recent examples, the Hotel Conquistador case, finally surfaced this past year, 1980. It involved a claim by the IRS that the value of meals furnished to employees free of charge must be treated as wages for payroll tax purposes. That meant the hotel, which gave its workers meals, had to include the value of the meals for its payroll taxes, a costly matter.

However, the Court of Claims said the Hotel Conquistador was right, the IRS wrong. Those meals were not subject to FICA and FUTA taxes. The IRS appealed to the Supreme Court.

I had been following the case, and so was particularly interested to learn that the Supreme Court denied certiorari, would not hear it. I was given the news last January, hot off the wire, by an ABC radio interviewer in New York, where I was going on various radio and TV programs to talk about the first edition of this book, just then published.

When I arrived at the studio, he told me about the decision, waving his news wire, and suggested that we might discuss it on the show.

Good idea, a nice news peg. To confirm my own hunch, I called a friend at the IRS National Office in Washington.

"I just heard about the Conquistador case," I told him. "What are they going to do?"

"Us?"

"Yeah."

"Tell 'em to stick it," he replied. And that's just what the IRS has done, and quite officially.

A few weeks later, the IRS issued a revenue ruling explaining why the Court of Claims was, quite simply, wrong. Employers are still responsible for those taxes, it said, and the IRS will hold them responsible, Court of Claims notwithstanding. Their attitude is: If you don't like us, sue us.

(Just to give you an idea of evolution in the world of taxes,

just before we went to press with this edition, the 5th Circuit
Court ruled in favor of the IRS over this same issue. I'm certain
that is not the end of the matter, so stay tuned.)

Not long after that, at a quasi-public Commissioner's Advisory Meeting, one of those periodic sessions the Commissioner
has with leading tax experts to discuss current tax questions and
problems, I heard Kurtz reaffirm that the Hotel Conquistador
decision was wrong and the IRS was not going to abide by it.

Just to show he and his agency can be consistent, at least, he
said the same thing to a more public gathering in June at a
breakfast meeting of the U.S. Chamber of Commerce. Respond-
ing to a question on the case, Kurtz told the assembled business
leaders that the IRS would not pay any refunds that were being
claimed as a result of the Conquistador decision, because the
court decision "does not represent what the law is." At least as
the IRS sees it.

Interestingly, the Commissioner also referred to other cases
on the same issue that were in the appeals courts and district
courts, as if to say the IRS will win those and then the law will
be once again correctly interpreted.

So, you can take on the IRS in the courts, but you had better
be prepared for an extremely long, extremely expensive legal
fight. They certainly are.

And you might also be prepared to lose, even if you win.

Can they send me to jail?

As we move through this book, we'll see where and for what
kinds of infractions the IRS can punish you.

But the big question is, of course, whether they can send you
to jail.

The answer is, only if they can prove in court a criminal act
on your part.

That means fraud, or willfully hiding income from them,
evading the payment of taxes, concealing property from them,
falsifying or destroying records, perjury, that kind of thing.

They cannot send you to jail if you make a mistake and misinterpret the law about medical deductions, and take more than you are legally entitled to. In that case, or where you have deductions that don't hold up when an agent audits you, what they do is recalculate your taxes and add some kind of penalty, plus interest.

Let me tell you something that is basic to their strategy, and important to your peace of mind: the IRS would rather get your money than send you to prison. Normally.

If you are a member of the Mafia, that does not hold. Or if the IRS has substantial evidence that you are *willfully* trying to defraud the government—if they find the $250,000 you stashed away in the bank in the Bahamas—and they also think that making a public example of you will scare other high rollers, then they will try to put you away.

Otherwise, the Service makes assessments and penalties. They might hit you for 5 percent of your taxes as a penalty, if you haven't paid what you are supposed to. Or, if you are supposed to pay estimated taxes and don't, 12 percent on the amount of underpayment. Or, if you don't file your tax return when it's due, 5 percent of the amount of tax, plus an additional 5 percent for each month or fraction of a month, up to a maximum of 25 percent.

They are not in any way eager to get into criminal litigation. You see, in criminal, for the first time in the whole tax process the rules of the game shift. In criminal, the burden is on them to prove that you are guilty. In other words, the law works just the way you always thought it was supposed to—presumed innocent until proven guilty.

As you can imagine, if you're a smart young tax lawyer, there is no better place in the universe to get experience and attention than the Chief Counsel's Office. That's the name of the legal offices of the IRS in Washington, D.C. After a few years, the knowledge and skills acquired are convertible into extremely lucrative positions in the legal/corporate community.

They are good and they pick their criminal cases carefully. When they decide to go into court on criminal charges, they are very certain they will win. In 1979, the IRS initiated some 9800 criminal investigations, and of those cases that actually end up with indictments, the IRS expects to win nearly all of them, and they are not being unrealistic.

But there is yet another kind of semi-legal power the IRS possesses that is even more disturbing to me because it is a power that is above the law. It is their administrative power.

The IRS actually has the power to clean out your bank account, sell your car, sell your house, without any judicial determination that you owe them 10¢ in taxes.

It's true. If they decide that you owe them more taxes and they can't get you to pay or to respond to their calls, letters, visiting Agents, they can apply their sweeping collection authority, and once they start the collection process, it is practically impossible for you to stop them.

Commissioner Kurtz described the awesome scope of this authority quite clearly to his own employees in a recent issue of the IRS internal newsletter: "The Service has extraordinary collection powers. There is no other agency of government that has the power to collect debts, to levy on property, to sell property prior to a judicial proceeding."

He went on to tell his employees: "I cannot overemphasize the importance of not using those powers in ways that appear improper and will cause adverse publicity. Even within the bounds of that which we may be technically empowered to do, we should be sensitive and use tact and discretion."

Whether the Commissioner is concerned more with the IRS's image or with the application of justice is hard to tell.

It is my experience that in fact the IRS uses its super collection powers with great care. At least they used to. In 1979, they filed 371,000 Notices of Federal Tax Lien and 465,000 notices of levy against taxpayers' wages, salaries, and other property. IRS actually seized taxpayer property 5,723 times.

They move in to wipe you out when they decide they have no other choice. They can't get you to respond in any way to their claims that you owe them more taxes. They have called repeatedly, sent letters and telegrams and Revenue Officers to your home, place of business, club, or neighborhood bar where you hang out. Those IRS people are armed, expecting the worst from you.

But you won't answer any of their messages, and if the RO finally does catch up with you and tells you face to face that you owe the IRS money, you tell him where to go, maybe even take a swing or a shot at him.

So they move, and a few days later when you get home you find your car is gone and a SOLD sign on your front lawn.

Perhaps you were guilty. Perhaps you owed them every penny they claimed. And perhaps not.

Supposing they made a mistake. We all know, and the IRS admits, it is not infallible and makes thousands and thousands of mistakes every year. "We are only human, after all," Commissioners tell Congress annually, when pressed. "Of course we make mistakes." Last year, Commissioner Kurtz spoke of "200,000 unhappy and aggravated taxpayers," people with problems and complaints not handled well by the IRS.

When you consider the volume of returns, if there were only a 1 percent rate of error, we're talking about 900,000 taxpayers who could be the innocent victims of IRS mistakes.

Supposing that by mistake they switched your Social Security number with sombeody else's. And they came after you, and even though you showed them and protested that they were wrong, the computer still kept coming up with your number.

Or supposing that in fact you did owe them more taxes, but you also owed a lot of other folks, and the strain was driving you crazy. You were working day and night to pay everybody off, and you just couldn't face the IRS one more time.

And supposing the amount you owed them was $4000. Even though they are technically correct, and you have not cooperated with them, where is the justice in their selling your home for, say, $50,000 in order to collect $4000?

Where is the justice indeed? While I do feel that in the majority of cases the IRS has been justified to act with "extreme prejudice" when it has done so, why should there be such a chance of plain human and/or computer error?

Last year, I was very pleased to offer testimony to the House Oversight Subcommittee of Ways and Means during its investigation into the IRS and the abuse of power.

My proposal to it was a very simple one: before the IRS is allowed to use its super collection powers, require it to obtain a court's permission to do so. In that way, through a quick, simple hearing with a judge, an independent third party could help assure that some horrible mistake wasn't about to be perpetrated, that someone wasn't about to be destroyed, or a life ruined, by mistake.

Meanwhile, until there is some such legal restraint on the IRS, I have one modest piece of advice: don't ignore them. It can be dangerous to ignore the IRS.

If you owe them, or even if they claim you owe them and you dispute the claim, don't ignore them. Answer their letters and calls. As painful as it might be, think about how much worse things could get.

And above all, don't forget that they would much rather get your money than send you to jail.

Talk to them. It might astonish you, but they can be reasonable. More reasonable than your bank, at times. They'll work out all kinds of payment plans with you.

If you do talk to them and find them unreasonable, or find their computer intransigent in its error, turn to your congressman or senator. The IRS fears Congress, as I said. A call from the office of your congressman or senator will freeze the great monster in its tracks. It will at least give you a chance to sort things out with them.

But if you ignore them, you are doing the one thing that is certain to deeply wound and anger the monster, and then . . .

Beyond all the information and advice I'll give you in this book, I want to take you inside where I was, and where part of me still is. Any time I hear or read about a new tax matter, a ruling, a regulation, a case, whatever, part of me automatically thinks about IRS strategy. What are they after? Who are they trying to get? Why are they doing it? And what can I do for myself and how can I do it?

I want you to begin to develop those kinds of instincts. By showing you how they think, who Harry the Auditor really is, what his training is, how his tax mind is shaped, as I do in Chapter 7, I hope I can help you sharpen your reflexes. And when, in Chapter 8, we look over Harry's shoulder and tap into his thoughts as he reviews your return and prepares his strategy to audit you, you ought to get some practical insight on how to cope with Harry.

And I especially hope you get something else, something a bit less tangible perhaps, but more important. I hope you are finally able to shake that nameless fear of the unknown. That you are able to regard the IRS clearly, even coolly, and say: "Okay, if I push my accountant to let me take that damn trip as a business deduction, I'm going to be kind of heavy in 'Travel and Entertainment.' . . . Is it worth it? Yeah, I think so. After all, I'm not really out of line much anywhere else."

At that point, you are finally taking charge of your tax life, which is after all a major part of your personal finances. And if you can have a real measure of control over that, life should become a bit more beautiful.

And what do you have against 7 regional and 58 district offices, 28,500 Agents and office auditors, 60,500 other full-time employees, a $2.3 billion budget, computer banks, and all the mind games they play?

You have a Marvin.

Marvin is your accountant, and though he might not look especially ferocious, he can save your life, especially if you know how to arm him properly.

Marvin is everyone's older uncle. Though he sometimes tries your patience, you have trusted him completely for years. He knows taxes, he lives simply, he has seen an awful lot with his now tired eyes. Marvin loves his wife and two children, and though he never says it, he doesn't really approve of how you throw your money around, or the way you live in general. Your accountant is genetically cautious. He is also bright, at least when it comes to taxes. On other matters you consider Marvin a bit naïve, not really as bright and experienced as yourself; but then, you aren't paying him to advise you on those other matters.

This year, as every year sometime after January 1, a bell went off in your head and you called Marvin "to do your taxes." Perhaps the reminder was a raise in pay, or some free-lance work coming up, a divorce-marriage-baby, some major event in life that tells you, as we'll discuss in Chapter 13, that somehow your tax situation is going to be different this year. Or maybe, by now, you call by reflex: a new year, a new tax return.

So Marvin gives you the date, and warns you, please, this year, to save time, have all the income slips and forms with you so we don't have to go calling all over town, and also the checks for medical deductions together in one pile.

The weekend before your appointment you have wasted, angrily sorting out all your checks for the year, matching American Express chits with hopelessly faded lunch dates on your calendar, and concocting white lies.

"That trip to Ft. Lauderdale certainly ought to be deductible," you start saying to yourself. "Yes, of course I saw my mother. What kind of son would I be if I went to Lauderdale and didn't see my eighty-year-old mother? But the real purpose of that trip was business. If I was going to invest in Florida land, I needed to see what I was buying. Think I'm going to pay $2500 for an acre of swampland?"

You have been confecting. You rehearse first in the privacy of your mind. In a few days you will try the part out in Marvin's office. Marvin is a very critical audience, but you know that Marvin's office is merely an out-of-town tryout. The Broadway opening will come when you speak those same smooth lines to the audience of an IRS auditor, a performance you profoundly hope you are never commanded to give.

You keep your appointment, and for a painfully long afternoon you answer all of Marvin's questions, feed him all your canceled checks and frayed receipts, conspire and argue. You conspire on the little things and argue over the big ones.

"How much for charity this year?" he asks, glancing at last year's return.

You pretend to be looking for canceled checks, the ones that will verify the imaginary extra $300 you gave to Dartmouth this year, and that special contribution to the hospital, and those benefit tickets you bought, and all the rest.

"Okay," Marvin says, "let me see what you got."

You hand him one check to the Dartmouth Alumni Fund for $200, a very dirty receipt from the ASPCA for $25, and a raffle ticket.

"That's all? That's all you got?" Marvin asks.

"I don't know where I put . . ." you reply, peering into your briefcase.

"Okay, okay," he says, looking back to last year's forms. "We had, last year, including your wife's cash contributions to church, we had $789.00. About the same this year?"

You are still bent over, pretending to look for those checks. "Yeah," you reply, with a note of resignation in your voice, as if it might actually prove to be more, if only you could find the evidence. "Yeah, I guess it's about the same."

"Perhaps a bit more?" he asks, knowing that this year you and your wife have more income to declare than last year, and so you are going to be allowed a higher level of deduction for charitable contributions.

"Oh, yeah," you answer nodding, "definitely a bit more."

"$846.00," he says, writing it on his worksheet.

Throughout this conversation, your eyes have never met his.

That is conspiracy. Though it might give you a criminal rush at the time, you have stolen peanuts. So little, in fact, that the IRS is not going to waste its time with the item on your return. (As I explain in Chapter 4, a charitable deduction can be one of the safest deductions you can take.)

So Marvin gives you that, but when it comes to the big stuff, he is less cooperative. He doesn't want to give you that trip to Florida. He positively recoils at the idea of deducting for an office in your home. He becomes almost nasty when he tells you that just because your wife sold two travel articles to *The Christian Science Monitor* for $80, you are not entitled to a $1900 deduction for a trip to England.

No, on the big stuff, everything with Marvin is a tug-of-war. In fact, each year it gets worse. Each year, as you think you know more and more about what you're entitled to, those tugs-of-war get decidedly more irritating. You begin to wonder if Marvin is working for you or the IRS.

There are grounds for your concern. Alas, Marvin has perfectly understandable conflict-of-interest problems.

If your name is Rockefeller, and Marvin is on your payroll, business or personal, at $100,000 a year, you have less to worry about. Your interests are Marvin's interests.

But if you are paying him $300 to $1000 a year, he is working for you, but he is also working for himself. Not that Marvin is a dishonest fellow, any more than you are. But he knows the rules of the IRS game much better than you do. With that knowledge, the part of him that is self-employed wants to avoid an audit almost more than you do.

First, Marvin knows that an audit is going to take a lot of his time. A day, two, three, who can tell? And he knows that he can't possibly charge you for all of that time. Some of it, but not all. So, while an audit may be profoundly traumatic for you, for Marvin it is uneconomical, which is for him slightly worse than profoundly traumatic.

Also, Marvin doesn't want trouble with the IRS. At all costs, he wants to keep out of the "Problem Preparer's Program." You can be sure he knows about that one.

But short of making the list and losing his business, Marvin knows the IRS can make his life difficult.

They can hit him with a battery of fines. Any mistake he makes in calculating your return can cost him $100, a nuisance fine the IRS has come up with. Marvin's a careful fellow, but anyone can make an honest error, especially if he's doing scores of returns, day in and day out, from the beginning of January through April 15, and beyond.

This last year there was an epidemic, a positive plague of negligence fines on accountants and preparers, especially in the New York area.

For any kind of error or miscalculation, or in cases where a taxpayer didn't have all the documentation for every single item, Agents were blaming the accountants and slapping $100 fines on them.

As usual with the IRS, the real purpose of this nastiness was more than met the eye. They weren't simply saying to tax preparers everywhere—and you can be sure that tax preparers all over America knew what was happening around New York —they weren't simply warning tax preparers to be careful, to take more pains with each return.

They were threatening them, intimidating them.

Imagine how Marvin might feel in an audit if he knows that Harry the Auditor is under secret orders to mete out as many negligence penalties as possible. Under those circumstances, Marvin might be a little less willing to fight quite so hard with Harry during the audit. And, as we'll see in Chapter II, if Marvin doesn't push and pull with Harry in the great confrontation, it could cost you real money.

But with a negligence penalty imminent, hanging over Marvin's head, invisible to you perhaps, but as real to him as a mallet, imagine how that could dampen Marvin's will to win.

Even worse, when the penalties were first established in 1976, Agents would hit Marvins with them right in front of their clients.

"I'm going to disallow that trip," Harry would tell Marvin. "You have no proof that was a business trip. He went to Florida to go fishing. And so far as I can see, he's not in the fishing business."

"Now, be reasonable . . . "

"And what's more, you're responsible. You should not have taken the deduction on the return to begin with, because you could see for yourself that he had no adequate proof that the trip was for business. And without such documentation, you can't take the deduction. You're responsible. You have to check your client's claims, check his proof."

"Excuse me, Mr. Harry," Marvin says, flushing at this double humiliation. "I'm well aware of what my responsibilities as a tax preparer are, as I have been for over twenty-five years. And I've fulfilled them. I checked my client's documentation and I found it fine. Quite adequate. You choose to call it 'inadequate.' I disagree. I say those plane tickets, hotel bills, are adequate because we know he was investigating real estate possibilities in the Fort Lauderdale area. You're asking for copies of letters to real estate brokers setting up appointments. My client told me, just as he's told you, he didn't bother to write. He went down there, knowing from friends and associates that the real estate market in the area was good for buying, and he called the brokers they recommended to him from his hotel room, and made his appointments."

Harry shakes his head. "Sorry, disallowed," he says. With absolutely no malice in his voice, he adds, "And there's a negligence penalty for you. $100. You'll get a notice."

What Harry was trying to do by embarrassing Marvin in front of his client was to intimidate him, force him to be much more conservative and strict with you. Along the way, he was also trying to make Marvin into an investigator and enforcement agent for the IRS.

There have been a number of penalties applied because Harry disagreed with Marvin's interpretation of a particular aspect of the tax law. For an honest difference of opinion, in other words, Marvin got fined.

Happily, accountants and other preparers have fought back. They have gone to their congressmen and senators, they have gone to the Commissioner of the IRS, and they have fought these penalties in court. In fact, something more than 80 percent of all these negligence penalties have been tossed out on appeal.

Still, that figure might not be much consolation to Marvin, because so many of those overturned cases were fought, financed, and won by big accounting firms. Chances are your Marvin is working alone, perhaps has a partner, maybe has hired a special assistant to lend a hand at tax time. He can't afford $2000 to fight a $100 negligence fine. He can't afford the legal fees, or the time and energy the fight drains. He says the hell with it. Let's give the bastards their $100, and be done with it.

Caught again. If Marvin pays, his name goes into what the IRS calls "a central file." Of course, that is not to be confused with the nonexistent Problem Preparers List. But in fact, by paying the fine he didn't deserve in the first place, Marvin is on his way toward making the big list.

Because of the outcry, the IRS has begun to back down a bit and set some controls on the use of this particular weapon.

Singleton Wolfe, who has recently retired, but who in 1979 was still Assistant Commissioner/Compliance and, as such, one of the most powerful people in the entire Service, cabled all Regional Commissioners, District Directors, and Service Center Directors special orders.

ALL REGIONAL COMMISSIONERS, DISTRICT DIRECTORS & SERVICE CENTER DIRECTORS INTERNAL REVENUE SERVICE

(MSARD; MSASC)—WE HAVE RECEIVED COMPLAINTS THAT SOME EXAMINERS HAVE PROPOSED RETURN PREPARER PENALTIES AS A MEANS OF INFLUENCING PREPARERS TO SUPPORT THE EXAMINERS' PROPOSALS IN INCOME TAX EXAMINATIONS. UNDER NO CIRCUMSTANCES WILL AN EXAMINER DISCUSS OR PROPOSE A PREPARER PENALTY AS TO INFLUENCE PREPARERS TO SUPPORT THE EXAMINER'S PROPOSALS IN INCOME TAX EXAMINATIONS. IN ADDITION, PROCEDURES OUTLINED IN IRM 426(27).6 IN PROPOSING PREPARER PENALTIES ARE HEREBY REVISED AND CLARIFIED. IF DURING THE COURSE OF AN EXAMINATION IT BECOMES EVIDENT TO AN EXAMINER THAT RETURN PREPARER CONDUCT PENALTIES (IRC 6694(a) or (b)) SHOULD BE CONSIDERED, TAX AUDITORS AND REVENUE AGENTS WILL DEVELOP THE FACTS TO A POINT WHERE IT APPEARS THE PENALTY SHOULD BE PURSUED AND WILL THEN DISCUSS THEIR FINDINGS WITH THEIR GROUP MANAGERS BEFORE DISCUSSING ASSERTION OF THE PENALTY WITH THE PREPARER. GROUP MANAGERS WILL MAKE THE DETERMINATION AS TO WHETHER THE PENALTY WILL BE PURSUED. THE MANDATORY REVIEW OF ALL PREPARER CASES WILL BE MADE PERSONALLY BY THE CHIEF OF REVIEW STAFF OF OR FOR EACH DISTRICT OFFICE. IRM 426(27) WILL BE REISSUED IN ACCORDANCE WITH IRM 1254. IN APPEALS, PROTESTED WORK UNITS INVOLVING IRC 6694(a) or (b) PENALTY ISSUES

WILL BE ASSIGNED TO GS–13 APPEALS OFFICERS TO ASSURE
HIGH QUALITY AND CONSISTENT DECISIONS.

S. B. WOLFE

ASSISTANT-COMMISSIONER

(COMPLIANCE)

So there are now some checks on Harry. Even Kurtz has
admitted that something is wrong. Losing that many cases on
appeal, he allowed, meant that perhaps his Agents needed a bit
more guidance in the fine art of defining "the line between
inadvertence and negligence."

Meanwhile, the effect of the campaign, even the presently
diminished campaign, has been precisely what I believe the IRS
was after in the first place: it has caused a number of Marvins
to stop doing returns altogether, and put a lot of small preparers
right out of the tax return business. Not worth the added worry
and expense to them. They can use their knowledge of accounting and their talents as tax advisors in other ways, not be
harassed, and still make perfectly decent livings.

Which is fine with the IRS. If Marvin stops doing your
return, you'll be faced with the choice of paying more, perhaps
retaining a large firm, which is more advice and expense than
you really need, or moving down the scale to some H&R Block
type. Many more people will choose to pay less, the IRS knows,
and they also know that the franchise preparers will be much
less imaginative and even more conservative than Marvin.
Fewer deductions for you. Fewer problems for them.

Nuisance fines probably still bother Marvin even more than
the possibility of a big problem. He is fully aware that if he
knowingly commits fraud with and for you, he is liable to a fine
of $5000 and/or up to five years in prison. But he's not going
to do that. If you tell him about income you've earned, he's
going to declare it. If you don't tell him about it, and the IRS
finds out, you'll be the one to pay the fines and perhaps be sent
to Lewisburg.

Marvin is always aware of what the IRS people really want

him to do, which is to help them rather than you, as much as possible.

Commissioner Kurtz went so far as to say that he'd like to see all tax preparers flag questionable areas on any returns they fill out. In other words, you are supposed to pay Marvin to do your return in order to save you every tax dollar he knows how, legally, and then he's supposed to attach a note to your return, saying:

> Dear IRS,
> Better take a very close look at the following items: Casualty loss, deduction for automobile for business purposes, and, of course, the interest-free loan to a brother that I've written off as a long-term loss. Don't hesitate to let me know if I can be of any further assistance.
>
> Sincerely,
> Marvin

Incredible as it might sound, that is Kurtz's position—Marvin as part-time IRS employee. If there are questionable items on your return, Kurtz maintains, chances are good your return will be selected for an audit, and Harry the Auditor is going to find and examine those questionable areas, anyway. So why don't we save time and money—taxpayers' money, at that?

All of this, the fines, the prison sentences, the Problem Preparer's Program, the harassing, have an understandable effect on Marvin—IRS salvos in its Hundred Years' War with your accountant. Marvin has hardened somewhat with time, just as has Harry the IRS Revenue Agent, his front-line opponent. Marvin has also learned that the veteran who is still standing after years of battle is the smart, cautious veteran. Don't take unnecessary risks, Marvin says to himself. Don't be brave above and beyond the call of duty. Collect fees, not medals.

Which is just how the IRS wants him to think. So Marvin is forced into something of a balancing act. A bit of fairness and risk for you, a pinch of caution for himself. When in doubt, be careful, be safe, which is his natural tendency and character anyway.

That's why, on the big items, you're getting a tougher tug-of-war every year. Something might be good and safe for Marvin, but not so good for you. To be sure, he might keep you from being stupidly reckless, but he might also cost you hundreds, even thousands of tax dollars.

In my opinion, you can measure the value of a tax advisor by the kinds of intelligent risks he is willing to take on your behalf. My own position is: Take everything the law entitles you to. The IRS might not like the law as it is, or like you for taking full advantage of it. And they might come after you, challenge you and Marvin to apply the damn law for them. So you and Marvin have to be prepared for that, and that means that if you take a deduction, you've got to have all the documentation and backup they will ask for. Be prepared, in other words, to defend in an audit what you have done. And be prepared to win it.

Chances are, after your racking session with Marvin, what you end up with is time spent, a headache, very mixed feelings about Marvin, and that continuing fear of the dreaded IRS.

You mail off the return.

And then, instead of feeling better, you feel worse.

<table>
<tr><td>3</td><td># Into the Pipeline</td></tr>
</table>

3	Into the Pipeline

Depending on where you live, the postman will deliver your return to one of ten regional service centers—Atlanta, Kansas City, Austin, Holtsville (N.Y.), Fresno (Cal.), Memphis, Ogden (Utah), Andover (Mass.), Philadelphia, or Cincinnati. Once there, your return enters what is known at the IRS as "the pipeline."

A Service Center is a complex that looks like a standard industrial park: office buildings, storage areas, and computers, lots of computers.

There are people here too, but at this stage of things people are not very important. They really are servants to the computers, keeping them fed and healthy.

A human being does, however, receive your envelope, open it, stamp it "received" with a date, and sort it according to type: individual return, corporate, partnership, etc.

A human being also makes the first inspection of your return, looking to see if, according to Line 66 on your return, you owe money.

If you owe, say, $212.19, he makes sure the check you've enclosed is made out for that amount.

If it is not, your return is immediately sent to "verification," and other human beings in that department will send you a letter, quickly, informing you of the error and telling you to send another check for the required amount, plus interest. Just a form letter with the blanks filled in.

Many people make innocent errors when writing checks to the IRS and many more make not such innocent ones, and at the Service we thought we could always tell the difference. We collected a whole catalogue of stalling tactics created by people who owed taxes, but didn't have the money on hand to pay.

Some might send their check, but date it for the wrong year.

Others forgot to sign the check.

Some people blamed us. They would pretend to be irritated with IRS bureaucratic inefficiency: "If you would please search your files," they would write, "I am sure that you will find my check. I certainly sent it to you, along with my return. If, however, after a thorough search you are unable to locate said check, please inform me, and I will, of course, issue a new one to you."

One of the most common stalling tactics is to pay with a check—all properly signed and dated—but for the wrong amount.

I had a client not long ago who owed $2144.00 in taxes. He had made a minor killing in the market on a tip, and I'd warned him that his normal withholdings were not going to be enough. But rather than put anything aside, he played another tip. When it came time to file his return, he didn't have the cash. So instead of attaching a check for $2144.00, he sent one in for $144.00—an innocent and clever mistake, he thought.

As it turned out, my client was very lucky. His ploy did give him a couple of extra weeks. During that time, his stock rose a full point—better than dropping ten. At least my client had the money then to pay the taxes and the interest charges. But he might have found himself short of funds, with the IRS knocking on his door, perhaps slapping him with a 5 percent penalty, or even civil fraud.

When I learned about his charade and questioned him, he

applied what I call the familiar *Titanic* Defense: Women and
Children First. "I have to think of my kids," he replied. "Know
what colleges cost today?"

But let's assume that you are strong enough to resist such
temptations and have enclosed your check for the right amount.

These checks used to sit around awhile, but now they are
deposited quickly into a U. S. Treasury account, so don't count
on float time with that check. I've been told that the IRS will
even fly checks from Service Centers to clearing banks for
same-day deposits, if the U.S. Treasury itself is short of cash.

Your return, meanwhile, moves along to another human
being. This one edits it and codes it for the computer.

Then it is punched into the machine.

This is where the IRS starts looking at what you've sent them
and what you've told them very closely.

For our purposes, it's best to think of the computer operating
on two levels.

On the first level, it will examine your return for simple,
honest mistakes.

On the second level, it will pass judgment on how good an
audit prospect you are. Here we get into important matters, the
sophisticated and, as yet, top-secret TCMP data on how the
computer selects returns to be audited, or at least recommends
that human beings consider them audit potential.

Let's take it a stage at a time.

First, the computer is going to check your return to find out
if all the addition, subtraction, multiplication, and division is
correct. Every single return in the United States is checked for
plain old math, and if there are mistakes, the computer discards
the return. "Spits it out" or "kicks it out" are the common
terms.

If that happens, your return will be adjusted, and you'll get
a letter with a refund check, or a bill, and an explanation of
what went wrong. Here's one place not to worry. You will not
be thrown into jail for sloppy arithmetic.

The computer will also decide if you owe an estimated tax

penalty, and if so, how much. Perhaps you should have been making quarterly payments and didn't. If that was the case, the computer will figure a penalty and a bill will be sent to you within a couple of weeks.

Or perhaps you didn't have enough withheld from your regular paychecks. Or a large capital gain on which you did not pay any tax at the time may have the same penalty.

One note of caution: The computer can make mistakes too. With estimated taxes, for example, there are four special exceptions that relieve you of having to pay on a quarterly basis. So if you get a letter from the computer asking for money, call Marvin before you send off a check.

The whole area of estimated taxes is yet another instance where the IRS wants to make tax preparers into part-time IRS employees. The Service has asked tax preparers to figure out what the estimated tax penalties should be, and then in effect collect the money for them. "After all," the IRS says to Marvin, "you know, even before you've finished meeting with your client, if there's going to be an estimated tax penalty—as soon as the t/p tells you about the big raise she got, and also tells you, no, she didn't increase the withholding from her paychecks. If she had done that, she wouldn't have had anything left of the raise for herself . . . At that point, Marvin, you know there's going to be a penalty. And as soon as you've done the return, you can easily calculate what the amount will be. So why not help us a little bit here?"

The IRS actually tried to force Marvin, by decree, to perform that service for them, on your time and money. But once again, Marvins of the tax world resisted and screamed so loudly that the Service backed down. For now, at least.

The computer also checks for other errors, honest or reasonably honest mistakes, that the IRS knows are especially widespread—the kind the Service has instructed the computer to catch and sort out before going any further. These vary from time to time, but, currently, they include the following:

• The computer is programmed to check that what you declare on Line 8 for wages and salary agrees with the W-2 forms
you've attached to your returns.

• The computer will check to see if you've remembered to
use the 3 percent deductible when figuring your medical expenses. People still overlook that.

• The computer will look for returns that take "partial exemptions." Many people claim they provide, say, 40 percent of
their mother's support and so they take only 40 percent of the
$1000 exemption allowed for a dependent. The problem is, nei-
ther the IRS nor its computer recognizes or allows "partial
dependency exemptions."

• The computer will inform taxpayers that, contrary to common understanding, taking deductions for nonbusiness utility
taxes, or driver's license and automobile fees, are not allowed.
T/ps often think these are like state, local, or sales taxes, and
they are wrong.

• The computer is also programmed to catch the mistakes
that crop up on many returns simply because people use the
wrong tables when they figure their final tax bill. Up at the top
of the return, the taxpayer has marked, correctly, "Single." But
when he or she is trying to figure out the tax from the tables
the IRS provides, the person looks at the wrong table and pays
according to the tax scale for "Married, filing joint return."

For any of these and other similar errors, the computer kicks
out the return, an adjustment is made, a letter goes out.

When I was with the IRS, there used to be a staggering
number of sloppy errors on returns. But now, with pocket
calculators costing $10 or $20, and the payment tables from the
IRS expanded to show how much you owe for up to $40,000
of taxable income, these mistakes are less common.

What does the first level of checking by the computer tell us?

In fiscal 1979, the IRS received 140 million tax returns of all
types.

Of those, 90.8 million were returns for individuals, and 6
million of them had mistakes in arithmetic.

Of the individual returns, 2.2 million had mistakes in which people cheated themselves. An average of $159 per return. Out went the checks.

On the other hand, the computers found that 3.8 million taxpayers had erred against the government. An average of $241 per return. Out went the letters.

Surprisingly, of the 90.8 million individual returns, the computer cited 69 million for refunds, not for any of the errors mentioned above, but because people had too much withheld from salary or wages or had overpaid in similar ways. Average refund was $518.

At the IRS, we liked those millions of t/ps, some three-quarters of all the individual taxpayers in America, who had more money withheld from their paychecks than the law required of them. They kept our cash flow moving nicely.

Of course, the overwithheld also provided us with further proof that taxpayers are stupid. But if they wanted to lend us their money interest-free, that was their problem.

Actually, what people are doing is forcing themselves to save. They don't miss the extra $10 a week. And then, in the spring, after filing their return, they get a check from the government, a lump sum they wouldn't otherwise have, and which can help pay for a nicer summer vacation.

In any case, if you claim a refund, the IRS will mail you a check once the computer has completed its first level of examination and it's sure you haven't made any of the simple errors. They are mailed on Fridays. If you receive a refund check and it is not for the amount you expected, there should be a form letter of explanation on its way. Check and letter are mailed separately, so give the letter about two weeks to arrive. If you still haven't received it by then, call your local IRS office. They can immediately trace it by plugging into the computer. They can tell you the day it was mailed or, if it hasn't been, its exact status. Generally speaking, if you file your return early, say, in January, you can expect that it'll take about four weeks before you receive your refund check. If you file in April, as I recommend, it might take ten weeks or so.

That's assuming all goes well, not always a safe assumption with refund checks. 42 percent of all the complaints that reached Problem Resolution Officers last year were related to refund checks.

I got a call from a salesman in Philadelphia recently with a refund check problem that offers a fair sample of the ways the IRS can infuriate you on this one.

The man was due a refund of $1800. Months went by and it had not come, so he called his local IRS office. A clerk punched into the computer and told him it had been mailed out to him, in fact four weeks ago to the day.

"Well, then, something's wrong," the man told the clerk. "Can't take four weeks for a check to reach me. It must have been lost or stolen. What do I do now?"

"You'll have to fill out the necessary papers," the clerk told him. "And then the Secret Service and our special investigators will investigate."

"Secret Service?" the salesman said, somewhat appalled. "Good Lord. I don't understand."

"Theft of a federal check, sir," the clerk informed him. "That's a federal offense. We've got to investigate."

"That's the only way I can get my check? The only way I can get my money from you people?"

"Fill out the forms, sir, and we'll investigate."

"Well, how long do these things take?" he asked. "I mean, quite frankly, I can use the $1800."

"You'll receive your money eventually."

"What do you mean 'eventually'? Next month? Next year? When?"

"Assuming the investigation proves you are right, you'll receive your money in one to four years."

"One to four . . . I don't believe what I'm hearing. Are you kidding?"

"Certainly not, sir. Where shall I send the papers?"

"One question."

"Yes, sir."

"How much interest do you pay on that money you owe me over one to four years?"

"Interest, sir?"

"You heard me. I said 'interest.' "

"To the best of my knowledge, no interest," the clerk replied. "Now, if you don't mind, where should I send the papers? There are a lot of other taxpayers with problems waiting."

"Oh, I see, I see. You're a busy man. Well, I don't want to take up your precious time. You don't have to bother sending me those forms, mister. Just stuff 'em any old place that's convenient. I'll get satisfaction on this from my congressman."

"What did you say?"

"I said, this is an outrage. You lose my refund check, my own money which you owe me, and then you expect me to wait one to four years to get it, with no interest. Are you out of your mind? This is a damn outrage and I don't have to put up with it. The hell with you. I'll get satisfaction from my congressman."

There was a pause. Then the clerk said, "I wouldn't do that if I were you . . ."

"I beg your pardon?"

"We can make life miserable for you," the clerk told him. "You go to your congressman, and I assure you, this will take that much longer before we resolve your problem."

"What's your name, mister?"

Click.

There is a happy ending. The salesman did go to his congressman, and he did get his refund check rather quickly. (The National Office says it takes four months, not four years for new checks of this sort to be issued.) He didn't get the clerk, unfortunately, because he never had the man's name.

There are several lessons and morals from this horror story.

First of all, the source of the salesman's problem, as he and I figured out in our conversation, and as the IRS clerk could have just as easily, was that the man had moved. When he had filed his return, he had taken the preprinted label off the income tax package the IRS had sent him and us all at Christmas time, and corrected the address on it. Most certainly, some key puncher in his Service Center didn't pick up the corrected change.

So when the IRS sent him his refund check, they sent it to his old address. He had left a forwarding address for all his mail with his local post office, which worked for all other mail, but not his refund check. If those checks are "undeliverable," the U.S. Postal Service will not forward them. At the IRS's request, they return them to the IRS.

The IRS is sitting on tens of millions of dollars in "undeliverable" refund checks, having the use of all that money interest free. To their credit, they do pay lip service to propriety. They maintain stoutly that they're merely trying to protect taxpayers' refunds. They're taking no chances, they say, waiting to be notified of the correct change of address.

If you have a new address, notify the IRS Service Center where you file your return, and do it in writing. Remember, the IRS is required to send refund checks only to your last known address.

As for those preprinted labels, I'm often asked whether it's wise to use them or not. To begin with, they will not in any way increase your chances of an audit, as some people seem to believe.

They are simply coded with information that makes it easier for the IRS to process your return. So if the information you read on them is correct, my advice is to use them. By all means use them. Because you can then eliminate the chance that some low-grade clerical type will make a mistake punching that basic data on you into the system.

However, if any of the information on the label is incorrect, destroy it and write the correct stuff on your tax return.

A final lesson: If you're confronted with a difficult and/or stupid and/or threatening clerk, as the salesman was, don't waste time.

Go immediately to the IRS Problem Resolution Officer in your local IRS office. He's a new creation, a recognition by the National Office that too many t/ps are furious with the treatment they receive all too often at the hands of IRS personnel and that t/p fury is too often justified.

The Problem Resolution Officer has a certain amount of power, and he can cut red tape.

But if you still don't get satisfaction there, do exactly what the salesman did. Go directly to your congressman or senator. Above all, the IRS fears members of the House Ways and Means Committee and the Senate Finance Committee. So if you have a representative or senator on one of those committees, you're really in luck. But even without that special clout, a call from the office of any representative or senator to the IRS will bring fast action.

Whether you have to go that infuriating route or not, if you do receive a refund check, it doesn't mean you won't be audited. An IRS auditor may come after you months or even years later. In most cases, the law allows them three years from April 15 of the year you filed to complete an audit. The audit might, in fact probably will, result in your having to give back some of the refund. But at least you will not have had to wait for your money, which can be no small consolation.

When you are to receive a refund and Marvin does anticipate an audit, he should try to give you some estimate of how much you'll have to return.

Obviously, Marvin will advise you to put that money aside.

Obviously, you will not do what he says.

Once the computer in the Service Center is finished reviewing your return for basic information, checking all the items I mentioned, it records all the information on your return on computer tapes.

These tapes, from the 10 Service Centers, are then sent to Martinsburg, West Virginia, the electronic nerve center of the IRS.

In this heavily guarded computer complex, where even IRS employees require special passes to get in, all the tax returns in the nation are rated, evaluated, and graded, according to secret formulas. The grades derived from the formulas show the IRS who has the "highest audit potential."

The IRS programs the computers to tell them who is telling the truth, who is stretching it. Who is cheating the most and where, on which items. Which deductions are the most distorted, and by how much. Who is taking deductions or claiming losses that we think are fishy. Who has structured business deals that we ought to look at closely. In short, the computers are programmed according to the Discriminant Functions System, the DIF. Which in turn is based on all of the detailed, revealing information gathered from the Taxpayer Compliance Measurement Program, those monstrous TCMP audits out of *1984,* in which each item on your return is questioned and verified.

There is other data, what the IRS calls "statistical experience," that helps the Service program the computer—the information gathered from tax returns over the years from all over the country, all over the world.

They know for example, that in 1974, Napa County, California, produced 9218 joint returns filed by people earning $15,000 or more. These people averaged deductions for just under 4 dependents—themselves, plus 2 children. They also reported average adjusted gross incomes of $23,746. And they declared on the average $20,045 in wages, another $3,122 from dividends, and $1,484 in interest.

Sorting things out that way, the IRS begins to get a profile of what is "normal" for various categories for Napa County, California.

Obviously, such profiles are broad sketches, and open to fairly broad distortion. Supposing all those wine makers in Napa have shared ideas about what special deductions they are entitled to as small agri-businessmen, battling nature and the giant agri-conglomerates, and the majority of them have their taxes done by a handful of accountants who specialize in advising wine makers?

In that case, what the profile might reveal is a common and accepted pattern of erroneous judgment, rather than the clear and honest picture of finances that is needed if the "norms" are going to be valid.

This is where the TCMP comes in. It was designed to eliminate the distortion of any broad profile. When they have finished dissecting those 55,000 TCMP returns, they can say to the computer, "Self-employed business consultant living in the southwest, making $35,000. Be on the alert for the following items. Watch out for medical expenses. Look very closely at deductions made in connection with independent work, especially when it supplements salaried jobs. Bartering. Business gifts. For some reason, taxpayers are going crazy with business gifts. Entertainment for business purposes . . ."

From the TCMP data, the IRS decides what is "normal," not only for each important item on the return, but how it varies according to income classes, as well as geographic location. It costs more to live in San Francisco than Little Rock, and the "norms" are designed to reflect the difference. Which means the computer is going to be quite finely tuned indeed.

The TCMP is also invaluable to the IRS in planning general audit strategy. From the sample, the IRS learns which income classes are the most honest, and which cheat the most.

TCMP surveys, for example, showed that 92.8 percent of all individual taxpayers reported all the taxes they owed. The balance reported taxes, but not all of them.

There were vast differences in compliance among classes. For individuals filing personal returns with adjusted gross incomes (AGI) of between $10,000 and $50,000, 96.1 percent reported what they actually owed. But with individuals filing business returns with the AGI under $10,000, only 57.2 percent reported fully.

That largely confirms what we knew at the IRS: small businessmen have big distortions on their returns, partly because they can't afford costly tax advisors, and partly because they are in the habit of scrambling and juggling to keep their businesses going, and the tax return is just one more piece of juggling.

Big businesses have a high voluntary compliance rating average of 95.5 percent. They retain some of the most expensive and competent tax pros in the country to compose their returns.

Still, they are hardly spared. The IRS maintains a list of about 1,300 major companies, and it audits every one of those companies. Whole squads of auditors move into the offices of the 1,300 companies. It costs the IRS some ten percent of its auditing resources to do this, but the feeling has always been that it's well worth the investment. An annual audit will certainly help to keep folks honest. And, of course, if the Service can catch Exxon in even the slightest error, what it recoups is huge.

The "norms," the "truth," as they are derived from the TCMPs, are the heart of the Discriminant Functions System, the DIF. It is the DIF that weighs and evaluates every important item on your return, on every return filed with the IRS, measuring it against those "norms."

Each measured item on your return then receives a numerical grade, plus 10, minus 7, etc. Some items are also examined and graded for their relationship to others.

Taking your return, let's assume that you are married, have two children, and are earning $40,000 a year. Let's also assume you reported that last year you paid $8640 in interest on the mortgage of your home, and that you live in Montgomery County, Maryland.

The computer has been told that Montgomery County is an expensive place to live. Nevertheless, according to its information, what you claim to be paying is more than what it would expect. Its norm is $5040. So the difference is worth, say, +20 DIF points.

"But that's grossly unfair," you say. "I mean, if I actually have to pay $8640 to my bank for the interest on my mortgage, then I'm entitled to a deduction of that amount, no matter what the damn computer and its DIF consider normal."

Right you are. And if that's what you really paid, that's the deduction you will get.

Simply because the computer gives you points, and when it adds up your points, it says, "This guy is ripe for an audit," does not necessarily mean that you will be audited. Nor does it mean if you are audited, you will have to cough up more dough.

In the end, a human being at the IRS decides whether the computer is wise in its judgment. And a human being decides whether to pursue you.

If your mortgage interest had amounted to less than the norm, you would have received minus points, a DIF credit, which can balance out some other area of your return.

With some items, if you are graded above normal it can kick out the whole return. For example, because the IRS has never trusted taxpayers when it comes to business-related "Travel and Entertainment" expenses, the computer is especially sensitive to those items and the amounts you claim there.

Similarly, the computer will shudder if you claim substantial business expenses that were not reimbursed by your employer, another extremely gray and sensitive area so far as the IRS is concerned. Since 1976, any time you take deductions for "Office in Home," the computer grumbles. And the newest computer agitator is "Vacation Home," when you use it part of the year and rent it out the rest. (More on these and other dangerous deductions in Chapter 5.)

So one of the risky items alone, or a combination of items where you are scoring above normal, could place you over the predetermined DIF "cutoff score" and spit out your return. After it's through grading, the computer adds up the total. The higher your score, as the IRS puts it, "the greater probability of tax error."

There are two extremely important refinements to the audit selection process this year, and both are going to make life tougher for people heavy with deductions.

It used to be that for audit selection purposes the computer examined your return on the basis of your Adjusted Gross Income.

That's the bottom line on the first page of your Form 1040, and you reach it only after adding up all sources of income—wages, interest, dividends, everything—and then making a few adjustments. If you have some business losses that you document on Schedule C, you subtract those here. If you have some long- or short-term capital losses, which you spell out on Schedule D, also subtract those here.

Further, before determining your AGI, you might deduct a moving expense, a payment to an IRA or Keogh retirement plan, or alimony you paid, among other things.

Finally you hit Line 31, and the figure you come up with there, after the above adjustments, is your AGI.

You still might have itemized deductions to take and all kinds of additional adjustments to make on that AGI figure before you reach the real bottom line, your taxable income.

But even at the AGI stage of things, you can imagine that for some people, their AGI is considerably lower than the amount they started out with, before there is a single subtraction or adjustment.

Some taxpayers started out with $100,000 earned during the year, but after they got finished subtracting for various tax shelters and a handful of other adjustments, their AGI was down to $10,000.

Nothing illegal, mind you, but it was very confusing for the IRS computer. Since the computer was categorizing returns according to AGIs, it meant that the wheeler-dealer who opened with $100,000 was now being lumped together with the rural schoolteacher when it came to audit consideration, and rural schoolteachers are a very unappealing group to the computer. As we know, and the computer knows, the more income to start with, the more promising the t/p is as an audit candidate.

Now all that is changed. Now in rating you as an audit candidate, the computer will start right at the top with something called Total Positive Income.

How much income did this t/p have before he took a single loss, made a single adjustment, subtracted a single penny for any reason whatsoever? the computer asks as it scans your return.

The figure it comes up with is your Total Positive Income.

And from now on, that figure will determine your income level for audit selection purposes.

They started using this technique in 1979, but in 1980, for the first time ever, all federal income tax returns will be graded this way.

The other important change is a most logical modification and, I think, a reflection of the times.

It has to do with whether you, as an individual t/p, are considered a "business" or a "nonbusiness" when the returns are sorted for audit classification in Martinsburg.

Most individuals, of course, are in the nonbusiness category. And it is in that category that their chances for audit are higher. A person who is in the nonbusiness, wage-earner classification with an income in the $100,000 range has a 1 in 10, or 10 percent, chance of being audited. That's high.

A business with an income of $100,000 stands only a 1 in 30 chance of being audited.

The reason for the difference is that the IRS knows that a business operating at that level promises much slimmer pickings than a healthy corporate giant, and as we know, their auditing resources are limited.

An individual who reports that kind of income, on the other hand, might well be worth real attention.

Until now, whether you were dumped in the "business" or "nonbusiness" pile depended on whether or not you filed a Schedule C along with your Form 1040.

If you filed a Schedule C Profit or (Loss) Form, Business or Profession (Sole Proprietorship), your return was stacked with "business." They classified you that way even if the major part of your income was actually from salary, not from an unincorporated business, like free-lance consulting.

Your audit chances were greatly reduced, then. If you showed $95,000 from salary, and $5000 additional income on Schedule C for consulting, you were treated as "business," and your audit chances were cut to only 1 in 30.

Starting this year, however, the computer is asking, What's the primary source of income on this return? As it scans the return, it weighs "salary" of $95,000 against "consulting" of $5000, and labels you a "nonbusiness" candidate for audit consideration, and a good one.

In fact, this new classification system is so logical, you might wonder, even if you don't welcome it, why this hadn't been done sooner.

My guess is that though Schedule C was a kind of hole in the system, until now it didn't matter much. Until now, people either worked for employers, and received wages and salaries and W-2 forms, or they worked for themselves, and filed accordingly. But now, hordes of people are doing both, holding salaried jobs and doing independent work in order to live decently. So, as times have changed, the IRS, or perhaps more accurately its computers, is changing with them.

A piece of advice that will cut down your chances of getting audited: the later you file your return, the lower your chances of being called in. File between April 1 and April 15.

I know this is precisely the opposite of what the IRS asks of you. A good citizen and a nice little t/p files early. The people at the Service push the idea that if you file early, you'll get your refund early.

It does make life easier for them to have the flow of returns spread out. But I have learned that, because of the way the DIF works, the later the better would make life easier for you.

You see, as the tapes with the information from the returns reach Martinsburg, they are fed to the computer in batches. The IRS doesn't wait until April 15 to do it all at once.

The DIF "cutoff scores" are on a kind of sliding scale. Let's say it takes a basic 240 points to kick out your return. But that is relative to income category, as well as the number of returns in each category the IRS wants to audit. Remember, the IRS has a national audit strategy, and it has limited resources.

So, if they are going to audit only 3 percent in the category of "Individuals, $10,000 to under $50,000," the computer will be programmed to select the top 3 percent, providing they have at least the required 240 DIF.

Which means that statistically your chances of not being selected are better if your return is being processed when there are more returns for it to be compared with.

File in February, and your 240 DIF might just be close to the head of the thin class.

File during the first two weeks in April, when the great bulk of returns have already come in, and your 240 might not be enough. In that batch, it might be necessary to have 260 DIF points to be selected.

To the best of my knowledge, this bit of information, known to a certain number of IRS people, had never been published before the first edition of this book came out in January 1980.

I have no illusions about the impact any single book can have. So I must confess I was astonished and absolutely delighted when I learned what happened up in New York around April 15 last year.

What happened was that so many people in the New York City area, where the book had happily sold out many times over, filed between April 1 and April 15 that the computer at the Holtsville Service Center broke down. Overload. Holtsville handles all returns from New York City, surrounding counties, and all of New Jersey. The thing had a nervous breakdown.

Two accountants in New York, both former IRS Agents who still have strong contacts within the Service, told me that the people at Holtsville were blaming the collapse on "that damn book."

Of course, it's impossible to be absolutely certain of what causes a great event like that, but I do know from my friends in the National Office that the IRS was truly upset with the piece of advice.

And I do know that they quickly leaked some counter-advice of their own, again playing their media game. "Warning to last-minute income tax filers," their leak said, in one form or another. "The IRS is so disturbed by recent books and articles claiming that returns filed near April 15 have a lower chance of being audited that they are going to take special steps to examine all such returns more closely than ever."

My advice this year? File as close to April 15 as you can. You will still cut down your chances of being audited, for the very same reasons I gave last year.

Though human beings, as we'll see, do make the final decisions regarding audits, the selection and sifting process obviously is structured around DIF. About 75 percent of all the returns from individuals that are selected for audits are spit out by the computer after it has totaled the DIF points.

The other 25 percent result from a number of reasons, many of which you have no control over:

• The IRS might audit your partner, and during the process decide that, in order to have a clear picture of his affairs, they need to compare them with yours.

• There might be a major crime task force descending on your area of the business world, and your return could get swept into the investigation, even though you are not involved.

• You might be paying alimony, and taking it as a legitimate deduction. But your ex is not declaring it as income, calling it "child support" instead. And that is not deductible by you, or taxable to her. So you may be very pleased to hear that ex has been called for an audit. But the pleasure will be shortlived.

• Or that ex might not be collecting the alimony or child support she feels she's entitled to, and calls the IRS with information about a second brokerage account you maintain. Some other person who is out for you might call the Service and become an informer. If his charge against you checks out, your return may be pulled and you will be audited, even though the computer found you a model citizen.

• The company you work for might be audited, and the IRS finds expense-account abuse. As a high-ranking employee, you'll get audited.

About now it might have occurred to you, as it does to most people when I first tell them about the TCMP and how the DIF system works, that life could be made much happier if you could get your hands on the table of norms for your region of the country. Then all you'd have to do is "fine-tune" your return, deducting just so much, but no more.

I'm afraid I have to tell you that there is no greater secret in the IRS than DIF, and it was always my understanding that no one person, not even the Commissioner, had all of the numbers and formulas. It's like the design of a super-weapons system, where no single person is entrusted with more than a part of its workings.

Of course, that might change now. The Freedom of Information case I mentioned in Chapter 1, in which the Longs sued to gain access to TCMP data, could unlock the great secrets. I wish them well, but I'm not going to hold my breath.

The computer program is fully updated and refined every two years, though the IRS can and does feed new instructions into the system constantly.

The IRS is always running tests and surveys to keep themselves current. Recently, I learned they surveyed returns to see if people receiving state tax refunds were reporting the money as income. When people don't, a high audit potential obviously exists, and they want the computer to know.

They've also had a mini-TCMP checking on child care credits. From Atlanta, Holtsville, New York, and Fresno, California, they've selected 6000 returns that took this credit. The letters have gone out to these taxpayers asking them to prove that they claimed the credit correctly, to show that they also paid Social Security taxes and withholding taxes, where applicable, for the people performing the child care work. Not a large sampling by any means, but enough, they figure, to tell them whether this item is worth their paying much attention to.

In addition to all the TCMP and other data, agents in the field are also continually sending information for the computer to the National Office. Whenever agents begin to see a rash of a certain kind of t/p activity or an abuse of a particular sort, they inform National Office.

I know they continue to encounter an alarmingly great wave of tax protesters fed by the Proposition 13 mania, and the computer has been warned to watch out for those returns.

Also, agents have reported a considerable amount of questionable reporting in connection with tax shelter partnerships. (More in Chapter 6.)

Once the computer has finished examining and grading your return, if it decides that on the whole you have been fairly honest, at least of "average" honesty, the IRS probably won't audit you for that year's return.

However, if the computer has graded you high and cited you for having high audit potential, your return is batched with others the computer is recommending for audit and passed along to human beings for further examination.

It is at this point that the IRS audit strategy is orchestrated to cover all income levels, reach into all parts of the nation, touch all kinds of job categories.

Once the returns have been sorted accordingly, and a good balance among the various objectives of the audit strategy is achieved, the returns are sent to audit offices where they will be evaluated by human beings, yet again, before they are finally stamped for audit.

Are there dollar quotas for each office? No.

For each auditor? No.

When the National Office in Washington finally works out its strategy, it allocates manpower for audits to each regional office and decides how many returns for audit will be allocated to each regional office.

But the decisions are based on the audit objectives I've mentioned, and IRS logic.

Obviously, the IRS offices in Manhattan, Los Angeles, Chicago, Houston, Boston, San Francisco, Austin are expected to produce great amounts of audit revenue. That's where a great cross section of t/p classifications are going to be found.

But that is not the same as setting quotas. When I was in the National Office in Washington, D.C., I never heard of dollar quotas from anyone who knew. Nor have I heard of any since. In that sense, the IRS is not like other businesses. It does not call all the heads of branch offices to national headquarters every spring for pep talks. It does not say, "Okay, Bradley, last year you and your people up in Manhattan dug up $765 million in additional taxes and penalties" (as in fact the Manhattan office did, in 1978) "and this year we want to see a 10 percent increase. We're counting on you, Bradley, as our main man in New York."

It doesn't work that way. There are, however, other pressures on Bradley.

Bradley in Manhattan or Los Angeles or wherever knows that he is expected to produce. He will not get a raise in pay even if he increases his audit dollars. Remember, he is a government employee. He is earning about $50,000 a year. He has job security, but if he doesn't do what the National Office considers a good job, which includes handling the volume of audits and producing what the National Office considers a proper amount of audit revenue, then they can make life difficult for him.

He has job security, but that security could mean an IRS job, though not the same one he has and wants to hold on to. Bradley knows what all those Commissioners and Assistant Commissioners are saying year after year when they parade before the various congressional committees asking for bigger budgets. They are saying, congressmen, senators, every year we're getting more and more efficient. Every year we're getting more work done, greater results, at less cost (proportionately speaking, of course). So you can be sure that the few paltry millions more we're asking for this year will be a wise expenditure.

Translated by Bradley, that means handling an ever-increasing volume of audits, producing continually greater amounts of audit revenue—without a proportionate increase in his staff.

Can be tough to produce those minor miracles, Bradley knows, but if he doesn't, he also knows that the National Office won't give him very high marks, and then they can and will make life difficult for him.

If Bradley is running the Manhattan office, chances are he has lived in New York a long time and likes it there. He doesn't want to be transferred to Mississippi, and the National Office can do that to him. He doesn't want to be demoted to Assistant District Director, either.

Or, if Bradley is a District Director in Phoenix, he's probably also there because he likes it. Maybe even worked his way to Phoenix from some other district up north where the winters were starting to really get to him and his wife. The last thing he wants now is to be transferred back north. In fact, I would guess from my IRS friends that the worst threat these days is to be moved to Manhattan. Accurate or not, New York City does not have a good reputation around the Service as a place to live or work. Except of course with those Agents who were born and grew up there.

The point is that Bradley knows what the National Office can do to him. So Bradley does his job. He knows just what's expected of him.

Similarly, Bradley doesn't give dollar quotas to his auditors. He doesn't have to. They also know they have to produce. They want to be promoted to higher GS grades and salaries. How well they work as auditors is carefully watched.

What auditors have instead of quotas is pressure. Pressure to close cases fast, to make their own time pay off.

The law says the IRS has three years to come and audit you, and that's what usually happens. They can reach further back under some circumstances. If you've never filed and they catch up with you, they can open up your affairs back to the day you were born. Or if you filed but there was fraud, they have six years to audit you. Or if they audit you and you've used income averaging, they may go back and examine your returns for four years to consider their relationship to the return under scrutiny.

So if Bradley and his auditors haven't come for you within three years, unless there's something special, according to the law they can't come for you later, not for that old return.

In fact, though, because of the pressure on auditors to produce, Agents work on a twenty-six-month schedule for audits. They don't give themselves those three years but just twenty-six months from the time you file your return to complete, not just start, an audit.

Which is good news for you: if you haven't been called about a return you filed two years ago—which is to say your 1978 return, which was due April 1979—chances are virtually certain that you're clear on that one.

The first human being who will examine your return in your local district office is the "Classifier," Murphy.

He's an experienced examiner, and he also knows the limitations of the computer. He has the authority to overrule the machine, to examine your return, to decide the computer was wrong, and to toss your return back in the hopper. His decision will be based on his judgment that your return will or will not be worth an auditor's time. (Obviously, Murphy's job and skills are rather special. Just how special and just what effect "Classifiers" have on the whole audit process, the IRS is trying to find out. Since 1976, they have been running a study, and it's meant to be completed this year.)

Murphy will scan your return following the computer's complaints. He might agree with the machine that you have taken a higher "Travel and Entertainment" deduction than your business income merits. But then, when it comes to that deduction for the office in your home which the computer is really disturbed about, he does something the computer cannot do. He reaches for the note attached to your return by Marvin.

The note says: "Taxpayer claims the appropriate deduction for his office maintained in his residence pursuant to the applicable law and regulation which limit the deduction. The office is separate and apart from the rest of the home and is used exclusively for business on a regular basis."

Among other things, the language of Marvin's message tells Murphy that you have someone handling your taxes who knows what he's doing, which means to him, "If we go for an audit on this one, this guy, Marvin, will be there, which means we have a tougher time and a longer battle."

Murphy is beginning to wonder if it's worth it, worth the time of one of the auditors.

He screens your return again, now applying not only all the knowledge and instinct of his long experience, but asking himself seven key questions, which he has been told by National Office to ask:

(a) Is the income sufficient to support the exemptions claimed?

(b) Does the refund appear to be out of line when considering the gross income and exemptions?

(c) Is there a possibility that income may be underreported?

(d) Could the taxpayer be moonlighting, earning tips, or have other types of income not subject to withholding tax?

(e) Is the taxpayer engaged in the type of business or profession normally considered to be more profitable than reflected by the return?

(f) Is the taxpayer's yield (net profit) on his/her investment (equity in assets) less than he/she could have realized by depositing the same amount in a savings account?

(g) Is the standard deduction used with high gross and low net shown on a business schedule? Experience has shown that the incidence of fraud is greater on low business returns when the return reflects large receipts ($100,000 or more), a sizable investment, and the standard deduction is used.

After reviewing and satisfying himself on those points, Murphy does a rough computation. "On this one," he thinks, "we could disallow, say, $500–600 in deductions. And he's in a 30 percent bracket? Be lucky if we end up with $150. And with that Marvin there, he'd tie up one of our auditors for a whole day . . . Nope, nope, that's no way to run this office. Not worth anybody's time."

And he drops your return into the "safe" basket, to be filed away. No audit. Computer overruled.

But if Murphy feels, instead, that this return looks very promising, he passes it along to a Group Manager, to Jackson.

Jackson, the Group Manager, will review the Classifier's recommendation, and if he disagrees, he can send it back. But what is much more likely, Jackson will concur with the decision to audit. Then it is his task to assign the return to one of his auditors.

"How long will this one take?" Jackson asks himself, knowing the current workloads of his various auditors. He also considers the complexities of your case, matching it with the special talents of his Agents. Who would be especially good on this one, he asks, noting that, say, a knowledge of the furniture business would help? Different Agents have different specialties. Some have taken advanced courses in the IRS, others developed their expertise through years on the job.

He assigns it to Harry.

Harry has been an auditor for seven years, is a GS 11, and earns about $24,700 a year. In style, manner, dress, he resembles Marvin. In fact, one day, he might become a Marvin. He talks about it now and then with other Agents in his office, how two or three of them might leave the Service and open their own little office, doing tax and general accounting, each of them a partner.

Meanwhile, Harry likes his job pretty well, and is good at it. He knows that people make the mistake of underestimating him when he comes to an audit because he doesn't look very impressive, and they know he doesn't make that much money, often considerably less than they do.

Harry's not bothered by this sort of thing. That's the rich t/p's problem. He knows taxes, and over the years he has started to develop those special instincts the veterans talk about. He can now smell lies the way a vintner can smell bad wine. Whether the scent rises off the return as he's examining it, or hangs in the air of an accountant's office, he is getting so he can feel it, trace it, analyze it, and nail the smiling liar quickly, very quickly if the t/p has underestimated him.

Harry's real problem, as relentless as a headache that never goes away, is time. He has a regular caseload of about 20 cases, and Jackson, his Group Manager, is always on him to close those cases. Close those cases, close those cases. Trouble is, as soon as he gets rid of one he gets another.

When Harry gets your return from Jackson, he flips through it. In theory, he knows he can decide that the return is not worth the time and trouble, *his* time and trouble. But that means he has to disagree with both his Group Manager and his Classifier, so Harry rarely sends a return back.

However, he may find his alternative not very happy either. "Oh, for Chrissake," he says, "I bet the damn computer kicked this one out because of the $18,000 casualty loss this guy claimed. But I know who this guy is. He's the one who totaled his Mercedes right after his kid got the insurance canceled. I read about this guy in the papers."

Harry scans the rest of the return and sighs, and for good reason. He knows more about this taxpayer and this kind of return than the computer, the Classifier, or the Group Manager. He knows that there is less here than meets the eye. The machine and everyone up there might be certain that all these deductions, especially the casualty item, are way too big, but Harry knows that this taxpayer and his Marvin are going to be able to document and hold forth very nicely.

Harry is trapped between a rock and a hard place. He does not want to send your return back upstairs and he is certain of a tough match. One thing, though, he knows for sure: he better not go through the audit and recommend "no change." Because if that happens, he's going to waste even more time writing a big report, and he's going to be called on the carpet to explain. In short, Harry will have violated the judgment of his superiors, and been faulty in his own decision to boot.

"If you didn't think this was worth an audit, why didn't you say so?" he can hear them asking.

But since he cannot tell them the truth—"Because you guys would have had my ass for questioning your judgment"—he knows what he must do instead.

He must make this audit successful.

And that means, *some* change. He knows he will be better off giving you a few dollars rather than conducting the whole audit and coming up with "no change."

So he accepts your return for audit, and then begins to look at it closely, mapping out an audit strategy. (We'll do it with him in Chapter 8.)

Altogether, a rather impressive system. Indeed, the IRS would like us all to believe that it's infallible. Try to get away with anything and it'll nail you.

In fact, however, the system, TCMP included, is not infallible, and they know it. The big net comes with some holes. Let me tell you about a few of the larger ones.

For starters, there is nothing much the IRS can do about unreported income. In fact, it is the biggest problem they have.

Before you get carried away by your darker thoughts, understand what I mean by "unreported income."

Don't think that if you fail to report your salary or wages and conveniently lose your W-2 forms, you are going to avoid paying taxes. If you have received a W-2 form it means that your salary or wages were reported by your employer. And that information has been given to the computer and stored there, waiting for your return to come in. When it arrives, the amount reported and the amount you have declared are immediately compared. If there's a discrepancy, there'll be questions.

So forget that idea. The worst place to cheat on your taxes is on reported salary and wages.

In theory, almost every source of revenue you receive is reported to the IRS. Certainly, every employer, full or part-time, will send in the appropriate information slip. Every bank will tell them when they've paid you $10 or more in interest. Companies will report what they've paid you in dividends.

In reality, however, as we know, life and people do not always conform to theory.

One huge area that escapes the IRS system is cash business. Some of it is small stuff. The $30 a week you give the cleaning woman. You don't report that, nor does she.

But some cash businesses take in more than 30 bucks a week. The IRS figures that the tax take on the Mafia and other illegal operations would amount to something between $6.3 and $8.8 billion. Short of that and less dramatic, but still vast, are taxes lost through the workings of the "underground economy." Restaurant owners, waiters, taxi drivers, the housepainters who moonlight on weekends, giving you an especially good price. The mechanic you find at your Ford dealer's garage. He does the work you need on Sunday in his own garage, does it well, and charges you half of what his weekday boss asks. Cash. Independent contractors give the IRS fits.

Let's call that kind of unreported income "blue collar." Meanwhile, "white-collar" types are not without opportunities, though they are a bit more complicated.

Every time we receive a Form 1099 information slip from a bank, or a mutual fund, the piece of paper tells us the amount we have received—the dividends from stock, the interest on a bank account—and it also tells us that the information is being reported to the IRS.

And it is. In fiscal 1979 the IRS received 500 million 1099 forms.

Some 400 million were sent in on computer tape or discs. The rest arrived as little slips of paper, like the ones you got in the mail.

They have your social security number on them, which is how they're matched to your return. This is called the Information Return Program (IRP).

In theory, the 1099s, like the W-2s, should be waiting for your return in the computer. And like wages and salary, the two figures should be compared.

In practice, we have something else.

Of the material that was sent to the IRS on computer tape, 100 percent was matched against individual returns.

Of the stuff on paper, still only 15 percent.

The IRS simply did not have the hardware, manpower, or budget to process the other 85 percent of the paper slips.

What did they do with them? Store them away, in case they audit you? Nope. There aren't enough warehouses in America. They shred them.

It's a real problem for the IRS. Commissioner Kurtz told a group of us not long ago that they "don't know enough about unreported income. Large omissions can be detected. But small ones, $2000–$3000 in unreported income, are hard to find, even when doing a detailed net worth audit."

You can be sure the IRS tries. In the TCMP audits, extraordinary efforts are made to dig up any income you haven't reported. With regular audits, they will question you very, very carefully.

For the first time this year, auditors will be supplied with all the data off those computer tapes. Comparing that with your actual return, they might just begin to perceive possible omissions. On close examination, closer than the computer was capable of giving you, Harry the Auditor might be able to deduct and intuit and say, "There's got to be more income here somewhere. Got to be. I can just smell it."

Also for the first time this year, the IRS is rolling out the Combined Annual Wage Reporting Program. CAWR really means that the Social Security Administration is now sending to IRS all of the information it has on you. Feeding those tapes into their computers will make it that much easier for the IRS to compare what you tell them on your return with what you're really doing.

So they're trying. But the truth is, they don't expect to make much of a dent. There's still going to be 85 percent of those paper 1099s unmatched, a point the IRS makes strongly during congressional hearings at budget time. Congress listens each year to these repeated arguments for more millions, but knows that the IRS is a little like the Pentagon in that regard. There can never be enough money, because the enemy and the dangers are growing forever more menacing. Only difference is, the Pentagon's enemy-client is the Russkies, and the IRS's is us, the American taxpayers. Though, to their credit, I haven't yet heard the IRS try to make the case that their enemy is even more dangerous than the Pentagon's because theirs is right here at home, on American soil.

The IRS is also trying to do something about brokerage houses. They represent a big hole in the system because they are not required to report security transactions to the IRS. That reporting is up to you.

When I was with the IRS, we would fantasize about having access to tapes in brokerage houses that showed what their customers really bought and sold. Matching those figures with customers' returns would be a sure way to pick up undeclared small profits. But it was fantasy then, and still is.

We were trying then, and the IRS is still trying now, to get Congress to legislate withholding taxes on dividends and interest, which we knew was income people were very lax about declaring. But Congress would not, has not agreed. Too many old and retired people depend on dividends and interest to keep themselves afloat. Many Americans on fixed incomes couldn't make ends meet if you withheld chunks, Congress always told us. Okay, but to us it was still taxable income before it was anything else.

Kurtz does make a strong argument that many of the holes could be narrowed, if not completely closed, and much of the noncompliance wiped out if only there was withholding on every kind of income.

He points out, correctly, that 98 percent of all wages and salaries are voluntarily reported by taxpayers. And the reason, he maintains, again correctly in my view, is because people know that those earnings are being reported by their employers, and that one way or another, the IRS will compare what the employers report with what employees put down on their tax returns.

By extension, Kurtz says, "withholding is the backbone of the American tax system." Where there is no withholding but there is reporting, such as on dividends and interest, reporting levels by t/ps drop to about 80 percent.

And where there is neither withholding nor reporting, such as with independent contractors, the self-employed, moonlighters, free-lancers, compliance levels are around 60 percent.

What Kurtz and others in the IRS are deeply concerned over is not only missing revenue dollars, but the effect of all the conniving taxpayers on everybody else.

Quite simply, they know that if you are a person who pays all your taxes, you are going to be at first annoyed, then increasingly curious, if your neighbor tells you about all the money he earned in cash, free-lancing, off the books.

And this is especially so during a time when all taxpayers feel the terrible burden of higher and higher taxes, of higher and higher inflation, of having less and less to keep for themselves.

What truly scares the IRS today is the reverse ripple effect.

That is why they are going quite crazy over the so-called underground economy. Every meeting of the Commissioner's Advisory Council keeps coming back to it. Agents everywhere have been issued special battle orders. And at the National Office, a new Underground Economy Staff has been set up, handling among other things a two-year study of the semi-invisible enemy creature, complete with "secondary information sources," which is IRS for informants.

This creature, part real and part imaginary, has always been with us. The IRS has eternally issued pious pieces of fantasy, which they call reports, on the millions and billions of tax dollars they would be able to siphon into the U.S. Treasury if only they could tax the Mafia. Just imagine, they said only this past year, if we could tax prostitution, drugs, illegal gambling! Wow! $15 to $20 billion in tax revenue! We promise!

Plain silliness. They have no more solid idea of what those businesses gross than you or I do.

There is, however, a much less silly side of the underground economy and it has nothing to do with godfathers. It has to do with very average, otherwise law-abiding citizens who are growing angry. People who are saying, "The hell with it. I can barely make a living anymore, and damn it, I work hard. I'll be damned if I'm going to give 25 percent of all I earn to those goddamn bureaucrats."

I am thinking especially of people who are employed in perfectly legal jobs, but they are jobs where there is little or no withholding. Next time you hire a mover, after you get his estimate, ask him what that figure would be if you paid him in cash. Ditto for any of those cash and/or self-employed folks I mentioned earlier.

Last year, *60 Minutes* did a fascinating show on the underground economy, and what was especially amazing to me was the number of people who talked to Morley Safer, on camera, without trying in the least to hide their faces. They did withhold their own names, but otherwise there they were flatly telling more than 50 million viewers they simply didn't pay taxes, and here's how they did it, and why.

Toward the end of the show, Safer, standing in front of the IRS National Office in Washington, said that he had tried to get the IRS to discuss this whole phenomenon on the show, and they turned him down.

They had no choice. If they had allowed him to interview them, they would have had to confirm that there were millions of solid Americans, just like the folks Safer had interviewed on the show, who were not paying their taxes.

I am sure, by the way, that the IRS will track down the very people Safer interviewed. It's too flagrant an insult and challenge to them to ignore. (The producer of that particular *60 Minutes* segment told me that one of the people whom Safer had interviewed was called in by the IRS for a massive audit some months after the show. The man has had his problems with the IRS before, the producer told me, but this time he thinks someone recognized him on the show and reported him to the Service.)

But it's not that handful, of course, who matter in themselves. It's the ripple effect again. And the IRS is going to do whatever it can to crack down. They know, especially in these times, that if good t/ps begin to think that others are not paying their taxes and getting away with it, before long you will wonder why you should be the fool.

Add to this the IRS's realization that more and more t/ps are searching for legal methods of reducing their taxes, through devices like tax shelters, and you can begin to understand how the world looks these days from the higher levels of the National Office.

There's another hole in the great system. It is all those deductions that simply can't be monitored. Deductions that tend to make the rich richer.

You're a vice-president of a manufacturing firm in Toledo,

making $60,000 a year. Thanks to your expense account, you're living very well, even though you are in a 40 percent marginal tax bracket, after claiming all deductions and exemptions.

When you come to New York, on business of course, you bring your wife and put her down on your expense account. A legitimate business deduction, you say, since you have to take X, Y, and Z and *their* wives out to dinner, because that's how to develop good relations which lead to good business in our great free enterprise system.

If you don't bring your wife, you might invite an old friend to join you for dinner. So on your expense account his or her name becomes Mr. T. R. Thorpe, one of your company's attorneys in New York.

The company accepts it, and so does the IRS.

Officially, the IRS says that all tax laws are equally enforced everywhere. In fact, they are not. They can't be. How can they take your claim for a business dinner at The Four Seasons and check it? Can they call T. R. Thorpe, Esq., and ask him if he actually broke bread with you that night at The Four Seasons? Yes, they could, but imagine what would happen to the system as a whole if the Service tried to police all the expense account deductions claimed every year.

The only time the IRS pursues the more than slightly questionable claims like these is if it happens to send Harry the Auditor after you for other, bigger fish and in the course of that he decides that you really are a crook. If Harry thought he was on the track of something big, he would turn you and your case over to a Special Agent in Criminal.

There are other soft and luxuriant spots in the system. If the president of a large corporation owns an apartment in the UN Plaza building in New York, or, rather, the corporation owns the apartment, is the IRS really going to determine how often the apartment is used for business, and how often for personal purposes?

No. Partly because it's like the deduction for dinner at The Four Seasons. And also because that fine American and his company retain excellent lawyers. The IRS knows it wouldn't be worth its time and resources to fight lawyers like these over an issue like this. Other issues, certainly, where the stakes are higher.

As Marvin would say: "Your lawyers are not as good as those of the head of Decontrolled Oil Inc. And he doesn't even have to pay for them himself. No. You got two guys named Arthur and Richard, and even if they could win for you, which I doubt, you still couldn't afford the fight."

The truth is the rich do get richer. And, as one of them, John F. Kennedy, liked to remind us: "Life is unfair." So is the tax law.

Let me mention one other flaw in the IRS's perfect system, known in the Service as "audit lottery," or "audit roulette."

The fact is that a very small percentage of all the individual returns filed are audited.

Of the 90.8 million returns from individuals filed in fiscal 1979, only 2.28 million were audited. Which means only 2.16 percent, 22 out of 1000. This is even lower than it was in 1978, and for 1980 I have seen projected IRS figures going as low as 2.07 percent.

Let me show you your audit risk by income category.

1. Standard 1040 Form, no itemizing. 28.7 million returns. .67 percent audited in 1978; same for 1979.

2. Under $10,000 Adjusted Gross Income, with itemized deductions, nonbusiness return. 2.9 percent audited in 1978; 2.5 percent in 1979.

3. $10,000–$15,000 AGI, itemized deductions, nonbusiness. 2.6 percent audited in 1978; 2.25 percent in 1979.

4. $15,000–$50,000 AGI, itemized deductions, nonbusiness. 2.64 percent audited in 1978; 2.91 percent in 1979.

5. Over $50,000 AGI, itemized deductions, nonbusiness. 10.4 percent audited in 1978; 10.55 percent in 1979.

6. Under $10,000, business return. 3.28 percent in 1978; 3.28 percent in 1979.

7. $10,000–$30,000 business. 2.03 percent in 1978; 1.81 percent in 1979.

8. Over $30,000, business. 6.68 percent in 1978; 5.77 percent in 1979.

In addition, during 1979 the IRS audited

• 2.55 percent of all partnerships
• 4.19 percent of small corporations with assets under $100,000
• 7.94 percent of corporations with assets between $100,000 and $1 million
• 2.59 percent of small business corporations (a special classification)
• 18.5 percent of estate tax returns showing estates with assets up to $300,000
• 46.17 percent of estate tax returns showing estates with assets over $300,000.

Statistically, then, your chances of having to go through the procedure are not very high, though the odds vary from group to group. If you are earning more than $50,000 a year and are involved in some tax shelter investments, you have measurably increased your chances for an audit. Nevertheless, because of the limited number of audits that the IRS can handle, you still have a very good chance of being left alone.

The IRS has always been terribly aware of its limitations here. When I was with them, our feeling was that we could never audit enough people or businesses. Indeed, we thought the government was foolish and very unbusinesslike not to give us a larger budget, so we could hire and train more auditors. We had the figures that showed that such an investment would bring a solid return.

But beyond the profit motive is the IRS concern that so many taxpayers who really deserve to be audited cannot be. They slip through.

I've heard Commissioner Kurtz on this. In fact, I was a bit surprised at how strongly he put it. If more people knew what a small percentage we actually audit, he said, we'd have an enormous number of taxpayers playing what he called "audit roulette." They'd simply take their chances.

Which, of course, is one excellent reason why the IRS tries so hard to scare you into believing that it is omniscient, omnipotent, and omnipresent, why they try so hard to scare you into "complying voluntarily."

4 | 24 Safe Deductions

Now for specific relief.

There really are safe deductions. Deductions you can take and not worry about. They will not kick your return out of the computer, assuming of course you don't go crazy with them.

We were aware of some of these items when I was in the Service, but they never meant much to us. We were so clean with our own returns, the whole idea of being "safe" was alien to us. That's what the enemy worried about.

But once I got out, of course, the world changed. Clients began to say: "You were on the inside. What are they really after? Are there any deductions that are really safe?"

So I began to probe my IRS friends, who for these purposes were mostly auditors and ex-auditors, and started to compile a list. To be sure, I was met by a certain number of blank stares. After all, the official IRS position, which is ingrained on the brain of every auditor, is that there are no safe deductions. The t/p must prove everything.

That's true, if you want to be completely literal. And auditors and even ex-auditors can be completely literal.

But in the real world, even they admit there are safe deductions. Basically, these are deductions the IRS doesn't care that much about, in comparison with other items on your return. In some cases, the IRS knows it's a deduction that you can prove too easily—medical expenses, for example—and that you do prove it. TCMP data and audit experience show them that the level of "voluntary compliance" is high, and the documentation is there. So why bother, they say.

In other cases, the IRS knows you're cheating, but the amounts you're padding onto—the deduction for "professional journals," say—aren't worth their launching a whole audit. If you do get kicked out and audited for some other more substantial reason, Harry the Auditor might also check out a few of these "safe" items.

What governs the safety of all of these items is "normalcy." So long as they don't grossly violate the "normal" range of the DIF formulas, the computer will not blink.

Needless to say, Marvin will not be able to give you the top secret DIF "norms" for your part of the country. But there is something he can do which will give you a ball park figure.

There are two IRS reports he can refer to and extrapolate from, and if he's worth his fee, he will.

The first is Supplemental Report, Statistics of Income–1974, Small Area Data, Individual Income Tax Returns, Stock Number 048-004-01492-1, Publication 1008 (12-77). For sale by Superintendent of Documents, U.S. Government Printing Office, Washington, D.C. 20402, at a cost of $6.

It is a breakdown by state, county, and metropolitan levels for individual t/ps. The IRS doesn't publish this information very often, and 1974 was the last compilation. So it's dated, but when adjusted for inflation, it will provide Marvin with some guidelines.

The other report is Statistics of Income–1978. In this one, there are a number of interesting figures. For example, taking a national average in the 1978 calendar year, we see that individuals with Adjusted Gross Incomes of $30,000 to $50,000 deducted $502 for medical expenses, $868 for charitable contributions, $2879 for interest they paid, $3007 for taxes other than federal income taxes, and $612 for miscellaneous deductions.

If that's your income group, you can see how you compare. But don't get too clever. Don't take a look at these figures and say, "Hey, I was low $500 for the interest deduction I claimed. Nothing like a little fine-tuning . . . I always say."

That won't work. These are merely national averages. What's average for one part of the nation might not apply to your district. Beyond which, making up numbers for your return, even if you can slip them past Marvin, is a very dangerous way to live. You are inviting fraud, you are inviting jail.

However, these averages can provide you and Marvin with some general ball park figures. So if, for example, you have much higher medical deductions or charitable contributions than the averages for your category, you know that your chances for an audit are increased. If they are legitimate deductions, you have nothing to fear. Take the deductions, and if you should be audited, simply present your documentation.

The averages can also be an aid to tax planning. If you find as you compare your deductions with the national averages that you are way off the mark, extremely high or low on some items, talk to Marvin about it. Maybe he and you are overlooking something. He might not be giving you something you're entitled to or reminding you to keep receipts on an item.

In those ways, then, you might find the following 1978 averages of interest and use.

If you have an Adjusted Gross Income of $20,000 to $25,000, here were the national averages in your category:

Medical	$ 561
Interest paid	$2280
Charitable contributions	$ 570
Taxes (other than federal)	$ 1875
Miscellaneous deductions	$ 455

FOR ADJUSTED GROSS INCOME OF $25,000 TO $30,000:

Medical	$ 498
Interest paid	$2455
Charitable contributions	$ 643

Taxes (other than federal)	$2245
Miscellaneous deductions	$ 479

FOR ADJUSTED GROSS INCOME OF $30,000 TO $50,000:

Medical	$ 502
Interest paid	$2879
Charitable contributions	$ 868
Taxes (other than federal)	$3007
Miscellaneous deductions	$ 612

FOR ADJUSTED GROSS INCOME OF $50,000 TO $100,000:

Medical	$ 667
Interest paid	$4585
Charitable contributions	$ 1824
Taxes (other than federal)	$5309
Miscellaneous deductions	$ 1135

I have recently updated my list of safe deductions. Items slip from safe to not so safe or to dangerous if taxpayers start to get out of line and overly greedy. As we know, the IRS is constantly monitoring that sort of behavior and fine-tuning its own mechanisms accordingly.

Let me share my current list with you, and I hope it does for you what it does for my clients, which is to give them a chance to relax when we're doing their returns. They know that these are deductions and credits they can take without worry.

1. Energy tax credits.   This one is safe for two reasons:

First, the maximum credit you are allowed is only $300. That's not enough to the IRS for an entire audit. The averages for 1979 over the whole range of incomes from $10,000 to $100,-000 amounted to only $86 to $137.

Second, it's safe because it's still relatively new. The IRS has not yet had enough time to closely determine, through TCMP audits and other sources, how honest taxpayers are being with this item.

One warning: there are specific conditions attached to this credit, so if you are kicked out for something else, expect Harry to verify them; as we'll see in Chapter 11, if you don't meet the conditions, you'll lose the whole thing.

2. Charitable contributions.   This is two parts safe, one part risky.

On your return, you are asked first to list the amount for which you have receipts. This is safe. The IRS knows that most of you won't claim $3000 when the truth is $300.

The next line asks about cash contributions for which you have no receipts. Obviously, this one is your word against theirs. Yet this is still quite safe. Even if you should be picked for an audit, you have little to worry about here.

The aspect of charity that might bring you some trouble is contributing goods valued at $200 or more. That's the third line on Schedule A for charitable.

If the contribution and your deduction are less than $200, the IRS doesn't bother. You claim $100 of clothes to Good Will? Be their guest. But with the more valuable stuff, they care, and the sticky point comes with the estimated value of the gift.

If you really want to get rid of that Georgian tea set, or if you're finally going to give that piece of real estate to the University of Texas, you could have trouble, despite your good intentions.

You must be sure you have an independent appraisal of the gift. (The appraiser's fee is tax deductible.) But be prepared nevertheless for a fight from the IRS, even if your appraiser is the best in the business. They have their own appraisers, and if your deduction is substantial and they feel they can cut you down, they probably will try. Appraising, after all, is an art, not a science, and their appraiser could very well come up with a completely different figure from yours.

The IRS has sixty-four people in the National Office in Valuation, and they are very knowing in their fields. The head of the department is both a CPA and a licensed engineer. Under him are specialists in manuscripts, paintings, oil properties, land, antiques, among other areas. And the specialists have outside specialists who advise them. The art advisory panel consists of several dealers who offer their sense of the marketplace and their keen vision for $50 a day and plane fare. As an offshoot of that panel, in keeping pace with the marketplace, the IRS recently established another panel of experts just for prints.

Don't expect a flying squad of menacing experts to storm into Marvin's office in the middle of your audit just because you've taken $10,000 on the nineteenth-century writing table you gave to dear old Duke.

What will happen is that Harry will check it against his catalogue price. If that is, say, $4700, expect that Harry and Marvin will compromise somewhere in between.

But if the spread is much larger and you and Marvin aren't giving more than a few hundred bucks, then Harry might well figure that you are worth some special attention. Then he would bring in an expert from the National Office, fly him or her right there, and you will end up being allowed a considerably lower valuation and deduction.

How can that happen when you've gone to the trouble and expense of having your own expert make the valuation? Since there are experts and there are experts, the burden of proof is always on you the taxpayer, and in case of a tie, they win.

Still, you've got those first two categories of charitable giving where you don't have to worry. Why? Well, it's not as if you're really fooling the IRS. They know you say to yourself: "How can they tell how much I actually deposit as I leave church?" They also know that later in this discussion with yourself, you say: "Still, it would look a little suspicious if I claimed I dropped $5000 onto the church collection plate. That's $100 every Sunday, which is really a bit much, even for a true believer like me." They know, in other words, that the amounts you invent are hardly worth great efforts on their part to retrieve.

Still, they don't want things to get out of control. So what they do is play a little game with you, or rather permit Harry to play it. The idea of the game is to limit the total amount you can get away with.

They permit Harry to develop a Table for Charitable Contributions. This is not something Harry sits down and works out with the help of the computer in Martinsburg, which is then issued from on high in the National Office.

Rather, it is something evolved by Harry and all his local colleagues. Agents in each region of the country decide what is "normal" for their districts. Based on their data, their experience, their knowledge of the way people live in their districts, they decide how much is "normal," according to income levels. And that's what they and the IRS allow you to claim.

They don't have a written table, like the sales tax table, so don't ask Marvin for it. But the game works as if they did.

Let's say you're showing a joint income of $50,000. Well, if you earned that $50,000 in Atlanta, the local Harry may allow you to deduct around $500 for charities, and he doesn't much care how much of that you can document. That may be what he and his colleagues in Atlanta have decided is "normal" for someone with $50,000 in Atlanta to give away to charities.

But if you made it in Chicago, and live in Lake Forest, the Harry up there may allow you $750 without any trouble. Is that fair? Yes and no. Perhaps people in Lake Forest do contribute more to charities than people in Atlanta. Maybe it's social pressures, maybe they just have bigger hearts. Harry is not interested in the reasons why. He's got the numbers. If he's in New York, and you're a taxpayer living in Great Neck, Long Island, he may give you $1200 for the same $50,000 income.

3. Casualty losses. This one is kind of interesting because it used to be a dangerous item. Losses from accidents, storms, floods, and theft used to be closely watched by the computer and by Harry. But in recent years the IRS has found that taxpayers have plenty of documentation for whatever they claim, and they have also come to understand how to compute the deduction.

To do this, take the value of the loss before any insurance reimbursement, subtract what the insurance company gave you, plus another $100, and what remains is what you are allowed to deduct.

You may take this on your Schedule A alone, but it's a little safer to combine it with a Form 4684. On that one you have space to tell the Classifier exactly what the loss was, while on Schedule A all you're giving is an amount.

4. Professional journals.   A lot of people worry about this one and waste time deciding what's really professional and what's just for fun. Take whatever you think can possibly qualify. The IRS doesn't much care because the amounts are relatively small. (Of course, small amounts upon small amounts can become a nice set of deductions.)

5. Home phone.   Another one that worries people. This is not the same as an office in your home. You are entitled to deduct for the business use of your home phone, even without an office at home. And you don't have to be self-employed to do it. You might well be an employee and still have to use your home phone in connection with your job. If you aren't reimbursed by the company, you may deduct those costs.

Without any worry, take all your long-distance business calls, plus 10–15 percent of the balance of the bill. If you have a special business need, I suggest you get a special phone. If you have a supplier on the West Coast and you're in Boston, and it's best to reach him late in the day—that means you're calling him at 4:00 P.M. his time, which is 7:00 P.M. your time, when you're at home. Or you have salesmen on the road you want checking with you at hours when you're at home. Put a special phone into your home and deduct the whole thing. And don't worry about Harry tapping your line. He won't, not for these modest bucks.

6. Medical expenses.   Though these deductions can be very high, the IRS doesn't pay much attention to them. Over the years, they have seen that taxpayers really do spend a lot of money keeping themselves healthy and alive. And they also keep all the canceled checks and paid bills.

Moreover, since you may deduct only that portion of your medical expenses which exceeds three percent of your Adjusted Gross Income, the amount of medical being itemized above that figure is greatly reduced. If you have an AGI of $40,000, you have to show more than $1200 in medical costs before you may deduct a dollar more. And those are costs, of course, not reimbursed by any insurance plan.

While you don't have to worry that your medical deductions will kick out your return, there is one thing to watch out for, in relation to medical, if you are selected for audit for some other reason.

Harry might have to adjust your Adjusted Gross Income. He might be able to show that the short-term loss you claim is really long term, or that you have undeclared dividend income or something else that will increase your income, and eventually cause your AGI to be higher. In that case, the three percent medical floor is going to be higher. And your own medical deduction will be less, by that amount.

It's not anything to worry about when doing your return. Take the medical deductions and relax. If you subsequently hear from Harry for an audit, you and Marvin in your pre-audit strategy session (Chapter 9) can estimate what you might lose in adjusted medical deductions.

7. *"Other" medical and dental expenses.* This is the line on your Schedule A that comes after your deductions for doctor, dentist, and hospital bills. The form tells you to "Include hearing aids, dentures, eyeglasses, transportation, etc." And be sure to do it, without a twinge.

All very safe, even if somewhat special, and I know that many people hesitate to claim a number of medical deductions because they fear the treatments are too special, even exotic. Or they worry about having a combination of an unusual deduction and an unusually high amount.

I received a most disturbing letter a few months ago from a woman who had read this book last year, and she was terribly worried that she was inviting an audit. She had an infant daughter who suffered from a near-miss sudden infant death syndrome, that horrendous, mysterious disease in which babies simply stop breathing, die in their cribs for no apparent reason. The syndrome had been diagnosed by her pediatrician, and he had told her to buy a special monitoring device for the baby. It tracks the sleeping infant's breathing and, if it stops, sounds an alarm.

Imagine the extent of this woman's fear of the IRS and an audit, that on top of her deepest concerns for her daughter's life, she was writing to ask me if I thought she should take the expensive monitoring machine as a medical deduction. She knew it was a legitimate deduction, yet she feared that the machine was so special and so expensive that she would surely be kicked out by the computer. She couldn't rest.

Of course, I told her to be absolutely certain she took that machine as a deduction. And if she got called for an audit, not to give it a second thought. All she'd have to do would be to produce her bill of sale and her canceled check for the machine.

The undisputed range of these "other" medical and dental deductions is extremely broad.

Face-lifts, breast implants, thigh-tapering, are all rather special, but still very safe deductions. Birth-control devices for men and women, ditto. Acupuncture is deductible, and so is Laetrile, in states where it is legal. Contact lenses and solutions to keep them clean, extra pairs of glasses or contacts, prescription sunglasses, are all safe. Psychiatric and psychological care and treatment are, of course, quite deductible.

Also, don't overlook transportation costs for medical treatment. If you're seeing a psychotherapist three times a week and taking taxis there and back, it can add up.

You are also allowed 9¢ a mile, if you drive for medical care. The IRS won't question that. However, they did go to court to keep a taxpayer from deducting an additional 5¢ a mile for depreciation on his car, and the court upheld the IRS.

One piddling spot to watch: the IRS is supposed to allow you the cost of any babysitters you pay while you go for medical care. But they don't want to. They've lost this in the courts, but agents tell me they are still supposed to disallow that item, if they discover it in an audit. The issue hasn't yet reached the Supreme Court.

Babysitter costs are pretty small amounts, to be sure. My

advice is not to list them separately, but toss them in with some other medical expense. That way you receive what you're entitled to, and you don't get the computer all excited.

8. Sales tax.   The IRS takes your word for this one. To a degree, they are playing that control game again with you, only this time they actually issue tables so that Marvin can give you an "average" for your income level and state.

Be sure not to forget any major purchases you made during the year. You are allowed to add the sales taxes for cars, airplanes, motorcycles, boats, trucks, and motor homes onto the figure in the table.

And also be sure you give yourself enough income. The higher your income, the more the IRS table allows you for your "average." So be sure you calculate not only on the basis of salary and other declared income, but that you also include all tax-exempt income, such as the untaxed portion of a long-term capital gain, income from tax-exempt bonds, social security income, VA disability benefits.

Add it all up to determine your real income, then go into the charts for your "average," and add onto that your Lear jet.

9. Mortgage interest.   This might well be the largest single deduction on your return, but it is about the safest. Again, the IRS has learned that taxpayers are fairly honest when they claim the interest paid on their mortgages, and that they also keep the year-end summary sheets from banks and mortgage companies.

There is one aspect of mortgage interest that does disturb the computer, however. As we have seen, the computer is not very discerning at times. In the year that you sell or buy a house, especially sell *and* buy, you are going to have an abnormally large mortgage interest deduction. All the computer knows is that the item is above "normal" and out of line with your declared income.

For example, you buy a new house in January for $120,000 and finance $96,000 on an 11 percent mortgage, over 30 years. You'll be paying interest of about $10,300 a year. Let's further assume that you have to pay two "points" to the mortgage company on signing. (A "point" is a charge of 1 percent of the loan.) That's another $1920 you will deduct.

In addition, when you sold your old house, you paid a prepayment penalty on that mortgage of 2 percent. Since you still owed $70,000, that's another $1400 you pay and you deduct.

All of which adds up to an interest deduction for you in one year of $13,620, and that to the rigid machine is suspiciously high for your income.

Let there be no question about your taking the full amount. You do that. However, be aware that the figure might be high enough to kick you out, or penalize you with a high negative DIF score. So you are unavoidably increasing your chances for an audit that year. My warning is, be very certain about all the other deductions and credits you have for that year. Your least concern is the large mortgage interest. Harry will give you that with a glance at the supporting papers. But there are all those other items he'll want to examine, to make the whole audit worthwhile.

10. "Other" interest.   No concern here. The amounts usually aren't enough to entice the IRS.

Still, people tend to be careless and overlook what they are entitled to. Credit card charges, finance charges on personal loans, department store charges that you spread out and pay interest on, and of course any major purchase involving loans, like cars, boats, vacations.

Several auditors have told me they don't even bother with this one in an audit. If they see the taxpayer has credit card interest statements and the rest, and other items have already been fairly well documented, they pass right over your amount.

11. Moving expenses.   This is an extremely safe deduction that many people don't know about, and cheat themselves out of.

Basically, the law allows you to deduct what you spend, within certain limits, to change your residence for business-related reasons, if you move 35 miles or more.

There are no limits on the amount you may take for the cost of the movers, or what you have to spend to transport yourself and your family from old residence to new, including lodging and food along the way.

The IRS knows that you'll have a receipt from the mover, and your food and lodging expenses are relatively minor. So for all that, be their guest.

They will also allow you other expenses connected with the move, but here they have a $3000 limit. This covers travel and living expenses you incur while finding the new place, temporary living quarters, and expenses from the sale of your old place, like closing costs, commissions, legal fees, etc., and similar purchase costs of your new place.

The catch here is that you will easily exceed the $3000 ceiling for such items.

In addition to the 35-mile condition, there is also a "work rule." You must be employed for at least 39 weeks during the 12 months after you move. Or, if you're self-employed, you have to work for double that time, 78 weeks out of the 24 months that follow the move.

You take these deductions, by the way, for the year in which you make the move, on the assumption you will meet the "work" requirements. If you don't, you're supposed to let the IRS know.

You may not deduct moving expenses if you simply move to another home because you like it better. The move must somehow be related to work—a transfer to another office in the same company, or a change to a completely new company and a relocation. But if you qualify, this one is for thousands of dollars, and the computer couldn't care less.

12. Political contributions.   This used to be a deduction; now it's a credit. Either way, the IRS attitude is indifference because the amounts are so small. You are allowed a maximum credit of $50 if you're single, $100 for a couple filing a joint return. And during an election year, the IRS expects everyone to be claiming this.

13. Union dues.   Another small miscellaneous item a lot of people overlook. Again, too small for the computer's attention.

14. Dues to professional organizations.   Ditto. Often overlooked, even though some of these can be more than petty change. They can matter to you, in other words, even though they don't matter much to the IRS.

15. Capital gains and losses.   Another one where the amounts might be substantial, but the IRS has found a high degree of "voluntary compliance." Perhaps because the amounts are big, and taxpayers realize they can either be proved or not, people are honest.

The computer is taught, "if it's neat, it's fine." You have 100 shares of IBM stock which you sell after three years, fine. Loss or gain, doesn't matter to the IRS. It's all neat and provable.

But, as we'll see, when you get into matters like personal loans, or dates on transactions that come close to the "more than one year" holding period, the dividing line between long term and short term, then the classifiers and auditors get curious.

While the neat, clean stuff won't trip the computer, if Harry calls you in for other reasons, he'll ask to see your documentation on those.

16. Dividend exclusion.   The first $100 of dividend income you earn is not taxable. Your special incentive to invest in the American economy. If you're a married couple, and you own stock jointly, make that figure $200.

No problem with the computer for that deduction. However, by taking it you are informing the government that you do own some stock, and so, if you get audited, Harry will definitely ask you about those holdings, as well as the others he suspects you might have somewhere.

Starting in 1981, this will become a joint exclusion for both dividends and interest: $200 for single people, $400 for marrieds filing jointly.

17. Safe-deposit box rentals.   If you keep investment property, like stocks or bonds, in a safe-deposit box, you have a small deduction waiting for you for the rental charges.

Obviously, the $10–$100 a year you claim is hardly enough to agitate the computer.

But this is a deduction we always used to think at the National Office was devised by the Service for a very sneaky reason. They want to know if you've got a box and they're willing to give you this deduction in exchange for the information. They know that you might very well be keeping more than a few shares of stock in there. Let me remind you, if the IRS wants to get into your safe-deposit box to see what's really there, they probably will. I have known a lot of people who would rather not take this deduction for that reason. They don't want to tell Harry any more than they must.

18. Personal retirement plans.   The computer passes over IRA deductions, if your employer has answered "no" to the question on the W-2 forms, "Pension plan coverage?"

If the computer sees a Schedule C as part of your return, no problem with a Keogh plan deduction.

Average deductions in 1978 on IRAs for taxpayers in the $25,000 to $50,000 income range were from $1350 to $1450. For Keogh plans in that bracket, $2200 to $3300.

If your company has no pension plan, you may set up your own, an IRA, contribute up to $1500 a year, and deduct it. ($1750 if you're married and your spouse doesn't work.)

If you're self-employed, or have free-lance earnings in addition to your salaried job, you're entitled to the Keogh. With that, you may contribute up to $7500 in most cases and deduct it.

The only thing to watch out for here is that you really do qualify for one or the other. Be sure and check with Marvin. The IRS has won a number of court cases against people who made innocent errors, and the fines are severe. Basically, if you have been covered under a company-sponsored, tax-qualified retirement plan for any part of the year, even one day, you may not contribute to your own personal IRA for that year. You may keep open an account you've already started. But no contributions that year. As I said, check with Marvin on this one. It's a completely safe annual deduction worth hundreds of dollars to you, and beyond the tax advantages, these plans can become a splendid retirement arrangement, depending of course on what inflation does to the dollar by the time you retire.

19. Personal property taxes, state and local taxes.   These are so automatically paid and checked that the IRS doesn't question them. Withheld state and local taxes are usually listed right on your W-2.

If you live in an area where your local taxing jurisdiction does impose personal property taxes, just be sure you keep track. Where I live, it's $4.80 per $100 valuation, which means $384 on my $8000 car and $1152 on your Mercedes. And neither one of us wants to overlook it.

20. Real estate taxes.   Another nice deduction that's completely safe for obvious reasons; so easily documented, so little chance of error.

21. Alimony.   Put this down, the IRS believes you. You deduct what you pay your ex, and she or he is supposed to declare it as income and pay taxes on it. But child care is not deductible, nor does ex pay any tax on it.

Just remember that the terms of alimony must be spelled out in your divorce or separation agreement. It might seem unlikely, but there have been cases where money was being paid and considered alimony, but it was not written into the divorce papers. The IRS disallowed, and the courts upheld. Also, the courts have sustained the IRS when it has said that so-called child care was actually alimony. It was not specified in the divorce agreement as "child care." If Harry audits you and sees alimony, he'll ask to see the divorce decree.

One of the things Harry will check on that piece of paper is the date on it. You have to be extremely careful here. Alimony is only alimony, according to the IRS, when you have a legal obligation to pay it.

Saul Bellow, the Nobel Prize-winning author, recently lost a $15,000 deduction because of a day in timing. He had given his third wife a $15,000 payment as "temporary alimony" when they were getting divorced. He had agreed to the amount in a predivorce property settlement, and the whole thing was affirmed in the final divorce decree.

However, Bellow's ex cashed the check one day before the decree was entered. When he filed his return for that year, Bellow took the $15,000. The IRS disallowed it, claiming that it didn't satisfy tax law. And on the technicality of a day, a federal judge said the IRS was right.

Though Bellow argued that the payment as part of the predivorce settlement was a legal obligation, the judge ruled that he "was never under any enforceable obligation to pay a set amount of alimony . . . until after the payment was made."

22. Dependency exemptions. What you put down as dependents in your immediate family will not be questioned by the computer. However, if you claim "other dependents" and fill in those boxes, the computer will take note. I have heard of Agents calling taxpayers to clarify that single matter.

23. Self-improvement. This one used to bother the IRS a great deal, but finally taxpayers learned the limits involved.

If you take courses that are related to your present work, you may deduct the cost of them. You may not deduct courses that are unrelated, that are intended to teach you a new business and allow you to shift jobs. The IRS doesn't care about your argument that you'll then be able to earn even more money and pay them even more taxes. Present occupation only is allowed.

Of course, at times, the way you define "occupation" can make all the difference. The IRS recently went to court with a taxpayer who had put his occupation down as "Executive/Administrator" and had then deducted the cost of getting an MBA degree. The court upheld the taxpayer. However, if you take courses simply to make you a more intelligent, better person, that's strictly your business. You like music, take the music appreciation course, but don't expect the computer or Harry to allow that one.

24. Tax counseling.   The fee you pay to Marvin for tax services and advice is deductible, as is the cost of this book.

Let me pull all of these together into a check list for you. Take it into Marvin's office in March when you go to do your return. Be sure he covers you on each of these. Though some of them might not be all that much in themselves, remember that they can add up. For example, you might have noticed that several of these will be listed under "Miscellaneous deductions" on your return. Consider some average national deductions for 1978 on that item:

$20,000–$25,000	Adjusted Gross Income		$455
$25,000–$30,000	"	"	"	$479
$30,000–$50,000	"	"	"	$ 612
$50,000–$100,000	"	"	"	$1135

As I said, these things can truly add up. And remember, when you take them you don't have to be looking over your shoulder. They are safe.

24 SAFE DEDUCTIONS
1.   Energy tax credits.
2.   Charitable contributions.
3.   Casualty losses.
4.   Professional journals.
5.   Home phone.
6.   Medical expenses.
7.   "Other" medical and dental expenses.
8.   Sales tax.
9.   Mortgage interest.
10.   "Other" interest.
11.   Moving expenses.
12.   Political contributions.

ALL YOU NEED TO KNOW ABOUT THE IRS   96

13. Union dues.
14. Dues to professional organizations.
15. Capital gains and losses.
16. Dividend exclusion.
17. Safe-deposit box rentals.
18. Personal retirement plans.
19. Personal property taxes, state and local taxes.
20. Real estate taxes.
21. Alimony.
22. Dependency exemptions.
23. Self-improvement.
24. Tax counseling.

5 | 18 Danger Zones:

The Prime Issues

There used to be a Prime Issues List, an actual secret written list of tax items that deeply disturbed the IRS. If you were audited and you had claimed one of the items on the list, you were in trouble. Until November 1974, Agents were ordered to show no mercy toward anything on the list that they encountered during an audit. It was an absolute position. If you hit one of those items, Harry was told, disallow it. Completely. If the t/p doesn't like your decision, don't discuss it. No haggling, no compromises. Either the t/p accepts your ruling or he can take the whole thing to court. Which, of course, was right where the IRS wanted to see it. One way or another, they were going to eliminate and disallow these items. Either Harry would do it or they'd find some federal judge to do it for them.

With the Freedom of Information law, the IRS got nervous about an official, physical list. So items on it became unofficial and invisible. For a few years, the thing was maintained mentally and orally, but enforced as always.

Now the list has come somewhat out of the shadows. It is called, a bit more respectably, the Appeals Coordinated Issues List. On it are still those issues the IRS feels most strongly about, but currently there is a special administrative maneuver in the way they reveal their feelings. You will still know their wrath, and you will still have no choice but to accept their arbitrary decision or go to court. But now there is a new, a higher, level of wrath.

It all starts out the same. You are audited, and there are certain items on which Harry will give no ground. He disallows the deductions completely. You and Marvin argue, offer to compromise, plead and beg, but Harry simply shakes his head. "Sorry. Nothing," he says.

At the end of the audit, he gives you an estimate of what your revised tax bill will be, and you and Marvin agree with all his decisions, except for, say, his intransigence on your interest-free loan to your sister, and your tax shelter losses. On those, he has disallowed everything.

You and Marvin assert your rights and appeal the audit, or rather, those two specific conclusions of the audit. You go to an IRS appeals officer. He or she is a person with real power. They can negotiate with you, to settle and close a dispute. Their job and authority is to close cases, quickly, and that's what they do.

That is, unless you come to them to argue over Prime Issues on the Appeals Coordinated Issues List. Then you discover that this normally flexible, fairly reasonable appeals officer is just as adamant and uncompromising as Harry was. "Accept the IRS interpretation," he tells you, "or take us to court. . . . Yes, yes, I know you have made a perfectly reasonable settlement offer, but I'm afraid I can only repeat what I just told you. On these two issues, either accept our interpretation or . . ."

Voilà, you have made the Prime Issues/Appeals Coordinated Issues List. The IRS pretends that in this way they are able to treat "an issue of wide impact or importance frequently involving an entire industry or occupational group, large groups of partners, shareholders, creditors, beneficiaries, employees, contractors, or other parties, which the Director, Appeals Division, identifies for coordination because of the need or desirability for consistent treatment by the Internal Revenue Service."

They only want to be fair, they say. All t/ps are to be treated equally. But their effort at even-handed justice does not extend to their telling you what's on the list, though they claim they will someday soon.

I don't know every item on it, though my information is that all but one or two of the issues relate to tax shelters. I do know, however, that every item I identify in this chapter as being part of the list is indeed on it.

So that you can have a fuller picture of what all the "danger zones" on your return are, I've also included in this chapter a number of other problem areas which are not on the list, but which will increase your chances of being audited. As a practical matter, I consider all of these items as things to be approached with caution.

Emphasis and the amount of attention the IRS gives to the various items shift. On December 4, 1978, for example, it issued the IRS Compliance Program Guidelines for fiscal 1979 to all technical personnel, which includes our friend Harry.

The main points for him as an auditor were these. Unchanged from the year before were special emphasis on:

• tax shelter programs
• corporate "slush funds"
• completion of all income tax return audits within the 26–27-month audit cycle
• violations by preparers

New items included the following:

• Focusing on "abusive tax shelters" by scrutinizing Form 1040, Schedule A for such things as charitable gifts of tax shelter property, Schedule C, and Schedule D for "Silver Straddles," and capital gains as opposed to ordinary income.

• Special attention to Travel and Entertainment deductions, as well as fringe benefits and perks for business executives, including disclosures of those made to the SEC on Forms 10K and information found in public documents such as proxy statements, annual reports to shareholders.

• Identify "tax protesters" for "appropriate examinations

and investigations." Pay special attention to those who file
so-called Fifth Amendment returns, which are blank, or make
arguments for a lower tax according to their interpretation of
the gold-silver standard. Also, watch for taxpayers who claim
"vows of poverty," or claims of ministry on the basis of a
mail-order ordination.

• Faulty family estate trusts being used to shelter taxes.

Last year, Harry received orders regarding three additional
areas marked for special examination and the sternest treatment (all of which we'll look at closely in this chapter):

• *Vacation homes,* which the t/p uses part of the time, rents
part of the time. A high-priority issue with the IRS this year.

• *Non-filers.* As part of the broadening war against the "underground" economy, "invisible" or "disappearing" taxpayers,
tax protesters—all elements the IRS is now furiously pursuing.
They believe that somewhere between 8 and 12 percent of the
people who should be filing tax returns are not. Once again,
here they shudder at the reverse ripple effect, as well as the loss
of revenue, of course.

• *Financial losses.* The IRS doesn't like financial losses on
the part of its constituents. Those are sad numbers. The IRS
likes happy positive numbers. So, a new campaign to fight the
sad negative reports, such as those business losses you claim on
Schedule C, or certain kinds of losses on investments.

What this means for you and Marvin is that there are some
18 areas of your taxes the computer and Harry will pay special
attention to. That is not to say that you should not take a
deduction in those areas, if you and Marvin believe you are
entitled to it. You definitely should, but you must be especially
well prepared to defend it.

Bear in mind that what the IRS considers, and what I used
to consider, a tax-cheating scheme, might be entirely legal.
What is a reasonable and prudent investment for you that
allows you to reduce your taxes may be viewed by the IRS to
be a rotten device worthy of a tax cheat.

Here, then, are the current danger zones.

1. Tax shelters.   As long as I can remember, shelters have infuriated the IRS, even when they are set up absolutely according to the law as Congress wrote it. The point of tax-sheltered investment is to encourage people to invest in socially desirable parts of the economy. When Congress wanted to encourage more housing, for example, or the preservation of historic buildings, or drilling for more oil and gas, it allowed special tax benefits. Shelters.

A simple example is that you and three others buy an apartment complex, each of you investing $100,000. With the $400,-000 cash, you borrow the rest and your partnership buys the complex worth $8 million. You use the rent from the apartments to pay the mortgage payments to the bank.

Your tax advantage comes in the depreciation you are allowed to figure on the buildings. You are allowed to use the depreciation deduction to offset any other income you might have.

In reality, those depreciation deductions are largely artificial. True, the buildings do deteriorate with age, but their actual value might very well be going up. How often have you seen that happen when a neighborhood changes and improves?

When I first encountered hostility within the IRS toward shelters, I remember telling one older colleague, "The things are legal, though. We should get the law changed."

"Don't worry, we will."

He was right. A number of shelters were eliminated in the Tax Reform Act of 1976. But some still exist, and so does the IRS's attitude.

It announced loudly that anyone with investments in tax-shelter schemes should expect an audit. That's the scare ploy.

Commissioner Kurtz pared that down. He said they were now auditing about 1 in every 4 returns where shelters with "big losses" were involved.

My IRS friends tell me that "big losses" mean partnerships

that show tax write-offs of $25,000 or more a year. If you qualify, the odds for an audit are 1 in 4.

Of course, audit chances for people with much sheltered income will be further increased this year with the new audit selection system based on Total Positive Income, discussed in Chapter 3. Instead of judging your audit potential by your Adjusted Gross Income, which reflects shelter losses and other deductions, the computer now will rate you by Total Positive Income, which is whatever income you have to start with, before any losses or adjustments are made. Your Total Positive Income is most certainly going to be much higher than your Adjusted Gross Income, and so will your audit chances.

More than ever these days, the IRS is focusing its energy on shelters. They know that shelters are no longer just for rich folk. They know that a soaring number of average middle-class people are getting into shelters, legal and otherwise, as part of their desperate attempt to keep a bit of the money they earn from being dissolved by inflation and/or taxes.

On March 17, 1980, the IRS issued six rulings to cover and tighten a considerable range of shelter activity. They affect:

1. Advanced mineral royalties paid or incurred under minimum royalty provisions.

2. Intangible drilling costs for oil and gas, limited partnerships, and correct year of deduction.

3. Foreign gold mine and amount at risk.

4. Advanced mineral royalties with cash and nonresource notes.

5. Foreign tax-haven double trust with income for benefit of grantor.

6. Charitable contributions, establishing fair market value, especially for gems.

Also this past year, there was a major IRS campaign against phony tax shelter promoters, especially those pushing art and gem shelter schemes.

These things, which seemed to be springing up everywhere, usually work along these lines: A promoter offers you a bag of gems or a painting for $10,000. He promises you an appraisal that says those same gems, that same painting, has a fair market value of $100,000. You hold the junk for a year, he tells you, and he'll line up a museum, school, church, some legitimate charitable organization, who'll take the stuff from you as a contribution, and then you get to declare the $100,000 as a charitable deduction.

Life is not so magical, says the IRS. When they come to audit you for that huge charitable write-off, as they fairly certainly will, Harry will dismiss your work of art, your baubles, with a single wave of his hand. "You paid $10,000, you get $10,000," he'll inform you, "because that's the real fair market value of this trash, and that's what the law says you get. You got a problem, go talk to the guy who sold you this garbage. If you can find him. But don't bother me with it. I don't want to discuss it . . ."

There are two people at the National Office doing nothing but trying to monitor shelters. They spend all their time reading about new shelters, checking prospectuses, offerings, newsletters, special reports from the SEC, and then trying to devise ways to close them down.

And in IRS regional offices all around the country, there are other people tracking down shelters in their particular districts, driving out to see if there really is an oil field with drilling under way, just as that prospectus for Super Sure Strike, Inc., promises its investors. In my IRS days, a few of us who loved to fish often thought life could be awfully nice if you were assigned to the Denver IRS office and had to spend all your time checking firsthand and diligently on all those trout farms that are sold as tax shelters.

The IRS is putting additional money and people into the shelter part of the audit program, and it has convinced Congress to stretch the normal statute of limitations on these audits. A partner, just like anyone else, used to have to keep his personal return available for an audit for up to three years. Now he is responsible for the partnership schedule of his return for yet one more year.

2. Tax protests. "U. S. dollars aren't worth anything. There-fore I didn't earn anything, and have no taxes to declare."

That's an example of what some people actually scribble right across their return. They are angry about some aspect of the economy, maybe inflation or the devaluation of the dollar in relation to other currencies, and so they decide to send their message to the IRS. They ought to send it to their congressman. From the IRS, the only response they will get is a certain audit.

"The only legal tender is gold," other citizens write. "Since we are no longer on the gold standard, federal currency has no value." These taxpayers send payment for only part of what they owe, for a reason that is obvious to them at least.

Some people are still contesting the federal government's right to levy income taxes. "The Sixteenth Amendment is not constitutional," they inform the IRS.

The IRS does not regard these people as amusing cranks. They take them seriously and prime the computer for them. The real concern is that the numbers of protesters is expanding to dangerous proportions.

With that in mind, the IRS has programmed the computer to be sure to kick out the returns of protesters, and it goes after those people with a vengeance. They have them broken down into ten neat types:

• *Constitutional-basis self-incrimination.* "I'm not going to tell you what's on my return," these crazies write across the front of their 1040s. "I'd be incriminating myself, and that's a violation of my Fifth Amendment rights."

Others cite the Constitution, or claim to when informing the IRS that they have no legal basis for collecting taxes.

• *Fair market value.* "The dollar is not worth anything, so I'm not paying any taxes," these folk argue.

Or, the slightly more sophisticated among them state, "I'm reducing my gross income. That's only fair, since the value of the dollar is declining to practically nothing."

• *Gold standard.* "You can't tax me because I'm not earning gold or silver. You bureaucrats won't let me, yet that's the only damn thing left with any value."

• *Blank forms.* Some t/ps send in their tax return, write in their name, address, attach their W-2 forms, sign their names on the bottom, and leave the rest of it absolutely blank.

• *Nonpayment protest.* "Here's my return, but don't expect me to pay it. Not the way you're running this country."

• *Protest adjust.* "My taxes come to $1000, but I'm only going to pay $770, because 23 percent of my tax dollars go to defense, and I don't want any of my tax dollars, not one cent, spent for war."

• *Mail-order ministries.* These usually include papers of some church, a vow of poverty taken by the taxpayer, various certificates of ordination, a statement about separation of church and state. Many of these so-called churches are patently fraudulent schemes, invented for the sole purpose of evading taxes. Others, however, are not, even though they might be quite unconventional. The IRS is involved in several major court cases over the tax status of religious organizations that are suspicious to them, and constitutional rights will be defined before some of those cases are resolved.

• *Protester letters and cards.* These people don't send their returns, just notes or postcards with a neat message: "This is all you're getting from me, IRS. You waste my money, why the hell should I give you more? You want more, go print it."

• *Family estate trusts.* An elaborate mechanism to avoid paying taxes, which we'll consider below. Not to be confused with legitimate trusts. The IRS makes a clear distinction and, for the computer's information, lumps these t/ps in with "illegal tax protesters."

• *W-4—excessive overstatement of allowances.* The IRS contends that taking ten or more dependency allowances is questionable. The more exceptions you claim, the less your employer withholds from your regular paycheck. It all evens itself out in the end when you file your return. But the more allowances you take, the less cash there is flowing into the IRS each payday.

Tax protesters do get a bit excessive. Some have claimed on the order of 100 dependents.

The IRS has heard all the explanations for all of this behavior. They know all about inflation, a depressed economy, angry citizens, and plain old crazies. And they don't care about the reasons.

In January 1979, the National Office issued a supplement to the Agents Manual on illegal protesters and how to handle them. It made very clear the seriousness of the whole thing, and the priority to be given to these cases.

"Tax protesters' returns will be considered priority cases by the Examination Division," it says. "Those returns will be expeditiously assigned to an examiner and the examination will be initiated within 30 calendar days from the date of receipt in the district Examination Division.

"Group managers should consider the potential hazards to personal safety of Revenue Agents examining these returns. Meetings between the examiner and the protester taxpayer should be held, where practical, in a government facility. The group manager may make other arrangements to facilitate the examination when it would not compromise the safety of the examiner.

"These examinations must be completed as expeditiously as possible . . ."

They're not exaggerating. Stories about Agents being attacked during audits by protesters are fairly common now. I've talked with Agents who have handled protest audits, and though they didn't have to duck any karate chops or right hooks, they all found it very disagreeable duty. They were verbally attacked, constantly subjected to political speeches. The various ideologies, as confused as they were, didn't offend them. In any audit, Agents couldn't care less about political or constitutional issues, whether the argument is coming from a screaming lunatic or the most elegant, reasoned, expensive tax lawyer in America. What disturbs them is that their time is being wasted. The Agents I've talked to about protest audits all had more or less the same techniques for handling them.

They'd anticipate the first outburst and suffer it in silence. Don't say anything, don't answer any of the psychotic questions about subverting the Constitution, about destroying the gold standard, about welfare/Pentagon budget/foreign aid. Sit there, arrange your own papers, prepare for the actual audit.

The watch ploy, they noted, does not work with crazies. Does no good to start looking at your watch, hinting that time is fleeting and you are a busy person, a hint a relatively sane taxpayer might observe and respond to.

With a howling protester, what works is to let him blast his first furious salvo, get it off his chest, and as soon as there is a pause, as soon as he sags a bit, cut him off and start going down the blank return, item by item.

Then the routine is fairly predictable. The Agent asks for information on each item and the protester refuses to give him any information. After a few items, the Agent says: "Fine. Then I'll fill this out according to the information we have on you. And since I don't have any information regarding any deductions for you on any item, I'll just fill out the short form, and you'll take only the standard deduction we allow." At which point, the protester can stop protesting or the Agent cuts him apart. One way or the other, the protester will pay taxes, unless of course he prefers prison. And if he does, the IRS is happy to oblige.

3. Family estate trusts. These are not to be confused with legitimate private trusts. What we have here is a scheme which on the surface meets the law, but in fact does not pass the IRS test of being legal in substance as well as form.

In theory, you contribute all of your assets—house, cash, salary, cars, stocks, insurance, furniture, everything—and place them in a trust arrangement. The trust is then supposed to be the tax-paying entity, rather than you, since you purport to have nothing for them to tax.

Then you perform services as trustee. Since all of the trust's costs are, in theory, deductible, you have the trust pay all your personal living expenses as a cost of its administration.

In the last few years, there has been a proliferation of these creatures, sometimes called constitutional trusts, or pure trusts, particularly in the Midwest among doctors, dentists, farmers, and others with large land holdings. The IRS has lept on them, going to court over a dozen times, and winning every case. In one not long ago, a Nebraska doctor lost in the courts and had to pay the IRS $70,000.

In fact, the promoters are the only people who do benefit from these transparent devices. They charge anywhere from $2500 to $25,000 for their special services. That includes setting the thing up and giving you all the guidelines you will ever need, as they put it, to rebut the IRS, just in case you are challenged. Be assured that you certainly will be challenged, and your odds of winning are less than slight.

4. Mail-order ministries. This one is complicated, as I noted, because some so-called churches are, first, ways to evade taxes and, only then in passing, distantly related to religion. Others, however, are active religious movements with substantial followings, which also offers ways to avoid taxes.

Following some sort of ordination, the new minister takes a vow of poverty, swearing to give the church all of his worldly earnings. He or she gives his salary from an earthly job, dividends and profits from investments in temporal organizations like IBM, everything, to the church. In return the church provides all his daily needs, which means food, clothing, mortgage payments, car, tuition payments, doctor and dentist bills— everything the rest of us are scrambling to provide for ourselves. These churches have also been known to invest in the businesses of their ministers, or start businesses for them.

Separating the legitimate from the fraudulent is a problem the IRS has put to several courts. Constitutional issues are involved, the IRS realizes, and they also know that they can't permit these new churches to exist or spread. What is especially troubling to the IRS is their discovery that so many of the members of these churches and the new ministers are by no means criminal types, or on the lunatic fringe. They found middle-class garbage men up in New York in one mail-order church who are paying no taxes, and they found a major in the Marine Corps assigned to special duty at the White House who was the leader of a small new church group. (The Marine major, needless to say, was whisked out of the White House when his tax status surfaced last year. He maintained the purity of his commitment to his church, and also allowed that his once very promising career in the Marines—White House duty, after all, is for the select—was no longer very bright.)

5. Barter. The exchange of goods and services has spread around the country in recent years, as have the IRS's efforts to treat those cashless exchanges as income and tax them.

There is one kind of barter they know they can't do anything about. That's where a person who is, say, a lawyer does legal work for an electrician, and the electrician then rewires the lawyer's house in exchange.

The IRS has said that there is a dollar value on those services, and the lawyer and the electrician should be taxed accordingly. But the ever-realistic IRS knows it'll never hear about such cases, so it doesn't waste time trying to find them.

But they have instructed all their Agents to specifically question anyone they are auditing, who is self-employed, about barter activities.

There is another kind of barter activity that is very public, and the IRS is actively going after it. I am referring to the companies that bring people together for barter purposes and collect fees for their matchmaking. Some of these operations are well organized, with people contributing services and collecting credits that they can use, like money, for the services of others in the organization.

What the IRS is now trying to do is get hold of the membership lists of those clearing houses and associations. When they do, they will probably audit everyone on them.

To assist their Agents, the National Office issued a new ruling in 1980 on barter clubs, with instructions for Agents on how to assess the value of credits a t/p holds from a club, how to calculate the value of services received and compute the income tax on them.

6. Selected occupations.   As I noted, there are particular occupations that attract IRS auditors.

Doctors, dentists, airline pilots, well-to-do artists and writers, performers and entertainers, the self-employed, people in cash businesses, and independent contractors have long been given special attention by the Service.

Lately, they've included car dealers, construction contractors, real estate developers, and real estate agents in general.

With the real estate people, the IRS has generally found that record-keeping is awful and, frequently, that agents work in a gray twilight tax zone. As we know, the IRS likes things black and white, not gray.

Often an agent's company will treat him or her as an independent contractor, not an employee. That way, the company doesn't have to contribute to any retirement program, or pay its proportionate share of Social Security, or cover unemployment taxes, health benefit plans, life insurance, or bother withholding any money from what it pays the agent.

The agent, in such an arrangement, has much of the security and many of the advantages of working for a company—his office and related expenses are covered, expenses on the job are reimbursed, he even receives regular checks, which are called not "salary" but "advances against commissions." The agent also assumes a number of the tax advantages intended for truly self-employed people.

For many in the "special occupations" category, in addition to real estate agents, the IRS has found the same bad record-keeping. Also, with those kinds of work that lend themselves to it, they've found patterns of especially imaginative deductions.

In other cases, they want to make a big news splash and scare all the rest of us.

For a number of high-income professional categories, the

IRS employs a special tactic. It rents mailing lists. To be sure, they are the same harmless mailing lists a magazine rents when it goes on a subscription drive. Only the IRS uses them in order to match the names on them to its own computer lists, just to be sure that all of those highly trained and successful citizens are filing their returns.

If you happen to work in one of those jobs that the IRS loves to examine, learn to live with it. You're not going to change your job because of it.

One thing you might do: You might list yourself as "Executive" or "Manager" if you are with a company, even if the firm is your own. A doctor who incorporates, for example, is entitled to such a designation.

7. No preparer on a complex return.   If the IRS sees that you have taken several deductions, and let's say that you regularly buy and sell stocks, make pension plan contributions, have a share of rental property, and yet have done the tax return yourself, they are very likely going to audit you.

It's not that the computer cares whether you have a Marvin or not. But chances are that with your complex return and all of those complicated and perhaps dangerous claims, you will stand a higher chance of having the computer kick your return out anyway. Then, when Bradley the Examiner reviews your return, he'll see immediately that you've done such a complicated return by yourself, and he'll be bothered by it.

You might argue that you don't need to pay Marvin, that you can do it all yourself. You were always good in math. Bradley and the IRS are not impressed. They believe that a complex return requires a professional.

And to a degree, the courts have supported them. There was an aerial photographer who bought some special and very expensive camera equipment. He bought it in the middle of the year, though it wasn't delivered until the next January. He did his own return, taking a substantial depreciation deduction and an investment tax credit for the equipment, starting in July.

He got audited, and was told that he couldn't take the credit and deduction for that year because those tax breaks only start after the equipment is put into use, not from the time you start to pay for them.

He went to court and the court told him that the IRS was absolutely right. He had to pay back taxes, since the tax benefits were denied.

Not only that, the court slapped him with a negligence penalty. The judge said he had a complicated tax situation and he had not consulted with an accountant or lawyer, and any businessman should know better.

8. Having the wrong preparer   Not only will you increase your audit chances if you have done a complex return without a qualified preparer, but they will audit you if you happen to choose a preparer whose name is part of the Problem Preparer's Program.

9. Office in your home.   A new addition to the computer program came after the Tax Reform Act of 1976. The computer is now extremely wary of deductions for offices in the home. These always bothered the IRS, since so many t/ps were writing off the den because that's where they said they did all that work they took home from the office, not to mention the elaborate personal research done to play the market. Mostly transparent nonsense, the IRS knew, but now there is a law to confirm their suspicions. The 1976 Tax Act says that unless you use the space exclusively for an office, and a full-time office at that, no deduction.

I was astonished and amused during my IRS days when an employee at the National Office actually sued the IRS because his deduction for an office in his home had been disallowed. He claimed he needed the office at home because his work required a lot of library research and the IRS library wasn't open nights and weekends. There was real embarrassment and chagrin around the National Office, but I had to admire the fellow, even though I thought he was a little suicidal. He finally lost his case in the courts.

Knowing how pleased my old friends in the IRS were about

that new provision in the 1976 law, I made a special effort to find out if the computer had been set up to kick out a return if it so much as claimed an office in a home. Even if the deduction was legitimate, would that mean an automatic audit?

The answer I got was no. In and of itself, claiming an office at home will not kick out your return. But it will carry with it a very high DIF score.

If you are still entitled to this deduction, take it and attach a note to the return explaining your reasons. It won't do much for your case with the computer, since it can't read. Some computers do have the ability to read, but the IRS machine is in fact illiterate. However, our friend Bradley the Examiner, as we have seen, reads very well indeed. So your note could make the difference between an audit and no audit.

You should be aware that in addition to red-flagging your return by this deduction, you might have some additional troubles in the future if you've claimed an office at home and then sell your home.

I heard of one case in which a taxpayer had claimed an office in his home as an eighth of his house, taken the deduction, and on audit had it disallowed because he had another office in his place of employment.

The man sold that house for a profit, bought another, more expensive home, and so deferred all of his gain on the sale of the old house, just as the law allows and requires.

But the poor fellow got audited once more. This time the IRS once again disallowed his office deduction for the new house but, beyond that, told him that since he had claimed one-eighth of the old house for an office deduction, one-eighth of the gain on the sale of that house had to be taxed as a long-term capital gain. That portion could not be deferred.

When the exasperated and disbelieving man pointed out that his one-eighth deduction had been disallowed, and so they couldn't now tax him on that nonexistent office, the IRS said, pay anyway. When he argued that they were being illogical, unfair, arbitrary, and subjecting him to some kind of double jeopardy, they issued a new ruling just for him, which made their position logical, fair, and the model of even-handed justice. They told him that the gain on his residence is deferred only when it's a *personal* residence. One-eighth of the house was used for business, you told us. And even though we won't allow an office-in-the-home deduction, part of the home was still used for business. So the gain on that part, one-eighth, is taxed.

Another case became somewhat famous last year in New York, where a well-known writer got burned the same way, all because she was fortunate enough to benefit from the inflated New York co-op market.

In this one, the woman had bought a co-op for $40,000 and sold it three years later for $240,000, believe it or not, giving her a profit of $200,000. During those three years, she had claimed 25 percent of the small co-op as an office. She used it for a considerable amount of free-lance work, work she could not do at the magazine where she had a steady job and another office.

The deduction each year amounted to about $2000, or a total of $6000.

She bought a larger co-op, paying the inflated price of $325,000 it commanded. When she went to her Marvin, he had to tell her that even though she was buying up, she would not be able to defer all the gain, all of the $200,000 profit she had realized on the sale of her original co-op. She would have to pay a long-term capital gain tax on 25 percent of that $200,000.

She was aghast. First of all, she didn't have the $15,000 or so for that tax. Second, she blamed Marvin, which is to say that in effect she blamed Marvin for the soaring real estate values in New York City, for her profit, and she fired him.

How could you let me deduct $6000 and end up having to pay $15,000 in taxes? she screamed. It did Marvin no good to remind her that in fact he had argued with her each year over that deduction for the office in her co-op home. Or that he had little control over the New York realty market. In normal times, the profit his writer clients made on the sale of a co-op was a few thousand dollars, so their office-in-home deductions over the years far outvalued any tax they had to pay when they sold.

Interestingly, the writer knew a number of leading tax attorneys in New York, and called around for advice. She got advice, never the same from any two lawyers, and in the end sighed, screamed once more, and last summer did not rent a house in Easthampton so that she could pay her tax bill.

Marvin is presently advising all of his writer clients, and any others with offices in their homes, co-ops or otherwise, even when the offices are completely legitimate and fully qualify for the deduction, to get out of them. Go rent some space somewhere, he's telling them, we'll deduct it as a straight business expense, and we won't ever have to worry when you go to sell your home.

10. Travel and Entertainment.   This is a traditional sore point with the IRS. In my days their attitude was, and still is, that people cheat here, that an awful lot of T and E are personal, not business, expenses.

It is one deduction that I have always thought sticks deep in Harry's craw. After all, about the only expense account item he has is bus fare to Marvin's office for the audit session. Only normal, I think, that he's going to resent the two thousand dollars you are claiming for fancy dinners and trips to Bermuda.

There's nothing you can do about Harry's unconscious resentments. What you must do is have adequate documentation for all T and E. With it, Harry might still give you and Marvin a hard time, but what you can prove as a legitimate business expense, he'll have to allow. Without documentation he will tear your T and E apart with a special zest.

11. Income-splitting techniques.   These are complicated devices that allow you to deflect some of your income onto your dependents. They still have to pay taxes on that income, but presumably they are in much lower brackets than you, so their taxes are less, yet the benefits of the income still remain within the family. The gift-leaseback is a good example.

Let's say that you're a professional person, a doctor, and one who pays attention to what you earn and what you keep after taxes. You are especially concerned about passing along as much as you can to your children.

At the AMA convention a couple of years ago in San Francisco, where there was more talk about money, taxes, shelters and malpractice insurance than there was of medicine, you heard about a fascinating scheme from Walter, your medical school classmate. A little surprising that it came from Walter, because in the old days he didn't seem very concerned about the mercenary aspects of the profession. He loved medicine, helping people, wanted to live the way he wanted to live. Passed up a chance to get a big head start in Chicago, where his father had a substantial practice, because he wanted to breathe clean air, ski, hike in the mountains. Walter moved to Denver. Well, now he admits that he's got air that's just as damaging as the stuff in Los Angeles, but he still skis and hikes, has a fairly satisfying practice, and—most interesting to you—he owns his own office building.

He went on at tedious length about that building, but two things stuck in your mind after that long evening. One was that Walter was somehow able to own, in addition to that building, his home, a condo at the base of Ajax Mountain in Aspen, a summer cabin on the Continental Divide—"simple thing, brook running by, couple hundred acres of nothing"—and a large collection of nineteenth-century American landscape paintings "which are someday going to make my children very comfortable indeed."

The other thing you remembered was a phrase: A Clifford Trust.

The week you got back, you called Marvin.

"Would it make sense for me to buy a building? Have my own building?" you ask tentatively.

"Building?" he replied. "Well, we'd have to look at that very carefully. Your name isn't Zeckendorf, you know."

You let that pass. Marvin's sense of humor is usually somewhat deprecating. Not insulting, exactly, but another way of saying, go slow, be conservative.

"Marvin, tell me, what's a Clifford Trust exactly?"

"You been to another AMA convention?" he asks.

"Never mind that, Marvin. Would a Clifford Trust, or something like that, make sense for me?"

"Clifford Trust? . . . Clifford Trust?" he says slowly. "Let me get out your file and I'll call you back."

Surprisingly, when Marvin calls back the next day, he allows in that endlessly qualifying way of his that in fact a Clifford Trust might not be a bad thing for you.

It takes a couple of years before you find the suitable building at the right price, but finally the whole thing comes together in life and on your tax form.

What you do, with Marvin advising along the way, is to buy a professionals' office building, and put it into a trust, called a Clifford Trust. You, along with any other tenants, pay monthly rent. You can't touch the rental income from any of the offices in the building for 10 years and 1 day. After that period, the building and its future rental income revert to you.

You have not only moved your own office into the building, but brought another doctor into your office as a partner. That helps to determine the rent, which you both then pay to the Trust.

Your bank is the trustee, and your children are the beneficiaries of the Trust, which means that they receive its income as it comes in. They have to pay taxes on that. But, as noted, they are in a much lower tax bracket than you, so they pay much less than you would if you were receiving the rental income on top of all your other income.

You have also convinced them to invest their newly found income in a college fund, which will make life that much easier for you some years down the road.

And, of course, you are entitled to the usual business deduction of the rent you pay for your office, even though you are paying it to your own Clifford Trust.

There is more to this tax-splitting technique, but those are the main points.

All entirely legal, if Harry decides three things in your favor.

First, he has to be satisfied that the trustee is independent. Your banker is OK.

Second, he has to agree that the rent you are charging yourself and your partner is reasonable, and not exorbitant. That, in other words, you are not shoveling money into the Trust and fattening your business-office deduction. Let's say he agrees that your rent is competitive for that space in that kind of building in that particular location of the city. (You and Marvin have been very careful that it is all of those things.)

Third, according to Harry, does this building and this trust make good business sense? If you can't convince Harry that it does, then Harry is going to say, "Sorry, this is simply a way for you to avoid paying certain taxes. And we do not consider that a good business reason. Avoiding taxes is not a legitimate business reason. If you are really trying to take some money and give it to your kids, then take some money and give it to your kids. You can give each of them as much as $3000 a year tax free. But giving it to them through this Clifford Trust, Doctor, sorry, we don't allow it."

In other words, you and Marvin have followed the form of the law to the letter, but you are not following the intent, the substance of the law. Not as Harry and the IRS interpret the law.

The IRS has been fighting gift-leaseback and other income-splitting techniques for years. They win a few, they lose a few, and they are continually in the courts over them. In any case, it's safe to assume that income-splitting is on the Appeals Coordinated Issues List.

12. Your children as payees of interest. On Schedule A, you have to list all the interest payments you have made and are therefore deducting. There is a line for "Home mortgage" and another for "Credit and charge cards." And then it says: "Other (itemize)."

If you list your children as recipients, "payees," or even anyone with the same last name as yours, expect an audit.

13. Interest-free loans to relatives. The IRS has lost major court cases on this one, but it continues to appeal decisions and it will audit you if you have made a substantial interest-free loan to a relative.

Why? What business is it of theirs, you ask, if you want to help out a relative?

They maintain it is their business because you are depriving them of taxes. The free use of money, the IRS contends, is unnatural. If you had put the money in a savings account or otherwise invested it most conservatively, you'd have income. And so, they argue, you should pay a gift tax on the value of the interest you could have earned had you charged interest to your sick old mother.

Or let's say you have a son or daughter starting a business and they need some help. A $25,000 loan can make a great difference to them, an amount you can manage. You're not in a position to give them the money, but lending is OK. In fact, you can afford to lend it, without interest. So you do. No stock, no equity interest, just a loan.

When you get audited, Harry will tell you you should have charged interest. That if you had left the money sitting in a bank you would have earned interest, and so far as he and the IRS are concerned, that $25,000 should definitely be returning interest income to you. And he'll figure out what the interest might have been and charge you a gift tax on that amount.

This, even though the Appeals Court supported the taxpayer in the famous Crown case in 1977–78, ruling that such loans were perfectly legal and tax free.

I'd better warn you, however, that this ruling is not good enough for the IRS. Until the Supreme Court upholds that decision, the IRS will continue to try to charge you a gift tax.

A footnote to this, helpful to any comprehension of logic and the tax law, and important to you if you are considering a loan to someone in your family:

The Appeals Court held that it was totally permissible to make a demand loan, bearing no or low interest. A demand loan is one where you the lender can call the loan at any time, "demand" it from the borrower, in this case, your son or daughter.

But what happens if you issue a "demand" loan and never "demand" it? Well, that's your business.

14. Family businesses. IRS mistrust of family financial operations extends to family businesses. Statistically, they have found that family and closely held businesses cheat an awful lot on their returns, make lots of mistakes because they can't afford or don't want to spend the money for good tax advice, and generally take the same proprietary attitude toward the income from their businesses as they do toward the businesses themselves: It's mine. All mine.

I remember an auditor telling me about one fellow who owned a furniture store. He had taken some of the furniture from his store for his new home. Natural enough. But he didn't consider that furniture as income. It was simply his stuff. It was his stuff on the floor of the furniture store. And it was his stuff in his house.

The auditor caught him easily. The man didn't know he was supposed to consider that furniture as income, figured at its fair market value. When the auditor saw that the man sold one home and bought another in the course of the tax year, he asked him how he furnished the new house.

"With my furniture, of course."

"From your store?"

"Of course from my store. Think I'm going to buy from my competitor?"

15. Death. We used to joke at the IRS that we'll even come after you in your grave. In fact, it is standard operating procedure for the IRS to audit the last two or three income tax returns preceding a decedent's death.

Grisly as it might sound, the IRS knows this is the last chance it will have to collect from that particular taxpayer, and it's going to make the most of it.

It's important, for that reason, that your executor know where your income tax records are kept, who prepared your returns, and any special tax situations you might have faced.

Estate tax returns also will be closely examined along with the returns of the last two or three years. Estates are complicated things, and for the IRS, full of matters of interpretation and evaluation. You say a necklace is worth only $500. The IRS might appraise it for $2500. Land? Houses? Paintings?

Recently, in auditing an estate, an agent went into a safe-deposit box with the executor of the estate and they found a collection of American silver coins. Together they added them up.

"I've got $984.50," the executor said.

"Right," the agent told him. "That'd amount to about $10,000."

"What? You just said . . . we just counted $984.50. How can that become $10,000?"

"I'll check out the exact amount. But everyone knows that silver coins minted before 1964 are worth at least 10 times their face value."

16. Vacation homes.   New on the list and a high priority for the IRS this year.

If you have a vacation home that you use strictly for your own pleasure, they don't care about you. But if you rent it out part of the year or all of the year, be sure and observe the complicated formulas and rules regarding how much you may deduct and for what. This is one to review with Marvin.

Basically, if you use the place for personal and nonbusiness purposes only, you deduct the same things you do with your primary residence—the real estate taxes you pay and all the interest on your mortgage.

In fact, if you use the cabin yourself but rent it out for two weeks or less, the IRS still doesn't care about you. You can take that income, tax free. Don't try in that case, however, to pretend you have a rental business going there which would entitle you to special deductions. All you can take are the real estate taxes and the mortgage interest.

It's with the other two categories that the IRS is edgy. Enjoy your little cabin. It's the gang from Fort Worth with their condos in Vail and Sun Valley, their A-frames near Lake Tahoe. There we find a mix of personal use and/or business rentals. The rub comes in the deductions.

If the place is a business, you can treat it like any other business property, claiming the full business deductions: real estate taxes and mortgage interest, of course, plus depreciation, insurance, maintenance, utilities, etc. You're allowed to use the business property yourself each year, for fourteen days or 10 percent of the rental time, without queering the deal.

There's yet another breed of rental home, one where you have a heavy mix of personal use and rental. In that case, you're allowed to take the special business deductions, but only in proportion to the amount of time the place is divided between personal use and rental business. If you use it yourself 25 percent of the time, then all the deductions are going to have to be calculated on a 25–75 percent basis. In addition, all of those deductions may not exceed the total amount of income you receive from renting.

As I said, check with Marvin.

17. Non-filers. As opposed to loud protesters, these people want to be invisible. They simply don't file returns.

Many get caught up in a kind of innocent psychological whirlpool. For one reason or another, they miss filing for one year. Then, instead of paying a small penalty and making it up, they avoid filing for another year, imagining that the IRS will come and electrocute them for having missed a year. And so it continues, the non-filing, year after year, until the pattern becomes entrenched and the fear grows absolutely crushing.

In reality, all that happens is a fine on the balance you owe. And you might not even owe anything. A young man came to me not long ago, terribly shaken. He was about to get married, he told me, and he knew that the following April he and his wife would file jointly. He confessed that he hadn't filed for five years, for the common reasons I cite above, and for five years he had been plagued with worry. Now all he could imagine was that come next April, he and his bride were headed for jail.

I assured him otherwise and helped him pull his returns together. The fact was that he had been employed during those five years, and his withholding had more than covered his taxes and the penalties. If you like happy endings, this young man received a refund in excess of $3000, a special wedding gift from the Internal Revenue Service.

The IRS, however, is not famous for its wedding gifts. To the contrary these days, it is disturbed by its estimate that some 8 to 12 percent of the citizens who should be paying taxes are not filing.

As usual, they aren't interested in why. They now have a major non-filer program going, matching information wherever they can get it. They're searching their own files to see who has disappeared from the ranks. They are getting tapes from the Social Security Administration and matching information on those tapes about wages and withholding with Social Security numbers. They're matching every Social Security number in the country with their own taped files, and if someone has a Social Security number but is not filing a federal tax return, they send out a letter asking for an explanation.

There are times, of course, when you can have one and not the other, when you can have a Social Security number and not have earned enough income to file, for example. But if the explanation is not forthcoming, the IRS will be.

18. Financial losses.   Another new one this year is certain kinds of financial and business losses. I'm not talking about simple losses you take in the market, but more complicated stuff.

Like that company you invested in and took ten shares of its stock. Nice people, lousy businessmen, and they've closed their doors. However, they haven't declared bankruptcy. Still, you know that place is finished and the stock is worthless, so you try to deduct your loss.

Harry won't allow that. Technically, legally, he reminds you, that company is still in existence, and you still own the stock.

"Yes," you say, "but the company is dead and the stock is worthless."

"Prove it to me," Harry says. "Ever see a company rise from the ashes? Happens all the time."

"I don't believe in miracles, Mr. Harry. This company is dead."

"If they declare legal bankruptcy," he says, "then you might be entitled to some loss. Or if you sell those ten shares and that results in a loss, then obviously you're entitled. Otherwise . . ."

"Mr. Harry, they don't seem to want to declare bankruptcy, and would you mind telling me who is going to buy ten shares of a dead company from me?"

"OK, let's move to the next item . . ."

If the next item on Harry's agenda in this audit is Schedule C losses, you're really in trouble. If you're filing a Schedule C, Profit or (Loss) from Business or Profession (Sole Proprietorship), your business had better have a reasonable expectation of a profit or Harry's going to call it a hobby, not a business, and disallow all your deductions in the supposed pursuit of business profit. If you show $1500 in expenses spent in order to earn $500 for free-lance consulting work, you're not going to get Harry to take that business seriously.

Finally, in this loss category, there are nonbusiness bad debts.

A man called me recently with just this kind of problem. He had a house built for him, and when the place was 80 percent finished, the contractor took the last 20 percent of the money and vanished. The owner got someone else to complete the job, for a new 20 percent. He took the original 20 percent as a loss, and an IRS auditor disallowed it.

The man is still fighting the case. One mistake he did make was not taking Marvin into the audit with him. I believe it's wise to take Marvin into any audit, unless it's a very simple affair (all of which we'll consider in Chapters 9, 10, and 11). Certainly, if you have any of the danger zone items on your return, you should not be confronting Harry in an audit alone.

To summarize, here at a glance are the danger zones:

1. Tax shelters.
2. Tax protests.
3. Family estate trusts.
4. Mail-order ministries.
5. Barter.
6. Selected occupations.
7. No preparer on a complex return.
8. Having the wrong preparer.
9. Office in your home.
10. Travel and entertainment.
11. Income-splitting techniques.
12. Your children as payees of interest.
13. Interest-free loans to relatives.
14. Family businesses.
15. Death.
16. Vacation homes.
17. Non-filers.
18. Financial losses.

6 | Where Does It Say
That the IRS Has to
Be Logical and Fair?

Prime Issues are hardly something to be cheery about, but at least you can grasp the issues involved and the way the IRS feels toward them. This is the way the game is played. You claim some paper losses from a shopping center investment, they are going to come after you.

But then there are other matters—and frankly, they verge on the mystical—when it seems that it is not the DIF and the computers that snare you, not even Harry, their human emissary. Instead, it seems as if you have been cracked by some transcendent force, so unfair and unthinkable is it all.

I am speaking of the countless inherent inequities of the tax law and the countless interpretations of the law by the IRS when it is at its most arbitrary and illogical.

In the IRS we were only too aware that Congress wrote the tax laws, not us. We were supposed to enforce those laws and collect the money.

In order to enforce them, the IRS must interpret them. And therein lies one of its real sources of power. It is a power that often makes the IRS look like a separate and sovereign government, not merely a branch of the Treasury Department.

We always used to say that the tax law was a living, changing thing. Indeed, that was part of its intellectual attraction to us, the way it was being reshaped continually by Congress, the courts, the public, and the IRS.

What remained constant in the Service was the paranoid attitude toward you, our enemy in the eternal war. It justifies a harsh and mean application of the law.

The result was, and is, that so far as taxes are concerned there is only one game in town; you must play, and the rules are pretty much made up by the IRS, which can and does change them as it goes along.

Here is a handful of cases that will show you specifically what I mean.

One of my favorite examples involves something most of us do every day, commute.

Let's say you live an hour outside the city where your office is. You take the 8:02 each morning to the office and the 6:14 each evening back home.

If you try to deduct the cost of that commutation ticket, it will be disallowed. Harry will simply tell you that going back and forth to your office is a personal expense, not a business expense, and personal expenses are not deductible. Let you have that one, next thing we know you'll want a deduction for the suit you bought to wear on the train and in the office.

Your next-door neighbor, however, is self-employed, and works out of her home. Most of her business is with clients in the city, the city where you work. And in fact two or three days a week she rides the train with you.

Well, every time your neighbor takes that train she deducts the cost of the ticket. Same train, for the same reasons: to earn her living. But she is allowed the deduction and you are not. Why? Because the law and the IRS say so.

You can argue with Harry all you want that you are also in the business of making a living. It will do you no good. If you are an employee, and you have to get to your job, the expense is not tax deductible. If you are self-employed, working out of your home, the cost of traveling from your so-called office to a client and back again is tax deductible. Fair? Hardly. Logical? No. It's just the law.

Uh, usually. Just this last year I received a call from a man who had read the first edition of this book, and who thought he understood something about commuting and self-employeds.

He worked for himself, and his office was attached to his home with its own private entrance. Indeed, one of the pleasures of being self-employed was that he had no lousy commuter train to mess with each morning. Simply walked next door.

He kept a special car for business traveling, and deducted all the expenses he was entitled to for that. But on audit, a portion of those car expenses was disallowed.

"I'm only going to allow 80 percent of that," the auditor told him.

"Why 80 percent? All my business driving is done with that car," he replied. "No personal driving. We have two other cars in the family for that. I'm entitled to the whole thing, 100 percent."

"Well, some of it has to be for commuting expense," she said.

"Commuting?" he said. "Excuse me, Mrs. Harriet, but that doesn't make any sense at all."

"Why not?"

"Because my office is attached to my house. I don't commute. Haven't for fourteen years."

"How do you get to your business car?"

"I don't commute to it," he answered, "if that's what you're thinking. I walk to the other side of the house and open the garage door."

She listened, shook her head, and wouldn't give in. Only 80 percent, she maintained. But she did agree to leave the matter open, and moved to the next item on the audit.

The man knew that the IRS could be totally illogical and arbitrary, but this one seemed too preposterous, and her willingness to leave it on the table made him wonder if in fact she was holding it out as a negotiating chip.

It turned out she was. As he correctly imagined, she was determined to come up with something from this audit. So she concocted the absurd idea that a man whose office is attached to his house commutes to it, and a little while later, she traded him back that 20 percent for a disallowance on another item, one with a touch more reality about it. The two amounts more or less washed out, the man was not punished for not commuting, and the auditor could report some change on the return, slightly justifying all the time she had invested in the whole process.

Supposing you decide that the cost of commuting is just one more reason to move back to the city. You sell your home and make a profit on the sale of the house you bought five years ago.

If you buy a home in the city that is more expensive, you do not have to pay any taxes on your profits, now. You defer taxes on the gain you made from the sale of your old house. Or, if you are fifty-five or over, according to the 1978 Tax Law, you might be able to exclude some or all of your profit from taxes.

But let's imagine that you decide you are really tired of owning. What you and your wife want now, especially with the kids grown up and on their own, is a rental, a nice apartment where you don't have to worry about fixing things that go wrong. In that case, you might have chosen a pleasant new way to live, but you are going to have to declare your profit on the sale of the house in the suburbs, and you are going to have to pay a tax on that capital gain.

If, however, all of the above were true, except that you sold the house at a loss, you would not be allowed to deduct the loss.

That's right, if you make a profit, you pay taxes, but if you sustain a loss, you may not deduct it.

Suppose you suffered a big stock loss, and you sold your house at a gain, then moved to a more expensive residence. The IRS won't let you use your profit from the house to offset your loss in the market. If you have a profit from the sale of your house, and buy up, you *must* defer the taxes you would normally pay on that gain. You can't say to them: "Look, I want to declare that capital gain this year, when I've got some long-term capital losses in the market." They won't listen. What you are proposing might be perfectly logical. That doesn't matter to them. What matters to them is that what you are proposing is good for you. They don't want that and won't permit it.

Many of us in recent years have stopped smoking, for extremely good reasons. We have read, or our doctors have told us, that if we smoke we will get cancer, develop heart problems, lung problems, and, generally speaking, kill ourselves.

The IRS is not moved.

If you spend money to break the habit, you may not deduct those expenses. Even if your doctor tells you to go to one of the clinics or courses, no deduction.

However, if you spend money for yourself or a dependent to be treated for drug abuse or addiction, or alcoholism, that is deductible as a medical expense.

The difference, according to the IRS? Watch closely. They maintain that drug and alcohol problems are medical problems in themselves. But smoking in and of itself is not a disease, it only *leads to* medical problems.

Question that, as I have during an audit, and you are simply told, "That is the IRS interpretation." Period.

You might be interested in knowing that although you may not deduct the cost of breaking the cigarette habit, which is to say, you may not deduct the cost of saving your own life, you are entirely welcome to deduct the cost of plastic surgery to make yourself look years younger. Or of a tummy tuck, to make yourself look pounds lighter.

However, if you're a heart-attack victim and you spend money for exercise equipment so you can give yourself a better chance of staying alive, don't expect the IRS to allow you any deduction for that equipment.

Often the law itself is written with illogical elements carefully set in it. In those cases, the IRS doesn't have to issue baffling interpretations. All it has to do is follow the letter of the law as Congress wrote it.

The wonderful energy credit is a fine example. The President said we should conserve energy, and asked Congress to allow people who spend money on storm windows, insulation, and the like in their homes to claim a tax credit for some of those expenses.

Congress said fine, all taxpayers who are also good citizens and save energy may claim as a tax credit 15 percent of the first $2000 they spend, up to a maximum of $300. Better than nothing, I suppose, and some kind of encouragement.

But, among other restrictions, Congress said that the house had to be built, or substantially constructed, *before* April 20, 1977. Which means that all new homes are excluded. Why? Because, in this case, Congress says so. And the IRS is delighted to support them.

There's an administrative ruling of the IRS that is especially mean, even for the IRS.

When Marvin is finished doing your return, he gives you some good news. He tells you that you have a tax refund coming of $3000. And you have a choice. You may have the IRS send you a check for that amount, or you may apply it toward your taxes for the coming year.

Naturally, your first reflex is to take the money. Marvin reminds you, however, that you're going to have a quarterly estimated tax to pay in a few months, so why not let the money ride? Again, being conservative, he thinks that you look on this as found money. And found money is to be spent on a great spring skiing holiday in Zermatt, maybe a quick detour on the way home through Paris. That's how Marvin reads your mind. Wasteful, he thinks, and what's worse, you never have any cash anyway, no matter how much you earn. You always have such a struggle to make those quarterly payments.

So this time Marvin pleads with special eloquence, and convinces you to apply the refund to next year's taxes. A happy man, he fills in Line 65: "Amount of line 63 to be credited on 1981 estimated tax . . . $3000."

For days the sheer virtue of it all almost makes up for a couple of weeks in the Swiss Alps. You have not only been prudent, you have been patriotic. You have lent the government $3000, interest-free.

Then a strange and terrible thing happens. A few months later, you receive a computer-generated notice from the IRS. There was a mistake on your return. It's one of those honest mistakes I told you about. There's no suggestion of fraud; they aren't accusing you of trying to evade taxes. It's just a simple mathematical error. In fact, it's a mistake Marvin made. He used the wrong table to figure your tax, or added incorrectly, or used the wrong column. As we know, the computer picks up those simple, honest mistakes quickly.

The form letter, disturbing as it is, at least is not a summons. You can see you are not going to jail for the mistake, for Marvin's mistake for Chrissake, but you have to pay some money. The miscalculation means that your refund of $3000 should have been only $1800. Which in turn means you have to pay the difference of $1200, plus interest and a penalty.

Painful, you think, but it could be worse, much worse. This is all paper money. Instead of getting $3000, you get only $1800.

You call Marvin and give him the news and he is appropriately contrite and apologetic. "What can I tell you? We all make mistakes," he sighs, then adds: "Don't worry about the interest and penalty. I'll pay that."

"Marvin, don't be ridiculous. You don't have to do that." You feel badly for him.

"Absolutely," he replies, "I couldn't do business any other way. I stand behind my work, and I'm a careful man. But every once in a while, I make a mistake, and I'm not going to have my clients paying for my mistakes. Fortunately, these occasions are rare. But when they happen it's my responsibility."

"Well, okay, Marvin," you say, "that's very good of you. Now what do I have to do, sign another form?"

"No, you don't need a form. Just send them a check for . . . for how much? $1200? Is that what you said?"

You shake your head and wonder what's happening to dear old Marvin. "Marvin, have you forgotten? We had a refund coming. You figured it to be $3000, and we were going to apply that to next year's taxes. Now they say the refund will be only $1800. I don't have to send them any check. Simply tell them to apply the $1800 against my next year's taxes."

There is a long pause on Marvin's end, followed by a moan and some coughing.

"Marvin, Marvin, are you all right?"

"Yes, I'm all right. But I'm afraid I have some bad news for you."

"What?"

"They won't do that."

"Do what?"

"Simply apply the $1800. You've also got to send them a check for the difference between the $3000 we claimed and the $1800 they came up with. You've got to send them a check for $1200."

"But that's crazy. I've got a refund of $1800 coming, even they say that. Why can't they apply that instead of the $3000 and be done with it? All they have to do is push another button on the computer."

"They already pushed the button. They applied the $3000 as we told them to. They've already applied that amount to next year's taxes."

"Yes, but that was before they knew, or we knew, that there had been an honest mistake. Now what they have to do is erase that figure and put in the correct one."

"They won't do it. You have to send them a check."

"But that's crazy, Marvin. Here I was trying to be a good citizen, paying my taxes early, and they're going to punish me for it?"

"What can I tell you? That's the revenue ruling."

"But it's the simplest kind of bookkeeping. Erase one figure and write in another. Don't make me come up with another $1200. That's outrageous."

"I guess the computer can't erase."

The truth is the IRS doesn't want to bother. What is money to you is administrative inefficiency for them. This way, they don't have to waste any human or computer time retrieving

your return and making the correction. And, after all, they
figure, it's your mistake. Your mistake in arithmetic to begin
with, and your further mistake to give them money before you
have to. If you're going to be that careless and stupid in the
great war, they will happily zap you.

The IRS, we know, is very suspicious of any financial dealings
between you and your relatives, especially if the dealings result
in any tax write-offs for you. This time, they do have the tax
law on their side. The law is quite clear that no deductions are
allowed for losses that you might sustain from sales or exchanges of property, directly or indirectly, between family
members.

At one level, that makes sense. It means that you, the father
or mother, can't take ten acres of property that you bought for
$1000 an acre, and sell it to your daughter for $100 an acre, and
claim a tax loss.

If you could, you would of course take the loss as a deduction, and the land would still be in the family.

That's not allowed. Unless, of course, your daughter is married, and you sell the same land, for the same price of $100 an
acre, to her husband, your son-in-law. In that case, you are
entitled to the tax loss, and the land still remains within the
family.

How come? For good reason, according to the IRS. The tax
rules list exactly who is a tax relative. Relatives are brothers,
sisters, spouse, parents, grandparents, children. In-laws are not
mentioned. So what you may not sell at a loss to your daughter,
you may sell at a loss to her husband.

Perhaps by now you know even before I tell you that you may
sell at a *profit* to *any* relative, blood or otherwise, and you will
be taxed on that profit. But even here the IRS has been known
to investigate—if they didn't think the profit was large enough,
if they thought you were being unbusinesslike or insufficiently
greedy with your relative.

Here is a dreadful story, which I'm afraid will pain anyone who owns any property and pays real estate taxes.

As you know, the law allows you to deduct the amount you pay for real estate taxes in the year you pay them. Indeed, for many people, this is one of the larger deductions they take. It is one of the joys of owning your own home.

Well, this is about a homeowner who, just like you, sent in a check every month to his mortgage company to cover the principal and interest on his mortgage and the local real estate taxes.

When he received his annual statement from the company, he checked over the figure for mortgage interest as one deductible item, and the amount for local taxes as another.

He took the deductions on his return, all pretty automatic, he thought, until the IRS notified him that they were disallowing part of his deduction for local taxes.

It seems that even though he had made his payments on time each month, people at the mortgage company had not. They had taken a couple months' worth of tax payments from him and others, and invested it. When it was time to pay local taxes with that money, they delayed. They were waiting for their investment to mature, figuring that their profits would easily cover any penalties for late payments they might receive.

When the investments paid off, they in turn paid the local taxes, and the small penalties. But our taxpayer was punished. They were two months late paying his taxes, even though he had faithfully paid them right on schedule. Nevertheless, the IRS said that only the amount actually paid to the local taxing authority during the year was deductible by the taxpayer, and the Tax Court and Court of Appeals sustained them.

One final case that transcends all others I know of as an example of how the whole tax system—the IRS, tax law, the courts —can work. Totally irrational.

Two men incorporated their finance business in Tennessee as a subchapter S company. We don't have to get too technical, but in a subchapter S, all of the company's profits and losses are passed directly through to the shareholders. If there are profits, the shareholders are taxed at the normal rate for personal income. There is no corporate tax on a subchapter S firm. But if there are losses, the shareholders may personally take any immediate tax advantages of the corporation's tax losses.

Obviously, if the shareholders of a subchapter S corporation have other sources of income, those losses are useful. And losses are common in the early years, while the company is being developed.

That's what happened in this case. There were losses, and the two owner-shareholders deducted them. Then the company got audited and the IRS said that the firm had not conformed to all the stringent requirements under subchapter S, and so all those deductions taken by the partners were going to be disallowed, retroactively.

The owners went to Tax Court. The Tax Court upheld the IRS. It said that the IRS had interpreted the law correctly, and the partners would have to pay the deficient taxes.

Or rather, it said that one of the partners would have to pay and the other would not. Their reason had nothing to do with differences between the owners, as you might imagine. The cases were exactly the same. The Tax Court's reason had to do with the fact that one taxpayer lived in Alabama, while the other lived in Missouri.

What difference should that make, you ask, to a federal law? Fair question. The answer is: The Golsen Rule.

According to the Golsen Rule, adopted by the U. S. Tax Court in the name of efficiency, the Tax Court will abide by the decisions of the Appeals Court of the district where a taxpayer resides, even though the Tax Court might disagree.

In this case, the 5th Circuit Court of Appeals in Alabama had already decided *against* the IRS on the same questions that were raised about another subchapter S company. And Alabama was where one partner of the finance company lived.

But the other unfortunate partner lived in Missouri, and the 8th Circuit Court of Appeals over there had not issued any such ruling.

Enter Solomon. The Tax Court said, the IRS is right. But applying Golsen, the one equal partner who lives in Alabama has to pay nothing. The other equal partner who lives in Missouri has to pay everything the IRS claims he owes.

A semihappy ending: The man from Missouri took the whole case into the 8th Circuit Court there, and won. Needless to say, he did not win on the same grounds as his partner from Alabama. The Missouri court didn't even agree with the Alabama court. They had other reasons for letting their citizen off, or, you might say, of granting him justice. But I can't imagine that he much cared, at that point, about matters like inconsistency in interpretation of the law, or equal justice under law. I'm sure all that mattered to him was that, at last and at least, he was equal to his equal partner.

From Section 601.201 (k)(1) and (2) of the Internal Revenue Service's Statement of Procedural Rules:

"The Service does not issue rulings or determination letters upon oral requests. Furthermore, National Office officials and employees ordinarily will not discuss a substantive tax issue with a taxpayer or his representative prior to the receipt of a request for a ruling, since *oral opinions or advice are not binding on the Service.* This should not be construed as preventing a taxpayer or his representative from inquiring whether the Service will rule on a particular question, or from discussing questions relating to procedural matters with regard to submitting a request for a ruling.

"A taxpayer may, of course, seek oral technical assistance from a district office in the preparation of his return or report, pursuant to other established procedures. Such oral advice is advisory only and the Service is not bound to recognize it in the examination of the taxpayer's return." [Italics mine.]

In other words, it is their written policy that anything they say may not be held against them. They will not be bound by any oral advice anyone from the IRS might give you, the taxpayer.

So if you have a question about a deduction, let's say, you

should feel free to call your local IRS office to get it cleared up. Then if the IRS worker tells you that you are entitled to take that deduction, and you do . . . well, don't expect that to mean anything.

If you are audited, Harry might well disallow that same deduction. It'll do you no good whatsoever to inform Harry that you took the deduction in the first place only after checking it with your local IRS office. He'll merely refer you to the written rule above: We're not responsible for anything we say.

Last year, at that same breakfast meeting I mentioned earlier, when Kurtz told the U.S. Chamber of Commerce that the Court of Claims decision on the Hotel Conquistador case "does not represent what the law is," he also shed light where it has been darkest for many taxpayers—on the endless proliferation of tax rulings and their infinite permutations.

To some of us, even solid tax professionals who spend all their time with the tax law, the process and the result are like a genetic nightmare, a monster that produces and reproduces itself, cloning and permutating, with no apparent control by human beings.

Not to Kurtz. He told the business leaders over coffee that it was the taxpayers who gained by having more and more IRS regulations. Because, he explained, the more IRS regs there are, the more guidance there is for interpreting the tax laws.

"We gain little from having regulations," he really said. "It is the taxpayer that gains."

7 | They Are Not Who
You Think They Are

Soon after I started at the National Office, my wife and I were at a party and someone asked me what I did for a living. Already I possessed that sense of organizational pride which is widespread amongst IRS employees, and I replied louder than I should have: "I'm with the IRS." Within minutes, I became the center of attention.

Some people wanted me to help them with their taxes. Others blamed me for the state of the economy as well as for personal financial problems. A complete stranger pointed at me and yelled, "Son of a bitch works for those bastards."

The lesson was clear enough, confirmed by my colleagues the following Monday.

"Never tell anybody you work for the Service," Dan said. "Are you crazy?"

It was an unhappy experience everyone had suffered, and it was one of the things that bound us together and supported our view of *us against them.*

The larger point, though, is that the conventional image you and other taxpayers hold of the people who work for the IRS is inaccurate. They are not a bunch of weird authoritarian types, but tax freaks with a limited sense of personal ambition, who want and need the security, structure, and discipline of the IRS. By character and personal compromise, they fit into the IRS system and do as they are told without much questioning. They are good soldiers who follow orders. They serve the IRS, and in return the IRS is very good to them.

Right from my first day, I felt comfortable with the work and the people at the IRS. There was an unexpectedly warm and friendly atmosphere, like belonging to a club. People were extremely nice, thoughtful, continually concerned for my wife, Debbie, when she was overdue with our first child. When Jennifer was born, folks I hardly knew sent us baby presents.

As I would learn, that special quality of family atmosphere is one of the things that is so seductive about the Service, and causes so many people to stay on and make a whole career of it. And this includes scores of people who didn't start out with that in mind, who began with the intention of spending a few years there, collecting those valuable IRS credentials, and then cashing in with a big accounting or law firm on the outside, or a major corporation. Many people, of course, do precisely that. But many never leave, for a mix of reasons, and the pleasantness of the place is one of them.

Meanwhile, no taxpayer money is wasted on interior decorating in the National Office. Most of us worked in large open areas divided by partitions, just as you might find in the accounting department of any large corporation. Not the best working conditions, but you get used to it, even the lack of privacy.

The Commissioner, who is appointed by the President, and the Assistant Commissioners, the eight powerful, permanent heads of divisions, who earn around $50,000 a year, have good-sized offices, but even those are quite plain, government-issue affairs. Somebody from the outside, corporate world with the same level of authority and power would be flatly insulted if he were assigned to such an office. Somehow, those things never mattered much to us.

As a Tax Law specialist, I worked under the Assistant Com-

missioner/Technical, and my job, basically, was to explain the
tax law and all the changing rules and regulations of the IRS
to agents and other employees of the IRS, and to the public as
well.

I had to take the laws, court cases, tax legislation, internal
IRS documents, and regulations, read the stuff, research and
analyze it, and then write about it in digest form, in language
that any Agent could grasp.

If there was a new regulation on casualty losses, I would go
back and research every position the IRS had taken on casualty
losses for twenty years and write about it so that an auditor in
the field could take his copy of the Index Digest System, flip to
"casualty losses," and in a couple of pages have everything he
needed to know.

Or if Congress passed a law which they issued along with
their committee reports explaining their "congressional intent," I'd take those, compare everything with previous law,
analyze the committee reports, and then write a tight descrip-
tion of the whole thing, along with an analysis of what the new
law would mean to the IRS.

The Index Digest, by the way, is printed by the Government
Printing Office, updated every two years, and you can buy a
copy from them if you feel the need. It would probably be more
useful as a gift to your tax advisor.

My group also wrote and put out all of the IRS's pronounce-
ments, and the weekly IRS Bulletin, which contains all of their
official rulings, procedures, and regulations.

While the IRS does not believe in telling you about your
rights, or anything else that might weaken its power over you,
it is delighted to inform you of new legislation or court decisions as *they* interpret them. We saw a version of this in the way
they make propagandists out of the press.

Beyond that, the policy was then, and still is, to tell the public
just enough to keep them from coming back and demanding
more. They are especially quiet about anything that might help
you. A change in policy, a new ruling or court decision that
could mean new deductions for you, maybe even a chance for

you to file amended tax returns to claim deductions that had previously not been allowed—such a thing might be mentioned in passing, buried in some press release. But you can be certain that no attention is called to it.

There was just such a case that concerned Medicare-related deductions. The IRS changed its mind. A friend who still works there mentioned it to me over lunch, and I called another friend, also a tax professional. He was astonished and furious. Though he follows the heavings and movements of the National Office as closely as I, he had not heard a word about this Medicare shift. And it affected him most directly. He had been disallowed substantial deductions claimed for the support of his mother because of the previous IRS Medicare position. He could now file amended returns worth thousands of dollars.

Of course if he hadn't heard the news of the policy change he might have lost all that money. Actually, with this fellow, since his life like mine is taxes, he would have found out eventually. But how will you learn of IRS doings important to your life? Only if you have a tax advisor. If he's at all professional and responsible, he will regularly read all the tax journals, newsletters, and IRS bulletins, with a trained eye, and sooner or later he will discover the new and useful policies.

The IRS did the same kind of whispering routine last year with a new deduction for clubs. Used to be that they'd allow you to deduct business expenses where they applied to your country club membership, and that one only. If you also belonged to a social club, and used it for business as well, they weren't interested. No deduction.

Well, on May 27 last year, Bulletin No. 1980-21 came out, and there, nicely buried on page 94, were two paragraphs. They said that dues and fees paid for membership in social, athletic, and sporting clubs, in addition to country clubs, were now deductible. And the deductions were retroactive to January 1, 1979. That could be a meaningful deduction, providing, of course, you file an amended return to take advantage of the retroactive ruling, providing, of course, that you learned about it in the first place.

In my IRS work, my group and I not only had to keep on

top of everything related to taxes, we had to understand the
needs and the real purposes of all the divisions of the Service.
We had to grasp how they thought, which is to say be attuned
to the whole nervous system of the IRS.

Often it was a matter of recognizing the difference between
appearance and reality. That's not so easy at first, and I was
especially fortunate from the beginning to work closely with
two old pros, thirty-year veterans, who were awfully savvy and
helpful.

I remember the first time I read a ruling that was so narrow
it didn't make any sense. I took it over to Gerry.

"Could you explain this one to me?" I asked him. "As I read
this thing, it can't apply to anyone."

He looked at it and nodded. "Read between the lines," he
said. "There's a company they want to stick. This clause about
not allowing loss carrybacks. Obviously, we got some company
that's been getting away with that one for years and we finally
caught up with them."

"The ruling has come down for that one company?"

"Why not?" he replied, with a slight smile.

I smiled too. We were pretty smart, weren't we? And pretty
tough, too, weren't we? Just a touch of the sense of battle, just
a touch of the macho that I was to feel in the Service. It's
something we never talked about openly, how we felt like such
tough guys. It was subtle. But you certainly knew the feeling
yourself, being on the side of the tough guys, and you could,
after a while, recognize it in the little smiles, which appeared,
for example, when a colleague told you about the case he'd just
heard about, where they sent a dentist to jail in Cleveland.
Finally nailed the guy.

"Finally nailed the guy" could serve as the motto for the IRS
because the Service can be so unbelievably dogged. I was reminded of how dogged not long ago, when Debbie and I went
to a retirement lunch for one of my old bosses, and the program
manager for one of the rulings groups filled me in on one case
I had forgotten about. They had not.

"Remember the Sylvia Porter case?" he asked me.

I shook my head slowly.

"You remember, it came up during your last few months here?"

I had been out of the Service for more than five years, and couldn't recall a thing.

"Sure you do. Remember, she had written a column about the sick relative and the hospital bed deduction?"

And then, faintly, I did recall some such case. "Oh, yeah. Gee, that was a long time ago."

"Well, we got her."

"You got Sylvia Porter?"

He smiled and nodded. "It was the one where she said, you have a sick relative living with you, you buy a hospital bed for them, a wheelchair, that kind of special equipment, you're entitled to a medical deduction. Then, a year, two years go by, the relative recovers. So, what do you do with a used hospital bed?"

"Give it to a hospital?"

"That's what she said. Give it to a hospital, and take a charitable deduction for the whole thing, *for what you paid for it originally.*" He shook his head. He even looked hurt. "That's simply not right, I mean it's not right to get a double, full deduction like that."

I recalled that when the article had just come out there was a lot of moaning around the office. It simply wasn't fair, getting a medical deduction when you bought the thing, and then a charity deduction when you gave it away. Even if it was legal, it just wasn't right. Well, it took five years, but at last it appeared that rightness would be served.

"We finally got the new ruling, just the other day," he told me. He went on to explain in exact detail the very complicated formula that had been devised, and which Sylvia Porter's readers now would have to follow, if they wanted to adjust and depreciate all their used hospital beds instead of taking two full deductions. He covered the tablecloth with his extremely involved computation. He was a very happy man.

Talking with him through lunch about the Sylvia Porter case and a half-dozen others reminded me of the old days. We were happy men when we were talking taxes.

Lunches were reunions and seminars. There were a few favorite places near the office we usually went to. The food hardly mattered to us. "Hey, I had a case come across my desk this morning . . ." someone would say, and we were off.

We had our own language, too, which of course heightened the sense of clubbiness. "Let me tell you about this new reg. Stupidest thing I ever heard of . . ."

We spoke of "regs," as in regulations; "procs," as in Revenue Procedures, the instructions published in the Bulletin for agents; "T/Ds," as in Treasury Decisions, regulations from the Treasury Department; and of course *you* were always a "t/p."

Some people are intrigued all their lives with very narrow aspects of the law. Others look through microscopes all day and love it.

For me and my friends at the IRS, then and now, it's taxes. I am told we can be very boring, alone or together. But we do enjoy each other. It's another thing that makes working at the IRS so seductive. You share that central passion with so many others just like you—new test cases; speculation about changes among the prime issues; arguing over the reasonableness of a new IRS position, whether it's really consistent with last year's ruling; the latest funny story about the auditor and the stubborn farmer; and we're very content.

The National Office was a good place for that kind of camaraderie because there was always time for the extra beer and the tax round table over crab cakes at lunch. You have your work to do, but there's very little pressure at the National Office.

There are several nice tangible benefits in the IRS, too.

First, you have great job security. It's practically impossible to be fired from the IRS.

The health plan is fantastic, the life insurance plan is good.

As for vacations, I started off with more than two weeks' vacation a year, and after three years, four weeks. That becomes more than five weeks a year after you've been there fifteen years. You're even allowed to accumulate vacation time up to a point, so I knew several veterans taking two to three months off at full pay. There's also a liberal sick-leave plan, and the credit union used to be one of the best I'd ever heard of.

The pay in the IRS is relatively good too. You might start in the National Office as I did at a GS 5 level, which today means only $12,266. But you'll move up quickly in level and salary, as I also did. There's an almost automatic cost-of-living increase every October 1, and when you rise to a GS 11 grade, you're earning a minimum of $22,486. Each "grade" promotion is worth between $2700 and $4600 a year. In the National Office, a regular "working grade" GS 12–13 middle level job pays between $27,000 and $33,000 a year.

Add to that and the other benefits the atmosphere, the commonality of interests, even of life styles. We were all paying off big mortgages on small suburban houses and rooted like crazy for the Redskins. There was a big bowling league, another for softball, and a lot of my friends there were avid golfers. They'd use vacation time to take afternoons off together on the fairways.

And, of course, whatever we decided to do, we were the good guys, the white hats. We knew the law and lived by it, and you didn't and tried to beat it. Morally, we felt very superior to all you t/ps.

We paid our taxes, every penny, or we stood to lose our jobs. We didn't have many unusual deductions, either, and wouldn't think of playing the shady games you do. We did our own tax returns, bosses traditionally doing them for their secretaries. And you can be sure we were rarely audited. The only time I was ever audited was when I was being considered for the job. Then IRS Internal Security, who checked me out, also had me audited as a part of their review. They audit every new professional employee. They came up with "no change" on my simple return, but the whole process took its prescribed toll on me.

People don't move much from one office to another, or rise from the field office in, say, Dallas to Washington. Usually if you want the National Office, you move to Washington, as I did, and you start there. IRS people don't want to move much. In that sense, the Service is quite different from large private corporations, where movement and advancement so often go hand in hand.

I have known a few exceptions, people who started in field offices as auditors, at a scale of, say, GS 5, and then worked their way up according to career plans they plotted for themselves. As auditors, they pulled themselves up to GS 9 or 11, then applied for and got transferred to the National Office. There they were able to move up to GS 13. That's a very high grade in the field, though the National Office is swarming with them. Like captains at the Pentagon. But the people I knew, after reaching 13, transferred back to the field, where they had real rank and power.

Generally people start in one place and stay there, moving up as time and slots permit. As a result, you find in Washington and the field alike a kind of entrenched professional bureaucracy.

You might moan seeing the words "entrenched professional bureaucracy," but I must tell you it is not necessarily a bad thing, especially when you consider the kinds of political pressures that might, and have in fact been applied to the IRS.

The President appoints the Commissioner. But in terms of our work, it mattered very little to us who was President. We never talked much about politics, though I would guess that most of my colleagues were Democrats.

To us, Presidents came and went, while we stayed on and did our work. That's very important, when you consider how we now know President Nixon tried to use the Service as a personal political tool. He had his own special list of enemy-taxpayers to be audited. And of course they were. At the time, word spread around the Service that political pressures were being applied by the White House. We knew there were special audit cases. It was troublesome, but there was a strong feeling that the effects would not spread, that the Service would not be politicized. And we were not.

There is a saying in the Service: If you stay five years, they've got you for life. I left just three weeks shy of five years, and one of the reasons I left was because I couldn't move up. There were no slots open immediately above me, and I could see that there were not going to be for years, unless someone died. I had other plans for myself and my life. I wanted more than the IRS could give me.

But if you don't have a lot of personal ambition, and indeed among the regulars in the Service there isn't a great deal, things can work out fine, just as they do in the Army. You move up as "slots" become open, as people resign, or, as is more likely at the upper levels, retire or die.

Do your work, keep your nose clean, be sure you contribute through the payroll plans to the United Givers Fund, the big federal employees charity, and buy Treasury Savings Bonds through the payroll, even though they are a perfectly dreadful place to put your money.

Play office politics carefully. Respect all of the clearly drawn fiefdoms that exist, and if you do get a bit of attention for a piece of work done unusually well, be sure to share the glory with your boss.

I remember a huge assignment I had, updating all of the research for the entire Index Digest System. Two of us worked very hard and closely under a woman, another thirty-year vet, and we did the job, swiftly and quite well.

She gave us plenty of thanks, which was all I expected, but a few weeks after I'd finished I was called into the boss's office, and told I was going to have my picture taken with the Assistant Commissioner that morning, in recognition of the great job I'd done. I wasn't even wearing a jacket that day, dress being informal at National Office, especially in the summer, and had to borrow a blazer two sizes too big for me. But we had the picture taken, and during the brief session I told Assistant Commissioner Gibbs how my boss had guided me through the whole complicated job. Which is known as winning points.

Pictures like this mean a great deal to some employees, especially the ones who intend to move on to private practice in a few years. Such things, hung on the walls of plush offices, can really push up the fees.

So even though it might surprise you, you can see that in many ways the IRS is not that different from a large private corporation, including the fact that the way to get ahead in both is not so much by excelling as simply by avoiding big mistakes.

Of course, there is one basic condition that sets the Service apart from General Motors. Power. GM cannot come in, go through your books and canceled checks, and destroy you in an afternoon.

Being different, the IRS requires certain kinds of people to fit into its system to make it work, and the system has some special demands.

To begin with, the IRS regulars did not start out being the "A" students in college. They completed college and probably majored in accounting, but they were the "B," maybe "C" students. The "A" students were snapped up by the Big Eight accounting firms. IRS people finished school and needed jobs and the IRS not only took them in, but gave them a happy place to work, a home. Quite naturally, they develop a special sense of loyalty toward the IRS, which wants only the good soldiers, those who do as they are told even when they don't want to.

That's important, essential in fact for the IRS system to work. From the beginning you learn that it's my IRS, right or wrong. You learn the tax law as they see it and as they teach it to you. And you follow it that way, even when you find their view as expressed, perhaps, in a ruling, illogical, arbitrary, distasteful. You don't question. You follow orders.

We could argue as much as we wanted over beers at lunch, but it was all academic, and almost completely technical. Very few personal or moral issues were discussed. And regardless of the position any of us took at lunchtime, when we got back to our desks, we had to shape the ruling as we were told to, strictly according to IRS policy.

Important IRS rulings, by the way, are not reached the way court rulings are, after an extensive airing of views pro and con, though the IRS would like you to think so and makes them appear that way. When the IRS issues an important ruling, they give the impression that they have considered (a) the basic issue, then (b) reflected on all of the facts of the present case, then (c) researched the matter fully, and (d) reached a "holding." Actually what happens is (a) the IRS considers the facts of the present case, (b) decides what they want to do, what their "holding" will be, and then (c) has some middle-level type pull together the research that will justify the position already reached.

Doing it the IRS way, being a good soldier, is also crucial to the audit system. Harry the Auditor must follow his orders. He must interpret the law as the IRS tells him to interpret it, and enforce it as they tell him to enforce it. That means he must follow the rulings and not question them, even when he thinks they are inconsistent, or bad law, or unrealistic and a waste of his valuable time.

There is constant friction between the National Office and all the Harrys out in the field, in the local offices. The National Office issues the rulings, and so far as Harry is concerned, they rarely reflect what's really happening in the trenches. In fact, relatively few people in the National Office have auditing experience. Still, on the whole, they have higher GS ratings than Harry, and what they say is law.

Not long ago, an agent from Los Angeles complained to me about a Revenue Procedure on gambling, a Rev. Proc., in our language. In this case, I learned, it came straight from the office of Singleton Wolfe, then Assistant Commissioner/Compliance, one of the two or three most powerful positions in the Service. Under him came Collections, Audits, all the functions and people that are going to get you. It is most unusual for an Assistant Commissioner to take a personal interest in a Rev. Proc.

In effect, this one says that if anyone wants to deduct gambling losses—and they may be deducted up to the amount of declared gambling winnings—the t/p must produce a diary that tells where and when the gambling took place, and the names and addresses of all the other players.

As the agent said to me: "Can you imagine going to Vegas, as a lot of people from LA do, sitting down at the blackjack table, and asking for the names and addresses of all the other players at the table?"

The effect of the procedure is to change the law. No one will produce those diaries, not legitimate ones at any rate, so no one will be able to deduct gambling losses legitimately.

For the agent who was explaining it to me, the thing was going to be a waste of his time. He knew the kinds of fights he would get every time he asked for a gambler's diary. And each fight meant that he had to explain the procedure, and lose time.

"If you want to keep gamblers honest," the agent told me, "you don't pass a ruling. You get smart. A guy comes in to me claiming $5000 lost at the track. Fine. Let me see your losing tickets. A certain number of those tickets better be in order, have consecutive numbers. And they better not have footprints all over them, 'cause then I know he just picked them up off the floor. That's how you handle them. That, or get Congress to write a new law. But this Rev. Proc . . ."

Still, there was nothing he could do. When it comes to rulings and procedures, he is allowed no discretion. He may not say, "Well, these particular gambling losses don't hold up, but I'll give you the rest of them." His discretion comes into an audit, when he asks himself, "Do I really believe this guy?" and the question concerns some allowable deduction where, say, there is insufficient documentation to cover all of it.

With gambling decrees from Singleton Wolfe, however, all an agent can do is hope that a lot of taxpayers will write their congressman, and take the IRS to court. Only then does the t/p have a chance to see the ruling changed so as to be consistent with the real world, with the world taxpayers live in. Not that the agent's interested in giving the taxpayers a break. He's interested in saving his own time. Meanwhile, ever the good foot soldier, he slogs on.

Sometimes, when agents have a ruling that makes life difficult for them, they try to work around it. One of them told me how he handled a case that involved a matter on the Audit Suspense List.

At issue was the practice of state troopers in New Jersey deducting the lunches they had to buy when they were roaming around the state on patrol. The IRS told them those lunches were not deductible and the matter went into the courts.

While the case was being fought, it was placed on the Audit Suspense List. That's a list of issues which the IRS is contesting in court. Every agent is given the list and told: "If any one of these items comes up on one of your audits, do not allow it. If the t/p protests, and his tax advisor says, 'But that's being decided right now in the courts, you can't simply disallow it,' discontinue that part of the audit, 'suspense it,' until the issue is finally resolved, even if it has to go all the way to the Supreme Court."

Nobody likes to "suspense" an audit. The taxpayer is left hanging, for months, maybe years.

So little games are played. In the case of the state troopers, the agent told me that he was handling an audit where a similar lunch deduction had been taken, while that item was on the Audit Suspense List.

"I told the t/p's accountant that I wasn't going to allow that deduction no matter what they said, did, promised, threatened, nothing. No way. But I indicated in the next breath that there were a few other items on the return, where maybe we could talk things over. The accountant was no dummy. He knew the damn thing was in the courts. But rather than try to make a federal case of it, another federal case, he nodded, quieted down his client, and we went ahead and finished the audit, one, two, three."

The Supreme Court, by the way, ruled that the troopers were not entitled to deductions for those lunches. Congress then went back and revised the law to give them their meals.

Sometimes friction between National Office and the field develops because agents don't think National Office fully understands what they need out there. Again, the gap between the command post and the realities of the front line.

When that happens, agents will take matters into their own hands. There was an agent in Oklahoma who wasn't satisfied with the ways and the weapons he had been given to catch people who use company cars for personal use and don't consider the car a form of income to be taxed. So he put together his own questionnaire, and whenever he came across a t/p who he suspected was using a company car for heavy personal use, or trying to write off his own car for supposed business use, he ordered him to fill out the questionnaire.

He had no right to order the taxpayer to do that. He had no right to draw up the questionnaire, even though it was a good one. Nine questions and the phrase, "Under penalties of perjury, I declare that to the best of my knowledge and belief the above information is true, correct and complete." Under penalties of perjury yet.

"Did you drive the vehicle from house to work and return? . . . Did you drive the vehicle on weekends or nonwork days for shopping, to attend church, to attend recreation events, or to make out-of-town trips? . . . Did any other members of your family drive the vehicle? . . . Was the company vehicle presented to you as an inducement or fringe benefit when you accepted employment? . . . If you were transferred to another job where you were no longer eligible to use a company vehicle, would you expect your pay to be increased to compensate for the loss of the vehicle? . . ."

As I said, good questions. But the agent had absolutely no right to do what he'd done. His case is not the only one I know of, either.

The Commissioner and his policy-making staff are aware that this sort of thing goes on, but they do nothing to discourage it, even though it means that the tax law is being unequally enforced. In Oklahoma, you'd have to fill out one of those extra legal questionnaires. In Michigan, agents have never heard of them.

Congress is always telling the IRS that the law is to be enforced in the same way everywhere.

If the IRS wants to crack down on people who abuse the use of company cars, fine. Then develop techniques in the National Office, standards of legality, maybe even fairness, and apply them throughout the country.

It's one of the results of the gap between National Office and field that has always troubled me. Like you, I am also a t/p. And I don't want some agent in my district abusing my rights in the name of what he considers efficiency.

The National Office not only interprets and shapes the law for Harry, it shapes and molds Harry himself. It trains him.

Harry comes to the IRS a college graduate who probably majored in accounting. As we have seen, he was not an "A" student.

When he first joins the Service, he is put through a special program of classes and on-the-job-training. The first phase runs for about six weeks.

I took the course so I could understand what auditors are supposed to do, and frankly, I found it quite boring.

There were about fifty in the class, and we met every day in a stuffy basement room in the National Office. Harry takes his training in a Regional Training Center, or a "satellite" center, and I know it wasn't much more interesting than mine was. The problem is the instruction; it's done by specialists from the Service with impressive experience and knowledge, but who as a rule can't teach.

The curriculum is basic tax law. From lectures, slides, films, Harry learns about credits and deductions, types of income and typical income tax problems, about dividends, interest, alimony, child care, royalties, minimum tax, maximum tax, self-employment. "This is a Schedule G for Income Averaging," the voice says. A projector throws one up on the screen and the instructor describes it, his pointer moving down line by line.

At the end of the course, Harry is supposed to be able to examine routine tax returns for individuals and small businesses. Nothing complicated.

By this time, he has also sat through a couple of introductory sessions on how to plan and carry out an audit.

Then he goes through another six weeks of observing and practicing what he has just been taught. "Hands-on" experience, it is called, or "OJT," on-the-job training. He is given actual returns to examine for possible audits, though they have been carefully culled beforehand. You don't have to worry that Harry the rookie is going to push the wrong button and send the Feds racing to your door.

Harry also goes along on some real audits and sits silently, watching the way a master works. Watching, talking with the experienced agents, that's how Harry really begins to learn his trade.

(And by the way, if the mature Harry shows up at your audit with someone else, ask who it is. Don't assume it's some little Harry-in-training. It could be a Special Agent, which means that Harry really thinks that you are a candidate for criminal prosecution. If it is a Special Agent, tell Harry, even if Marvin is there with you, that you want the audit postponed until you can get a lawyer to come with you. You have that legal right.)

After Harry is finished with "OJT," he goes back into the classroom for yet another six weeks. Now he learns about partnerships, routine corporation returns, and more complex tax matters, like loss carrybacks and shelters.

Another four to six weeks of on-the-job training follow, with Harry trying to apply what he studied in those classroom sessions.

Any additional formal training, Harry has to apply for later in his career. If he wants to move up to complex corporate tax cases, or estates, considered the classiest kind of work for an agent, he has to apply, and then, depending on his Supervisor's rating of him, and the openings, he might go back to specialized school.

The great majority of audits, by the way, are Office Audits. They are relatively simple matters, where three to five items are being questioned. The IRS sends you a letter, checking off the items they want to examine and sets up an appointment. Sometimes what the IRS wants can be done by mail, it's that simple; the verification of extraordinarily large medical expenses, for example.

Otherwise you go to one of the District Offices. There you meet with Harry, Jr., who is not as experienced as Harry, Sr. In his little cubicle, Harry, Jr., will do the simple audit of the specified items, with the whole thing being in most cases fairly swift and relatively painless.

To be accurate, we should call Harry, Jr., an Auditor, and Harry, Sr., a Revenue Agent. Let me call them both Auditors, since for our purposes that's what they both do.

Also, for our purposes in this book, I am assuming that your return and the audit it provokes (Chapters 8–11) are of a somewhat complicated nature, requiring the services of Harry, Sr.

During his basic training, Harry acquires a number of attitudes which will make him that good IRS soldier. Some are stated, some absorbed.

First of all, Harry is taught tax law, but only as the IRS sees it. There is little theory here, no gray areas, no Harvard Law School pacing back and forth with "on the one hand . . . on the other hand."

His work, Harry learns, is based upon Three Commandments, three Categorical Imperatives: Section 61 of the Internal Revenue Code, which defines "gross income"; Section 161, which covers "deductions"; and Section 262, which states the law as it applies to personal expenses.

Harry, the trainee, reads Section 61: "Except as otherwise provided in this subtitle, gross income means all income from whatever source derived, including (but not limited to) the following items:

"(1) Compensation for services, including fees, commissions, and similar items;

(2) Gross income derived from business;

(3) Gains derived from dealings in property;

(4) Interest;

(5) Rents;

(6) Royalties;

(7) Dividends;

(8) Alimony and separate maintenance payments;

(9) Annuities;

(10) Income from life insurance and endowment contracts;

(11) Pensions;

(12) Income from discharge of indebtedness;

(13) Distributive share of partnership gross income;

(14) Income in respect of decedent; and

(15) Income from an interest in an estate or trust."

As for what the law, and therefore what Harry will allow you in the way of deductions, Section 161 "Allowance of Deductions"—the Second Commandment—reads: "In computing taxable income . . . there shall be allowed as deductions the items specified in this part, subject to the exceptions provided. . . ." Included in the list are interest paid, taxes, losses, bad debts, depreciation, charitable contributions, expenses for the production of income, medical expenses, alimony payments, and so on.

Harry's Third Commandment, Section 262, says, "Except as otherwise expressly provided . . . no deduction shall be allowed for personal, living, or family expenses."

Harry has been trained to cite the Third Commandment during audit sessions when taxpayers ignorant of the law want to deduct expenses that are personal, like the cost of commuting to work, or life insurance premiums, or rent.

Harry's training makes the tax law simple. If it's income, tax it. When in doubt, tax it. If there are questionable deductions and credits, turn them down.

Harry also begins to develop an attitude toward national policy, which is that national policy is whatever the latest rulings say it is.

He is taught: "Harry, you follow the law as we give it to you. That's the way to get your job, your *important* job done. And the way to get ahead in the Service as well, Harry. You don't have the right or the power to change the law, so don't waste any time or energy on that. And we're not asking you to make any special interpretations of the law. We ask the Supreme Court to do that, Harry, if need be. You follow it as we interpret it for you. Otherwise you'll get hopelessly tangled up. Just imagine what would happen if you and all your colleagues out there in the field started to make your own interpretations, imposed your own judgments, your own morality on each audit case. Chaos. So just follow the law. And it's the IRS law, however it might appear to you, right, wrong, or indifferent. Apply it."

In fact, how the interpretations and rulings are determined doesn't much interest Harry. He doesn't have that kind of curiosity, and never did. He doesn't much care how or why the DIF formulas are computed, just so long as they aren't cockeyed and start kicking out every other return. Otherwise, all that matters to Harry is that, thanks to the computer and the judgments of Classifier Murphy and his boss Jackson, your return has landed on his desk.

Same for all the theory and abstractions of national policy. That's something they do way up there at National Office. It might be national policy to audit you in order to "scare" you into greater "voluntary compliance," but all Harry knows is he's going to pull your return apart, put it back together, and take your money quickly if he can. He develops a feeling of responsibility to the National Treasury to do that. But national policy means as much to Harry as "winning the hearts and minds" meant to a grunt in Vietnam.

Of course, the IRS knows that to get its job done, it isn't really necessary for Harry to be concerned with policy. His existence and presence are enough to deter you from doing something you might otherwise do. A barking dog is enough to scare off most burglars.

During his training, Harry also acquires a certain confidence, a feeling of superiority. It's part of the atmosphere at the IRS. Stories about taxpayer mistakes circulate endlessly. I remember one that struck me as hilarious. A young couple, both self-employed, filed a joint return. They were both required to file Schedule Cs for unincorporated businesses, and Schedule SEs for Social Security Self-Employment Tax. Instead, the couple had combined all of their income and deductions on one Schedule C, as if they were partners in the same business.

Well, that broke us up. How stupid could people be? Today, I don't think the story is any funnier than you do. As I've said, it takes a while to gain perspective on the place. But for Harry, the jokes will reinforce the opinion he has of you, which is quite low.

In fact, Harry is explicitly taught that he doesn't have to believe *anything* you fumbling taxpayers put on your returns. "The burden of proof," he is repeatedly told, "is on the taxpayer. Make him prove anything and everything you have reason to doubt. After all, Harry, if the return has been selected for audit, you know that something is wrong. The computer didn't kick out the t/p for the hell of it. The computer is programmed on the basis of all that solid TCMP data. When the computer spits, Harry, there's a good reason for it.

"Make the t/p prove his innocence. You have the power to do that, Harry, and the responsibility. Focus on the numbers on that return. Numbers are all that matter. Examine those, and you'll see for yourself where the t/p is guilty. And in the audit, Harry, remember it's going to be you against the t/p *and* his tax advisor. Two against one, Harry, so you'll have to be sharp, clever, and very tough to beat them."

By the time you encounter Harry in an audit session, he has been at it seven or eight years. During that time, he has been growing a black box in his head. That box is capable of handling most returns quite automatically.

Also, Harry might have the talents to move into private practice and earn more. But he might not have the ambition or the nerve to try it, not wanting to give up all the good, comfortable benefits that the protective IRS offers him.

Beyond that, Harry might have a special fondness for his job because it brings him something no outside position ever could. It gives him power and importance. When he is working as a Revenue Agent, conducting an audit of your return, it is probably the only time in his life when Harry the "B" student is top dog.

And when Harry takes some money away from you, gets it back for the government of the United States of America, he knows he is doing something important—winning a battle for the good guys.

So don't underestimate Harry. On the other hand, as we're about to see, you don't have to stand in awe of him, either. He is not Superman, nor is the IRS an infallible institution. If you know where they are coming from, there are ways to cope with and beat them both.

8 | The Audit: Harry

Prepares His Attack

If you're going to be audited, the day will come when you will hear from Harry. He might send an IRS form letter which will tell you that you have been selected for an audit and will tick off the specific areas of your return to be reviewed with you.

Or Harry might pick up the phone and call.

To get a call, of course, is more frightening, even though you will find Harry's voice controlled, businesslike, perhaps a trifle weary, like that of a middle-level bank officer calling to say you seem to have overdrawn a bit yet one more time.

Harry's tone, by the way, is deliberate. It's part of his training to be deferential but cool. He knows that his polite flatness will increase your nervousness, and perhaps, in the end, your honesty.

Try not to panic and hang up on Harry. People have and do. Harry doesn't take it personally. He is trained not to take anything personally. Hang up on Harry and he sends you a letter. Ignore the letter, and you edge toward disaster. Harry wants to meet with you, and he will.

As Harry considers your return and sketches his portrait of you in his mind, he brings to it the computer's findings, and, let us say, some seven years of experience. So his instincts and that sixth sense, the nose of a good cop, are rather nicely formed.

Harry also has something called the IRS Agents' Manual. The entire IRS Manual is actually composed of volumes upon volumes put together by the National Office to guide Harry very specifically in his preparation and execution of an audit, any kind of audit. If he has to audit a used-car dealer, for example, he's got about eighty pages telling him exactly what to check, how to proceed, step by step. Different manuals for different industries.

For you, he's got a book of about 225 pages. "Audit Techniques—Individuals and Partnerships." He might also use other sections of this Manual, e.g., "Estates and Trusts," "Corporations," etc.

First, let's take a look at the IRS's General Audit Standards for Harry (see next page). Then let's get to your return in particular. Here are Harry's broad guidelines, his marching orders, what he's going to try and find out about you, or your company.

What we have to tease out is how Harry will get specific within those guidelines. How he will try to get the information from you he wants. The Manual offers him direction in that effort, and Harry has his own ideas and techniques as well.

Let's tap into Harry's thoughts as he starts work, and as we go along, let's compare what he thinks with what the Manual tells him to do.

In his mind, Harry shifts back and forth from specifics to a bigger picture. The computer might tell him that your charitable deductions are far higher than the DIF norm. But what Harry wants to decide is whether they are normal for you, in particular; he wants to create a total profile of you and the way you live, the real you in the real world as he knows it, not as the computer breaks it down. Once he has that profile, he can decide whether the objections raised by the computer make sense and whether the numbers you've given him will support the way you live.

Chapter 200

Audit Standards

210 *(9-27-76)*   4233
General Standards

(1) An impartial mental attitude must be maintained in all affairs relating to an examination in order to assure a fair application of tax laws, regulations and rulings.

(2) Professional skill and ingenuity must be exercised in the performance of the examination and the preparation of the report.

(3) Issues should be raised only when in the agent's considered opinion they have real merit; never frivolously, arbitrarily or for bargaining purposes.

(4) The confidential nature of all information pertaining to any assignment must be rigidly observed.

(5) The Service's reputation for integrity must be maintained.

220 *(4-14-77)*   4233
Standards of Preliminary Planning

(1) Sound judgment should be exercised in selecting from assigned returns, those which are likely to contain areas of noncompliance, and where permissible, survey procedures should be employed to dispose of those which do not warrant further consideration.

(2) Advance planning of work schedules, with reasonable accuracy, is essential for the effective use of time.

(3) A general work plan should be formulated in each case, prior to contacting the taxpayer, which includes the development of issues suggested by the return and other information.

230 *(9-27-76)*   4233
Standards of Field Work

(1) Audits should normally be performed at the taxpayer's place of business because of the accessibility of the books and records, and to permit actual observation of taxpayer's business facilities and scope of operation.

(2) The use of accounting skills, tax knowledge and ingenuity should be directed toward recognizing and raising issues which relate to noncompliance areas.

(3) Adequate evidential matter should be obtained through inspection, observation, inquiry, analysis, and documentation to afford a reasonable basis for consideration of each issue with regard to the position of both the Government and the taxpayer.

(4) Workpapers should be legible, properly headed, indexed, and arranged in a logical and orderly manner.

(5) The position taken with respect to each issue should be supported by adequate authority.

240 *(1-20-77)*   4233
Standards of Reporting

(1) Reports are to be prepared in a complete, clear, concise, and legible manner in order that they may be easily read and understood.

(2) Workpapers should be used as a practical, professional tool to aid the agent in discussion of issues or questions with the taxpayer or his/her authorized representative, in orderly report preparation, and to provide generally a record of the audit procedures undertaken.

(3) Workpapers for the Coordinated Examination Program should follow the indexing format as outlined in Chapter 800.

250 *(9-27-76)*   4233
Standards of Public Relations

(1) Initial contact for audit arrangements should be made with the taxpayer and care should be exercised in explaining the type of records required.

(2) Agents must be fully cognizant of the proper sources for gathering information and of the rights of the taxpayer and his/her representatives.

(3) The necessary time and patience should be devoted to a discussion of any proposed adjustments to insure that the taxpayer has a proper understanding of the issues.

(4) Tact and discretion is required in pointing out errors in books and records in order to avoid discrediting an employee or representative of the taxpayer.

Chapter 300
Audit Techniques—Individuals and Partnerships

---

310 *(9-27-76)*   4233
Basic Techniques

311 *(9-27-76)*   4233
Individuals—Nonbusiness

Workpaper Reference

(1) Preliminary Analysis—Prior to contacting the taxpayer, scrutinize the return, prior examination report and other related documents, and prepare a list of items which suggest a need for special consideration.   *Worksheet A*

(2) Develop, as appropriate, through discussion with the taxpayer, prior agent's reports, the audit steps, or otherwise, sufficient information to know or reach informed judgments as to: *Worksheet B*

    (a) financial history and standard of living;

    (b) the real and personal property owned, including bank accounts, stocks and bonds, real estate, automobiles, etc., in this country and abroad;

    (c) any purchases, sales, transfers, contributions or exchanges of personal assets during the period;

    (d) the correctness of exemptions and dependents claimed;

    (e) the nature of employment to determine relationship with other entities and the existence of expense allowances, etc.;

    (f) any money or property received which was determined to be tax exempt or nontaxable income.

(3) Obtain records of all bank and brokerage accounts, other than business accounts. The bank and brokerage statements should be analyzed or test checked, as appropriate.   *Worksheet C*

(4) Obtain copies of other returns that require simultaneous examination. Make necessary inspection or verification.   *Worksheet D*

(5) Verify dividend and interest income. Other items of income and expenses should be analyzed, test checked, or scrutinized, whichever is proper. Detailed techniques for travel and entertainment should be followed, when auditing the account.   *Worksheet E*

(6) Determine allowability of foreign tax credit or deduction, and verify computations.   *Worksheet F*

312 *(9-27-76)*   4233
Individuals—Business and Partnerships

Items 1 and 4, of Individuals-Nonbusiness, are equally applicable in examination of partnerships.

(1) Discuss with the taxpayer or responsible official the following.   *Worksheet G*

    (a) Overall operations of the business, noting type of products manufactured or sold, services rendered, etc., and unusual events occurring during the period under examination.

    (b) Transactions with related taxpayers and with controlled foreign entities.

    (c) Accounting system employed and type of records maintained, noting any changes in accounting methods or procedures.

    (d) System of internal control. Determine the extent test checks will be required based on the adequacy of existing procedures.

page 4233-8   Tax Audit Guidelines, Individuals, Partnerships,
(9-27-76)   Estates and Trusts, and Corporations

*Workpaper
Reference*

1 Determine who makes the decision on whether an item is capitalized or expensed.

2 Ascertain the manner in which reimbursement to officers and employees must be vouchered and approved.

(2) Make a tour of the taxpayer's premises, where practical, noting operations in general, new construction, inventories, depreciable assets, etc.   *Worksheet H*

(3) Obtain records, workpapers, reports and documents, such as ledgers, journals, accountants' reports and workpapers, chart of accounts, procedural manuals and flow charts, partnership agreement, etc., which are necessary and may aid in the examination. Examine and make notes of any items which may affect the tax determination.   *Worksheet I*

(4) If the book and return income differ, prepare a reconciliation. Determine if differences have been properly handled.   *Worksheet J*

(5) Leaf through the general ledger, general journal and other books of original entry, and note accounts and items unusual in amount, source or nature. Significant entries must be analyzed.   *Worksheet K*

(6) Test selected transactions in the books of original entry for a representative period and trace such items to the source documents.   *Worksheet L*

(7) Examine capital and drawing accounts, inventory, travel and entertainment and other accounts determined to warrant further action. Detailed techniques for inventory and travel and entertainment should be followed.   *Worksheet M*

Harry's training conditioned him, as we know, to be detached. It's only numbers. That's terribly important and it can be both good and bad for you.

His personal prejudices and irritations, then, rarely get involved. He is not going to say, "This t/p, a woman t/p at that, and only thirty-five years old, and Jesus Christ, she's pulling down fifty a year. I'm going to get that bitch." None of that.

On the other hand, after a certain point the numbers have no reality for Harry. He doesn't really know what it is to earn $100,000 a year, can't even imagine it. So with that kind of return, it's all funny money. Take some here, give some there, it's all scratches on his pad. It is a quality that complements his other attitude: There is no flesh and blood on the other side of those numbers, merely another t/p the computer has snared. That allows him to be extremely dispassionate, a good way to be in mental battle.

Every return, we used to say in the IRS, is as different as every human being. Which makes it sound a bit as if your tax return was created by the Almighty, but the point is that each does remain unique. For our purposes, then, allow me to create a rough but realistic profile, which will give us earnings and deductions that should make sense to you, and which we can follow through the entire audit process. I'm composing on the return that was due April 15, 1980, for the tax year 1979, and we'll follow the tax law as it then applied.

Let's assume that you have a salary of $30,000. In addition, you pick up another $6000 in free-lance consulting work. Your wife has recently gone back to work, and last year earned commissions of $9000. You have two children, a daughter who is a freshman in college and a son in the eighth grade. So far, a joint income of $45,000.

You also show for income, $315 in interest. No dividend income. Harry is already suspicious.

He starts by turning the interest figures around. What does $315 mean? To Harry, it means a savings account of about $6000.

He looks back at your return, finds there is no entry on Schedule B reporting dividends and/or interest, which you fill out only when there's more than $400 to report.

So he knows that if you're honest, you've got only $6000 in the bank. Possible. From his experience, someone with $45,000 joint income, what he calls Economic Income, should have more in savings. Something is off. Unreported income? Excessive deductions? Let's see.

He glances at your Schedule C. It reports the income of $6000 from your work as a consultant, with deductions of $4018 in business expenses including $1515 for travel and entertainment.

Your wife's Schedule C shows her income of $9000, and deductions for business expenses of $7642, including car expenses of $1445.

It's totaled on Line 13, Form 1040: a net combined profit for you both in your self-employed activities of $3340. (If you had showed a loss there, Harry would have been extremely disturbed).

On Schedule D, you show Harry a long-term capital gain of $2000, but that is offset by a short-term loss of $4500. So there you (Marvin) have taken a net loss from your income of $2500.

On Line 14, he sees the capital loss: $2500.

And, on Line 18, you claim a loss from the rental of a property: $1655.

That makes Line 21, "Total Income": $29,500.

On Form 2106, Marvin has adjusted that figure by lumping together two more deductions: country club dues (for business purposes), $475; and employee business expenses (not reimbursed by employer), $525.

That makes Line 31, "Adjusted Gross Income": $28,500.

Harry is not disturbed by that number, but when he turns the page, and looks at Line 33, his eyebrows go up. There you have taken itemized deductions worth $16,420.

He turns with great interest to Schedule A and reads down the list of those deductions.

- Medical insurance premium: $150.
- State and local income tax: $1407.
- Real estate tax: $1284.
- Sales tax (from IRS tables): $310.
- Personal property tax: $500.
- Extra sales tax (for new car): $170.
- Home mortgage interest: $6600.
- Credit cards: $115.
- Car loan interest: $720.
- Charitable contributions: $4474.
- Casualty loss: $1800.
- Tax preparer's fee: $600.
- Appraisal fee: $150.
- Subscriptions to business publications and dues: $500.
- Education: $1010.
- Safe-deposit box: $30.

All of that makes Line 39, "Total deductions": $19,820.

You subtract from that what would have been the standard deduction for a married couple, if you had not itemized all your deductions: $3400.

And that leaves you with a net for deductions of $16,420.

Which leaves Harry whistling. Taking that from your Adjusted Gross Income of $28,500, Harry sees taxable income of only $12,080, and things aren't finished yet.

"Do you expect me to believe," Harry says, "that someone with forty-five gross, no tax shelters, except that rental loss, considering where this guy lives, two cars, that they can support a family of four on $12,000 taxable income? Out of $12,000 they're going to pay for food, clothing, the kid's college education, and the movies? There's a lot of money going out each month in this family. Where's it coming from?"

He glances at the rest. You have taken two tax credits: one for child care, $40; the other for energy, $300. Credits are subtracted from your computed taxes. On your $12,080 of taxable income, your tax would be only $716. Subtracting the credits brings it down to $376.

Your wife, however, has to pay $110 in self-employment tax, which brings the tax total up to $486.

You have withheld from your salary $4308.

Which means, as Line 63 shows Harry, that you have overpaid $3822.

And not being any dope, you are not going to lend the refund to the government, interest free. So Line 64, "Amount of overpayment to be refunded to you": $3822.

A refund in that amount will not in itself trip the computer. A refund of $100,000 or more, I can tell you, will not only kick out your return, but cause it to be reviewed at the highest levels.

Harry knows what kicked out your return: too much of everything, and he agrees. He's got lots of doubts.

In that extremely skeptical frame of mind, Harry checks the bottom of page 2 of your Form 1040. He wants to see who the author is. If he sees the signature of a "paid preparer," if he sees Marvin's signature, address, and social security number there in the box, it makes a great difference to Harry and his entire attitude toward your return. He will still have his serious doubts, but they will be of a different character.

With "charitable contributions," he will say, if you have done

Form 1040 Department of the Treasury—Internal Revenue Service **U.S. Individual Income Tax Return 1979**

For Privacy Act Notice, see page 3 of Instructions | For the year January 1–December 31, 1979, or other tax year beginning , 1979, ending , 19

Use IRS label. Otherwise, please print or type.

Your first name and initial (if joint return, also give spouse's name and initial) — *Lewis M. & Pat J.* Last name — *Taxpayer*

Your social security number — *000 00 0000*

Present home address (Number and street, including apartment number, or rural route) — *4318 Belvedere Rd.*

Spouse's social security no. — *000 00 0000*

City, town or post office, State and ZIP code — *Anytown, Mo.*

Your occupation ▶ *VP Marketing*
Spouse's occupation ▶ *Sales*

Presidential Election Campaign Fund

Do you want $1 to go to this fund? . . . . Yes ☐ No ☒

If joint return, does your spouse want $1 to go to this fund? . . . Yes ☐ No ☒

Note: Checking "Yes" will not increase your tax or reduce your refund.

Filing Status Check only one box.

1 ☐ Single
2 ☒ Married filing joint return (even if only one had income)
3 ☐ Married filing separate return. Enter spouse's social security number above and full name here ▶
4 ☐ Head of household. (See page 7 of Instructions.) If qualifying person is your unmarried child, enter child's name ▶
5 ☐ Qualifying widow(er) with dependent child (Year spouse died ▶ 19). (See page 7 of Instructions.)

Exemptions Always check the box labeled Yourself. Check other boxes if they apply.

6a ☒ Yourself ☐ 65 or over ☐ Blind
b ☒ Spouse ☐ 65 or over ☐ Blind

Enter number of boxes checked on 6a and b ▶ **2**

c First names of your dependent children who lived with you ▶ *Alice, Douglas*

Enter number of children listed ▶ **2**

d Other dependents:
(1) Name | (2) Relationship | (3) Number of months lived in your home | (4) Did dependent have income of $1,000 or more? | (5) Did you provide more than one-half of dependent's support?

Enter number of other dependents ▶

7 Total number of exemptions claimed . . . . Add numbers entered in boxes above ▶ **4**

Income Please attach Copy B of your Forms W–2 here. If you do not have a W–2, see page 5 of Instructions.

8 Wages, salaries, tips, etc. | 8 | **39,000**
9 Interest income (attach Schedule B if over $400) | 9 | **315**
10a Dividends (attach Schedule B if over $400) | | 10b Exclusion
c Subtract line 10b from line 10a | 10c |
11 State and local income tax refunds (does not apply unless refund is for year you itemized deductions—see page 10 of Instructions) | 11 |
12 Alimony received | 12 |
13 Business income or (loss) (attach Schedule C) | 13 | **3340**
14 Capital gain or (loss) (attach Schedule D) | 14 | **<2500>**
15 Taxable part of capital gain distributions not reported on Schedule D (see page 10 of Instructions) | 15 |
16 Supplemental gains or (losses) (attach Form 4797) | 16 |
17 Fully taxable pensions and annuities not reported on Schedule E | 17 |
18 Pensions, annuities, rents, royalties, partnerships, estates or trusts, etc. (attach Schedule E) | 18 | **<1655>**
19 Farm income or (loss) (attach Schedule F) | 19 |
20a Unemployment compensation. Total amount received |
b Taxable part, if any, from worksheet on page 10 of Instructions | 20b |
21 Other income (state nature and source—see page 10 of Instructions) ▶ | 21 |

Please attach check or money order here.

22 Total income. Add amounts in column for lines 8 through 21 ▶ | 22 | **29,500**

Adjustments to Income

23 Moving expense (attach Form 3903 or 3903F) | 23 |
24 Employee business expenses (attach Form 2106) | 24 | **1,000**
25 Payments to an IRA (see page 11 of Instructions) | 25 |
26 Payments to a Keogh (H.R. 10) retirement plan | 26 |
27 Interest penalty on early withdrawal of savings | 27 |
28 Alimony paid (see page 11 of Instructions) | 28 |
29 Disability income exclusion (attach Form 2440) | 29 |
30 Total adjustments. Add lines 23 through 29 ▶ | 30 | **1,000**

Adjusted Gross Income

31 Adjusted gross income. Subtract line 30 from line 22. If this line is less than $10,000, see page 2 of Instructions. If you want IRS to figure your tax, see page 4 of Instructions | 31 | **28,500**

*U.S. GOVERNMENT PRINTING OFFICE: 1979-0-283-335   E.I. 52-107-4467   Form 1040 (1979)

Form 1040 (1979)   Page **2**

Tax Compu-tation (See Instruc-tions on page 12)	32	Amount from line 31 (adjusted gross income)	32	28,500
	33	If you do not itemize deductions, enter zero	33	16,420
		If you itemize, complete Schedule A (Form 1040) and enter the amount from Schedule A, line 41 . . .		
		Caution: If you have unearned income and can be claimed as a dependent on your parent's return, check here ▶ ☐ and see page 12 of the Instructions. Also see page 12 of the Instructions if:		
		● You are married filing a separate return and your spouse itemizes deductions, OR		
		● You file Form 4563, OR		
		● You are a dual-status alien.		
	34	Subtract line 33 from line 32. Use the amount on line 34 to find your tax from the Tax Tables, or to figure your tax on Schedule TC, Part I . . . . Use Schedule TC, Part I, and the Tax Rate Schedules ONLY if:	34	12,080
		● Line 34 is more than $20,000 ($40,000 if you checked Filing Status Box 2 or 5), OR		
		● You have more exemptions than are shown in the Tax Table for your filing status, OR		
		● You use Schedule G or Form 4726 to figure your tax.		
		Otherwise, you MUST use the Tax Tables to find your tax.		
	35	Tax. Enter tax here and check if from ☐ Tax Tables or ☐ Schedule TC	35	716
	36	Additional taxes. (See page 12 of Instructions.) Enter here and check if from ☐ Form 4970, ☐ Form 4972, ☐ Form 5544, ☐ Form 5405, or ☐ Section 72(m)(5) penalty tax . .	36	
	37	**Total. Add lines 35 and 36** . . . . ▶	37	716
Credits	38	Credit for contributions to candidates for public office . . .	38	
	39	Credit for the elderly (attach Schedules R&RP)	39	
	40	Credit for child and dependent care expenses (attach Form 2441) .	40	40
	41	Investment credit (attach Form 3468)	41	
	42	Foreign tax credit (attach Form 1116)	42	
	43	Work incentive (WIN) credit (attach Form 4874)	43	
	44	Jobs credit (attach Form 5884)	44	
	45	Residential energy credits (attach Form 5695)	45	300
	46	Total credits. Add lines 38 through 45	46	340
	47	**Balance.** Subtract line 46 from line 37 and enter difference (but not less than zero) . ▶	47	376
Other Taxes (Including Advance EIC Payments)	48	Self-employment tax (attach Schedule SE)	48	110
	49a	Minimum tax. Attach Form 4625 and check here ▶ ☐	49a	
	49b	Alternative minimum tax. Attach Form 6251 and check here ▶ ☐ .	49b	
	50	Tax from recomputing prior-year investment credit (attach Form 4255) .	50	
	51a	Social security (FICA) tax on tip income not reported to employer (attach Form 4137) . .	51a	
	51b	Uncollected employee FICA and RRTA tax on tips (from Form W–2)	51b	
	52	Tax on an IRA (attach Form 5329)	52	
	53	Advance earned income credit payments received (from Form W–2)	53	
	54	**Total. Add lines 47 through 53** . . . . ▶	54	486
Payments Attach Forms W–2, W–2G, and W–2P to front.	55	Total Federal income tax withheld	55	4308
	56	1979 estimated tax payments and credit from 1978 return	56	
	57	Earned income credit. If line 32 is under $10,000, see page 2 of Instructions	57	
	58	Amount paid with Form 4868	58	
	59	Excess FICA and RRTA tax withheld (two or more employers) .	59	
	60	Credit for Federal tax on special fuels and oils (attach Form 4136 or 4136–T)	60	
	61	Regulated Investment Company credit (attach Form 2439)	61	
	62	Total. Add lines 55 through 61 . . . . ▶	62	4308
Refund or Balance Due	63	If line 62 is larger than line 54, enter amount OVERPAID . . . . ▶	63	3822
	64	Amount of line 63 to be REFUNDED TO YOU . . . . ▶	64	3822
	65	Amount of line 63 to be credited on 1980 estimated tax . . . . ▶	65	
	66	If line 54 is larger than line 62, enter BALANCE DUE. Attach check or money order for full amount payable to "Internal Revenue Service." Write your social security number on check or money order . . ▶ (Check ▶ ☐ if Form 2210 (2210F) is attached. See page 15 of Instructions.) ▶ $	66	

Please Sign Here

Under penalties of perjury, I declare that I have examined this return, including accompanying schedules and statements, and to the best of my knowledge and belief, it is true, correct, and complete. Declaration of preparer (other than taxpayer) is based on all information of which preparer has any knowledge.

▶ *Curtis M. Taxpayer* Your signature 4/14/80 Date ▶ *Pat J. Taxpayer* Spouse's signature (if filing jointly, BOTH must sign even if only one had income)

Paid Preparer's Information

Preparer's signature and date ▶ *Marvin H. Preparer*		Check if self-employed ☑	Preparer's social security no. ▶ 0-- :-- --
Firm's name (or yours, if self-employed) ▶ MARVIN H. PREPARER and address		E.I. No. ▶	ZIP code ▶ 4/14/80

Schedules A&B—Itemized Deductions AND Interest and Dividend Income

(Form 1040)
Department of the Treasury
Internal Revenue Service

▶ Attach to Form 1040. ▶ See Instructions for Schedules A and B (Form 1040).

19 79

08

Name(s) as shown on Form 1040

Lewis M. & Pat J. Taxpayer

Your social security number
000 00 0000

Schedule A—Itemized Deductions (Schedule B is on back)

Medical and Dental Expenses (not paid or reimbursed by insurance or otherwise) (See page 16 of Instructions.)

1 One-half (but not more than $150) of insurance premiums you paid for medical care. (Be sure to include in line 10 below.) ▶	**150**	
2 Medicine and drugs		
3 Enter 1% of Form 1040, line 31 . . .		
4 Subtract line 3 from line 2. If line 3 is more than line 2, enter zero		
5 Balance of insurance premiums for medical care not entered on line 1. . . .		
6 Other medical and dental expenses:		
a Doctors, dentists, nurses, etc. . . .		
b Hospitals		
c Other (itemize—include hearing aids, dentures, eyeglasses, transportation, etc.) ▶		
7 Total (add lines 4 through 6c)		
8 Enter 3% of Form 1040, line 31 . . .		
9 Subtract line 8 from line 7. If line 8 is more than line 7, enter zero		
10 Total medical and dental expenses (add lines 1 and 9). Enter here and on line 33 . ▶	**150**	

Taxes (See page 16 of Instructions.)
Note: Gasoline taxes are no longer deductible.

11 State and local income	**1407**	
12 Real estate	**1284**	
13 General sales (see sales tax tables) . .	**310**	
14 Personal property	**500**	
15 Other (itemize) ▶ *SALES TAX-NEW CAR*	**170**	
16 Total taxes (add lines 11 through 15). Enter here and on line 34 . . . . ▶	**3671**	

Interest Expense (See page 17 of Instructions.)

17 Home mortgage	**6600**	
18 Credit and charge cards	**115**	
19 Other (itemize) ▶ *CAR LOAN*	**720**	
20 Total interest expense (add lines 17 through 19). Enter here and on line 35 ▶	**7435**	

Contributions (See page 17 of Instructions.)

21 a Cash contributions for which you have receipts, cancelled checks, or other written evidence	**79**	
b Other cash contributions (show to whom you gave and how much you gave) ▶ *ST. MATTHEW'S*	**395**	
DARTMOUTH ALUMNI FUND	**200**	
GEORGIAN TEA SET TO THE	**3000**	
BROOKLINE RESTORATION SOCIETY		
SALVATION ARMY — 8 boxes of	**800**	
clothes, plus furniture		
22 Other than cash (see page 17 of instructions for required statement)		
23 Carryover from prior years		
24 Total contributions (add lines 21a through 23). Enter here and on line 36 . ▶	**4474**	

Casualty or Theft Loss(es) (See page 18 of Instructions.)

25 Loss before insurance reimbursement .		
26 Insurance reimbursement		
27 Subtract line 26 from line 25. If line 26 is more than line 25, enter zero . . .		
28 Enter $100 or amount from line 27, whichever is smaller	*See 4684 attac*	
29 Total casualty or theft loss(es) (subtract line 28 from line 27). Enter here and on line 37 . ▶	**1800**	

Miscellaneous Deductions (See page 18 of Instructions.)

30 Union dues.		
31 Other (itemize) ▶ *TAX PREP FEE*	**600**	
APPRAISAL fee	**150**	
BUSINESS PUBS & SUBSCRIPTIONS	**500**	
EDUCATION EXPENSES	**1010**	
SAFETY deposit box RENTAL	**30**	
32 Total miscellaneous deductions (add lines 30 and 31). Enter here and on line 38 ▶	**2290**	

Summary of Itemized Deductions   **A**
(See page 18 of Instructions.)

33 Total medical and dental—from line 10 .	**150**	
34 Total taxes—from line 16	**3671**	
35 Total interest—from line 20	**7435**	
36 Total contributions—from line 24 . . .	**4474**	
37 Total casualty or theft loss(es)—from line 29 .	**1800**	
38 Total miscellaneous—from line 32 . . .	**2290**	
39 Add lines 33 through 38	**19,820**	
40 If you checked Form 1040, Filing Status box: 2 or 5, enter $3,400 . . . . 1 or 4, enter $2,300 . . . . 3, enter $1,700	**3,400**	
41 Subtract line 40 from line 39. Enter here and on Form 1040, line 33. (If line 40 is more than line 39, see the instructions for line 41 on page 18.) . . . . ▶	**16,420**	

Schedules A&B (Form 1040) 1979	Schedule B—Interest and Dividend Income	Page 2

Name(s) as shown on Form 1040 (Do not enter name and social security number if shown on other side) | Your social security number

Part I — Interest Income

1 If you received more than $400 in interest, complete Part I and Part III. Please see page 9 of the instructions to find out what interest to report. Then answer the questions in Part III, below. If you received interest as a nominee for another, or you received or paid accrued interest on securities transferred between interest payment dates, please see page 18 of the instructions.

Name of payer	Amount

2 Total interest income. Enter here and on Form 1040, line 9 . . . .

Part II — Dividend Income

3 If you received more than $400 in gross dividends (including capital gain distributions) and other distributions on stock, complete Part II and Part III. Please see page 9 of the instructions. Write (H), (W), or (J), for stock held by husband, wife, or jointly. Then answer the questions in Part III, below. If you received dividends as a nominee for another, please see page 19 of the instructions.

Name of payer	Amount

Part III — Foreign Accounts and Foreign Trusts

If you are required to list interest in Part I or dividends in Part II, OR if you had a foreign account or were a grantor of or a transferor to a foreign trust, you must answer both questions in Part III. Please see page 19 of the instructions.

	Yes	No
A At any time during the tax year, did you have an interest in or a signature or other authority over a bank account, securities account, or other financial account in a foreign country (see page 19 of instructions)?		
B Were you the grantor of, or transferor to, a foreign trust which existed during the current tax year, whether or not you have any beneficial interest in it? If "Yes," you may have to file Forms 3520, 3520-A, or 926.		

4 Total of line 3 . . . .
5 Capital gain distributions. Enter here and on the appropriate line(s) on Schedule D. See Note below . . . . .
6 Nontaxable distributions . . . . .
7 Total (add lines 5 and 6) . . . . . .
8 Dividends before exclusion (subtract line 7 from line 4). Enter here and on Form 1040, line 10a . . . .

B

Note: If your capital gain distributions for the year do not include any gains before Nov. 1, 1978, and you do not need Schedule D to report any gains or losses, do not file that schedule. Instead, enter the taxable part of your capital gain distributions on Form 1040, line 15.

| SCHEDULE C
(Form 1040)
Department of the Treasury
Internal Revenue Service | **Profit or (Loss) From Business or Profession**
(Sole Proprietorship)
Partnerships, Joint Ventures, etc., Must File Form 1065.
▶ Attach to Form 1040 or Form 1041.   ▶ See Instructions for Schedule C (Form 1040). | 19**79**
09 |

Name of proprietor   _Lewis M. TAXPAYER_   Social security number of proprietor   _000   00   0000_

A Main business activity (see Instructions) ▶ _CONSULTING_   ; product ▶

B Business name ▶   C Employer identification number

D Business address (number and street) ▶ --
  City, State and Zip Code ▶

E Accounting method: (1) ☒ Cash   (2) ☐ Accrual   (3) ☐ Other (specify) ▶ ----------------------------   **C**

F Method(s) used to value closing inventory:
  (1) ☐ Cost   (2) ☐ Lower of cost or market   (3) ☐ Other (if other, attach explanation)   **Yes** | **No**

G Was there any major change in determining quantities, costs, or valuations between opening and closing inventory? . . | X
  If "Yes," attach explanation.

H Did you deduct expenses for an office in your home? . . . .   X |

I Did you elect to claim amortization (under section 191) or depreciation (under section 167(o)) for a rehabilitated
  certified historic structure (see Instructions)? . . . . | X
  (Amortizable basis (see Instructions) ▶   )

Part I   Income

1 a Gross receipts or sales	**1a**	_6,000_	
b Returns and allowances	**1b**		
c Balance (subtract line 1b from line 1a)	**1c**	_6,000_	
2 Cost of goods sold and/or operations (Schedule C–1, line 8)	**2**		
3 Gross profit (subtract line 2 from line 1c)	**3**	_6,000_	
4 Other income (attach schedule)	**4**		
5 Total income (add lines 3 and 4) . . . . ▶	**5**	_6,000_	

Part II   Deductions

6 Advertising	_250_	31 a Wages . .	
7 Amortization		b Jobs credit	
8 Bad debts from sales or services .		c WIN credit	
9 Bank charges	_50_	d Total credits	
10 Car and truck expenses		e Subtract line 31d from 31a .	
11 Commissions		32 Other expenses (specify):	
12 Depletion		a	
13 Depreciation (explain in Schedule C–2) .	_400_	b	
14 Dues and publications		c	
15 Employee benefit programs . .		d	
16 Freight (not included on Schedule C–1) .		e	
17 Insurance	_185_	f	
18 Interest on business indebtedness .		g	
19 Laundry and cleaning		h	
20 Legal and professional services .	_747_	i	
21 Office supplies	_340_	j	
22 Pension and profit-sharing plans .		k	
23 Postage	_48_	l	
24 Rent on business property . . .		m	
25 Repairs		n	
26 Supplies (not included on Schedule C–1) .		o	
27 Taxes	_80_	p	
28 Telephone	_285_	q	
29 Travel and entertainment . . .	_1515_	r	
30 Utilities	_118_	s	

33 Total deductions (add amounts in columns for lines 6 through 32s) . . . . ▶	33	_4018_
34 Net profit or (loss) (subtract line 33 from line 5). If a profit, enter on Form 1040, line 13, and on Schedule SE, Part II, line 5a (or Form 1041, line 6). If a loss, go on to line 35	34	_1982_

35 If you have a loss, do you have amounts for which you are **not** "at risk" in this business (see Instructions)? . . ☐ Yes ☐ No

Schedule C (Form 1040) 1979   Page **2**

SCHEDULE C–1.—Cost of Goods Sold and/or Operations (See Schedule C Instructions for Part I, line 2)

1 Inventory at beginning of year (if different from last year's closing inventory, attach explanation) .	**1**	
2 a Purchases **2a**		
b Cost of items withdrawn for personal use **2b**		
c Balance (subtract line 2b from line 2a)	**2c**	
3 Cost of labor (do not include salary paid to yourself)	**3**	
4 Materials and supplies	**4**	
5 Other costs (attach schedule)	**5**	
6 Add lines 1, 2c, and 3 through 5	**6**	
7 Inventory at end of year	**7**	
8 Cost of goods sold and/or operations (subtract line 7 from line 6). Enter here and on Part I, line 2 . ▶	**8**	

SCHEDULE C–2.—Depreciation (See Schedule C Instructions for line 13)
If you need more space, please use Form 4562.

Description of property (a)	Date acquired (b)	Cost or other basis (c)	Depreciation allowed or allowable in prior years (d)	Method of computing depreciation (e)	Life or rate (f)	Depreciation for this year (g)
1 Total additional first-year depreciation (do not include in items below) ——————————————▶						
2 Other depreciation:						
Buildings	7-15-74	80,000	400	SL ½ business use	25	400
Furniture and fixtures . . .						
Transportation equipment . .						
Machinery and other equipment .						
Other (specify)						
Totals		80,000			**3**	400
Depreciation claimed in Schedule C–1					**4**	
Balance (subtract line 4 from line 3). Enter here and on Part II, line 13 . . . . ▶					**5**	400

SCHEDULE C–3.—Expense Account Information (See Schedule C Instructions for Schedule C–3)

Enter information for yourself and your five highest paid employees. In determining the five highest paid employees, add expense account allowances to the salaries and wages. However, you don't have to provide the information for any employee for whom the combined amount is less than $25,000, or for yourself if your expense account allowance plus line 34, page 1, is less than $25,000.

Name (a)	Expense account (b)	Salaries and wages (c)
Owner		

Did you claim a deduction for expenses connected with:	Yes	No
Entertainment facility (boat, resort, ranch, etc.)?		
Living accommodations (except employees on business)?		
Conventions or meetings you or your employees attended outside the U.S. or its possessions? (See Instructions) . .		
Employees' families at conventions or meetings?		
If "Yes," were any of these conventions or meetings outside the U.S. or its possessions?		
Vacations for employees or their families not reported on Form W–2?		

SCHEDULE C
(Form 1040)
Department of the Treasury
Internal Revenue Service

Profit or (Loss) From Business or Profession
(Sole Proprietorship)
Partnerships, Joint Ventures, etc., Must File Form 1065.
▶ Attach to Form 1040 or Form 1041.   ▶ See Instructions for Schedule C (Form 1040).

1979
09

Name of proprietor	Social security number of proprietor
PAT J. TAXPAYER	000 : 00 : 0000

A Main business activity (see Instructions) ▶ SALES   ; product ▶

B Business name ▶

C Employer identification number

D Business address (number and street) ▶ _____
City, State and Zip Code ▶

E Accounting method: (1) ☒ Cash   (2) ☐ Accrual   (3) ☐ Other (specify) ▶ _____

F Method(s) used to value closing inventory:
(1) ☐ Cost   (2) ☐ Lower of cost or market   (3) ☐ Other (if other, attach explanation)

C

	Yes	No
G Was there any major change in determining quantities, costs, or valuations between opening and closing inventory? If "Yes," attach explanation.		X
H Did you deduct expenses for an office in your home?		X
I Did you elect to claim amortization (under section 191) or depreciation (under section 167(o)) for a rehabilitated certified historic structure (see Instructions)?		X

(Amortizable basis (see Instructions) ▶ _____)

Part I Income

1 a Gross receipts or sales	**1a** 9,000		
b Returns and allowances	**1b**		
c Balance (subtract line 1b from line 1a)		**1c**	9,000
2 Cost of goods sold and/or operations (Schedule C–1, line 8)		**2**	
3 Gross profit (subtract line 2 from line 1c)		**3**	9,000
4 Other income (attach schedule)		**4**	
5 Total income (add lines 3 and 4) ▶		**5**	9,000

Part II Deductions

6 Advertising	2500	31 a Wages		
7 Amortization		b Jobs credit		
8 Bad debts from sales or services		c WIN credit		
9 Bank charges		d Total credits		
10 Car and truck expenses	1445	e Subtract line 31d from 31a		
11 Commissions		32 Other expenses (specify):		
12 Depletion		a		
13 Depreciation (explain in Schedule C–2)		b		
14 Dues and publications	214	c		
15 Employee benefit programs		d		
16 Freight (not included on Schedule C–1)		e		
17 Insurance		f		
18 Interest on business indebtedness	828	g		
19 Laundry and cleaning		h		
20 Legal and professional services	285	i		
21 Office supplies	265	j		
22 Pension and profit-sharing plans		k		
23 Postage	120	l		
24 Rent on business property		m		
25 Repairs		n		
26 Supplies (not included on Schedule C–1)		o		
27 Taxes		p		
28 Telephone	1500	q		
29 Travel and entertainment	485	r		
30 Utilities		s		

33 Total deductions (add amounts in columns for lines 6 through 32s) ▶	**33**	7642
34 Net profit or (loss) (subtract line 33 from line 5). If a profit, enter on Form 1040, line 13, and on Schedule SE, Part II, line 5a (or Form 1041, line 6). If a loss, go on to line 35	**34**	1358

35 If you have a loss, do you have amounts for which you are not "at risk" in this business (see Instructions)? ☐ Yes ☐ No

SCHEDULE D
(Form 1040)
Department of the Treasury
Internal Revenue Service

Capital Gains and Losses
(Examples of property to be reported on this Schedule are gains and losses on stocks, bonds, and similar investments, and gains (but not losses) on personal assets such as a home or jewelry.)
▶ Attach to Form 1040.   ▶ See Instructions for Schedule D (Form 1040.)

19 79
12

Name(s) as shown on Form 1040   *Lewis M. & Pat J. Taxpayer*

Your social security number   *000 00 0000*

Caution: Columns f and g are not the same as last year. Most other lines have also been changed.

Part I   Short-term Capital Gains and Losses—Assets Held One Year or Less   D

a. Kind of property and description (Example, 100 shares 7% preferred of "Z" Co.)	b. Date acquired (Mo., day, yr.)	c. Date sold (Mo., day, yr.)	d. Gross sales price less expense of sale	e. Cost or other basis, as adjusted (see instructions page 20)	f. LOSS if column (e) is more than (d) subtract (d) from (e)	g. GAIN if column (d) is more than (e) subtract (e) from (d)
1 *Loan, Personal Lender declared Bankruptcy*	*8-1-78*	*4-13-79*	*- 0 -*	*4500*	*4500*	

2 Enter your share of net short-term gain or (loss) from transactions entered into by partnerships and fiduciaries after 10/31/78 . . . . **2**

3 Add lines 1 and 2 in column f and column g **3** *4500*

4 Combine line 3, column f and line 3, column g and enter the net gain or (loss) . . . . **4** *‹4500›*

5 Short-term capital loss carryover from years beginning after 1969 . . . . **5** (   )

Note: *If there is an entry on this line and line 7 or 19, see instructions for lines 7 and 19.*

6 Net gain or (loss), combine lines 4 and 5 . . . . **6** *‹4500›*

7 Enter your share of net short-term gain or (loss) from transactions entered into by partnerships and fiduciaries before 11/1/78 . . . . **7**

8 Net short-term gain or (loss), combine lines 6 and 7 . . . . **8** *‹4500›*

Part II   Long-term Capital Gains and Losses—Assets Held More Than One Year

9 *100 shs BP Mfg*	*4-1-78*	*4-3-79*	*7,000*	*5,000*		*2,000*

10 Enter your share of net long-term gain or (loss) from transactions entered into by partnerships and fiduciaries after 10/31/78 . . . . **10**

11 Add lines 9 and 10 in column f and column g **11**

12 Combine line 11, column f and line 11, column g and enter the net gain or (loss) **12** *2,000*

13 Capital gain distributions from transactions entered into after 10/31/78 . . . . **13**

14 Enter gain, if applicable, from Form 4797, line 6(a)(1) from transactions entered into after 10/31/78 . **14**

15 Enter your share of net long-term gain from transactions entered into by small business corporations (Subchapter S) after 10/31/78 . . . . **15**

16 Combine lines 12 through 15 . . . . **16** *2,000*

17 Long-term capital loss carryover from years beginning after 1969 . . . . **17** (   )

Note: *If there is an entry on this line and line 7 or 19, see instructions for lines 7 and 19.*

18 Net gain or (loss), combine lines 16 and 17 . . . . **18** *2,000*

19 Enter your share of capital gain distributions and net long-term gain or (loss) from transactions entered into by partnerships, fiduciaries, small business corporations, real estate investment trusts, and regulated investment companies before 11/1/78 . . . . **19**

20 Net long-term gain or (loss), combine lines 18 and 19 . . . . **20** *2,000*

Note: *If you have capital loss carryovers from years beginning before 1970, do not complete Parts III or V. See Form 4798 instead.*

Schedule D (Form 1040) 1979   Page **2**

Part III   Summary of Parts I and II

21 Combine lines 8 and 20, and enter the net gain or (loss) here . . . . | 21 | <2500>

Note: *Do not complete line 22 if lines 20 and 21 show a gain, and there is a net gain on line 7 or 19. Instead, complete Part IV.*

22 If line 21 shows a gain—
   a Enter 60% of line 20 or 60% of line 21, whichever is smaller. Enter zero if there is a loss or no entry on line 20 * . . . . | 22a

   b Subtract line 22a from line 21. Enter here and on Form 1040, line 14 . . . . | 22b

23 If line 21 shows a loss—
   a Enter one of the following amounts:
   (i)   If line 8 is zero or a net gain, enter 50% of line 21,
   (ii) If line 20 is zero or a net gain, enter line 21; or,
   (iii) If line 8 and line 20 are net losses, enter amount on line 8 added to 50% of the amount on line 20 . . . . | 23a | <2500>

   b Enter here and enter as a loss on Form 1040, line 14, the smallest of:
   (i)   The amount on line 23a,
   (ii) $3,000 ($1,500 if married and filing a separate return); or,
   (iii) Taxable income, as adjusted . . . . | 23b | <2500>

   Note: *If the loss on line 23a is more than the loss shown on line 23b, complete Part V to determine post-1969 capital loss carryovers from 1979 to 1980.*

Part IV   Computation of Capital Gain Deduction for Sales or Exchanges Before 11/1/78

24 Enter the smaller of line 20 or line 21 (or Form 4798, lines 8 and 9) . . . . | 24
25 If line 18 (or Form 4798, line 5) is a gain, combine lines 6 and 18 (or Form 4798, lines 1 and 5), and enter here. If this line or line 18 (or Form 4798, line 5) shows a loss or zero, skip to line 29 and enter zero on line 27 . . . . | 25
26 Enter smaller of line 18 (or Form 4798, line 5) or line 25 . . . . | 26
27 Enter smaller of line 24 or line 26 . . . . | 27
28 Enter 60% of amount on line 27 . . . . | 28
29 Subtract line 27 from line 24 . . . . | 29
30 Enter 50% of amount on line 29 . . . . | 30
31 Add line 28 and line 30. This is your capital gain deduction * . . . . | 31

32 Subtract line 31 from line 21 (or Form 4798, line 9). Enter here and on Form 1040, line 14 . . . . | 32

Part V   Computation of Post-1969 Capital Loss Carryovers from 1979 to 1980
(Complete this part if the loss on line 23a is more than the loss shown on line 23b)

Section A.—Short-term Capital Loss Carryover

33 Enter loss shown on line 8; if none, enter zero and skip lines 34 through 38—then go to line 39 . . . | 33
34 Enter gain shown on line 20. If that line is blank or shows a loss, enter zero . . . . | 34
35 Reduce any loss on line 33 to the extent of any gain on line 34 . . . . | 35
36 Enter amount shown on line 23b . . . . | 36
37 Enter smaller of line 35 or 36 . . . . | 37

38 Subtract line 37 from line 35 . . . . | 38
   Note: *The amount on line 38 is the part of your short-term capital loss carryover from 1979 to 1980 that is from years beginning after 1969.*

Section B.—Long-term Capital Loss Carryover

39 Subtract line 37 from line 36 (**Note:** *If you skipped lines 34 through 38, enter amount from line 23b*) . | 39
40 Enter loss from line 20; if none, enter zero and skip lines 41 through 44 . . . . | 40
41 Enter gain shown on line 8. If that line is blank or shows a loss, enter zero . . . . | 41
42 Reduce any loss on line 40 to the extent of any gain on line 41 . . . . | 42
43 Multiply amount on line 39 by 2 . . . . | 43

44 Subtract line 43 from line 42 . . . . | 44
   Note: *The amount on line 44 is the part of your long-term capital loss carryover from 1979 to 1980 that is from years beginning after 1969.*

* If the amount you enter on this line is other than zero, you may be liable for the alternative minimum tax. See Form 6251.

SCHEDULE E

(Form 1040)

Page 177 — THE AUDIT

SCHEDULE E (Form 1040) — Supplemental Income Schedule — 1979

Name: Lewis M. & Pat J. Taxpayer — SSN 000 00 0000

Part I — Pension and Annuity Income.

Part II — Rent and Royalty Income or Loss.
- 5a No 5b No 6a No

Property	(b) Rents	(c) Royalties	(d) Depreciation	(e) Other expenses	(f) Loss	(g) Income
A	2400		2100	1955	1655	
8 Totals	2400		2100	1955	(1655)	

9 Total rent and royalty income or (loss): (1655)

Part III — Income or Losses from Partnerships, Estates/Trusts, Small Business Corporations (blank)

Part IV
18 TOTAL income or (loss): <1655>
19 (blank)

Schedule E (Form 1040) 1979 — Page **2**

Part V — Property reported in Part II

Property Codes	Kind and location of property
A	Residential Frame, Anytown, USA
B	
C	
D	
E	

Part VI — Depreciation claimed in Part II. If you need more space, use Form 4562.

(a) Description of property	(b) Date acquired	(c) Cost or other basis	(d) Depreciation allowed or allowable in prior years	(e) Depreciation method	(f) Life or rate	(g) Depreciation for this year
Property A — Residential Frame	1-14-71	92,000	16,800	SL	20	2100
Totals (Property A)						2100
Property B						
Totals (Property B)						
Property C						
Totals (Property C)						
Property D						
Totals (Property D)						
Property E						
Totals (Property E)						

Part VII — Expenses claimed in Part II

Expenses (Description)	A	B	C	D	E
Advertising	$ 35	$	$	$	$
Cleaning	200				
Gardening	120				
Insurance	140				
Legal & Accounting	60				
Management fee	185				
Repairs - washer, dryer, Refrig. stove	375				
Repair Airconditioner	210				
Masonry work	150				
Taxes	480				
Totals	1955				

SCHEDULE SE (Form 1040) Department of the Treasury Internal Revenue Service	**Computation of Social Security Self-Employment Tax** ▶ See Instructions for Schedule SE (Form 1040). ▶ Attach to Form 1040.	19**79** 14

Name of self-employed person (as shown on social security card)	Social security number of self-employed person ▶	000 00 0000

PAT J. TAXPAYER

Part I — Computation of Net Earnings from FARM Self-employment

Regular Method

1 Net profit or (loss) from:
 a Schedule F (Form 1040) . . . . | 1a |
 b Farm partnerships . . . . | 1b |
2 Net earnings from farm self-employment (add lines 1a and 1b) . . . . | 2 |

Farm Optional Method

3 If gross profits from farming are:
 a Not more than $2,400, enter two-thirds of the gross profits . . . . }
 b More than $2,400 and the net farm profit is less than $1,600, enter $1,600 . . . . } . . . | 3 |

4 Enter here and on line 12a, the amount on line 2, or line 3 if you elect the farm optional method . | 4 |

Part II — Computation of Net Earnings from NONFARM Self-employment   **SE**

Regular Method

5 Net profit or (loss) from:
 a Schedule C (Form 1040) . . . . | 5a | 1358 |
 b Partnerships, joint ventures, etc. (other than farming) . . . . | 5b |
 c Service as a minister, member of a religious order, or a Christian Science practitioner. (Include rental value of parsonage or rental allowance furnished.) If you filed Form 4361 and have not revoked that exemption, check here ▶ ☐ and enter zero on this line . . . . | 5c |
 d Service with a foreign government or international organization . . . . | 5d |
 e Other (specify) ▶............... | 5e |
6 Total (add lines 5a through 5e) . . . . | 6 | 1358 |
7 Enter adjustments if any (attach statement, see page 29 of Instructions) . . . . | 7 |
8 Adjusted net earnings or (loss) from nonfarm self-employment (line 6, as adjusted by line 7) . . . | 8 | 1358 |
 Note: If line 8 is $1,600 or more or if you do not elect to use the Nonfarm Optional Method, skip lines 9 through 11 and enter amount from line 8 on line 12b, Part III.

Nonfarm Optional Method

9 a Maximum amount reportable under both optional methods combined (farm and nonfarm) . . | 9a | $1,600 | 00 |
 b Enter amount from line 3. (If you did not elect to use the farm optional method, enter zero.) . . | 9b |
 c Balance (subtract line 9b from line 9a) . . . . | 9c |
10 Enter two-thirds of gross nonfarm profits or $1,600, whichever is smaller . . . . . . | 10 |

11 Enter here and on line 12b, the amount on line 9c or line 10, whichever is smaller . . . . . | 11 |

Part III — Computation of Social Security Self-employment Tax

12 Net earnings or (loss):
 a From farming (from line 4) . . . . | 12a |
 b From nonfarm (from line 8, or line 11 if you elect to use the Nonfarm Optional Method) . . . | 12b | 1358 |
13 Total net earnings or (loss) from self-employment reported on lines 12a and 12b. (If line 13 is less than $400, you are not subject to self-employment tax. Do not fill in rest of schedule) . . . . | 13 | 1358 |
14 The largest amount of combined wages and self-employment earnings subject to social security or railroad retirement taxes for 1979 is . . . . | 14 | $22,900 | 00 |
15 a Total "FICA" wages (from Forms W-2) and "RRTA" compensation | 15a |
 b Unreported tips subject to FICA tax from Form 4137, line 9 or to RRTA . . . . | 15b |
 c Add lines 15a and 15b . . . . | 15c |
16 Balance (subtract line 15c from line 14) . . . . | 16 | 22900 |
17 Self-employment income—line 13 or 16, whichever is smaller . . . . | 17 | 1358 |
18 Self-employment tax. (If line 17 is $22,900, enter $1,854.90; If less, multiply the amount on line 17 by .081.) Enter here and on Form 1040, line 48 . . . . | 18 | 110 |

Form **2441**	**Credit for Child and Dependent Care Expenses**	**1979**
Department of the Treasury Internal Revenue Service	▶ Attach to Form 1040. ▶ See Instructions below.	21

Name(s) as shown on Form 1040

Lewis M. & Pat J. Taxpayer

Your social security number: 000 00 0000

1 See the definition for "qualifying person" in the instructions. Then read the instructions for line 1.

(a) Name of qualifying person	(b) Date of birth	(c) Relationship	(d) During 1979, the person lived with you for:	
			Months	Days
Douglas, (Son)	_11-1-65_	_Son_	_12_	

2 Persons or organizations who cared for those listed on line 1. See the instructions for line 2.

(a) Name and address (If more space is needed, attach schedule)	(b) Social security number, if applicable	(c) Relationship, if any	(d) Period of care From Month—Day	To Month—Day	(e) Amount of 1979 expenses (include those not paid during the year)
Chipawah Camp	_N/A_		_6-8_	_7-30_	_200_

To Figure Your Credit, You MUST Complete ALL Lines That Apply

3 Add the amounts in column 2(e)	**3**	_200_
4 Enter $2,000 ($4,000 if you listed two or more names in line 1) or amount on line 3, whichever is less	**4**	_200_
5 Earned income (wages, salaries, tips, etc.). See the instructions for line 5. An entry MUST be made on this line.		
(a) If unmarried at end of 1979, enter your earned income . . . . **(b)** If married at end of 1979, enter your earned income or your spouse's whichever is less . ▶	**5**	_1358_
6 Enter the amount on line 4 or line 5, whichever is less	**6**	_200_
7 Amount on line 6 paid during 1979. An entry MUST be made on this line . . . . ▶	**7**	_200_
8 Child and dependent care expenses for 1978 paid in 1979. See instructions for line 8	**8**	_—_
9 Add amounts on lines 7 and 8	**9**	_200_
10 Multiply line 9 by 20 percent	**10**	_40_
11 Limitation:		
a Enter tax from Form 1040, line 37 . . . . **11a** _7/6_		
b Enter total of lines 38, 39, and 41 through 43 of Form 1040 . . **11b** _—_		
c Subtract line 11b from line 11a (if line 11b is more than line 11a, enter zero)	**11c**	_7/6_
12 Credit for child and dependent care expenses. Enter the smaller of line 10 or line 11c here and on Form 1040, line 40 .	**12**	_40_

13 If payments listed on line 2 were made to an individual, complete the following:

	Yes	No
(a) If you paid $50 or more in a calendar quarter to an individual, were the services performed in your home?		
(b) If "Yes," have you filed appropriate wage tax returns on wages for services in your home (see instructions for line 13)?		
(c) If answer to (b) is "Yes," enter your employer identification number . . . . . . ▶		

Form **2106**	**Employee Business Expenses**	**1979**
Department of the Treasury Internal Revenue Service	(Please use Form 3903 to figure moving expense deduction.) ▶ Attach to Form 1040.	

Your name _Lewis TAXPAYER_	Social security number _000 : 00 : 0000_	Occupation in which expenses were incurred _MARKETING_
Employer's name	Employer's address	

Instructions

Use this form to show your business expenses as an employee during 1979. Include amounts:

● You paid as an employee;

● You charged to your employer (such as by credit card);

● You received as an advance, allowance, or repayment.

Several publications, available free from IRS, give more information about business expenses:

Publication 463, *Travel, Entertainment, and Gift Expenses.*

Publication 529, *Miscellaneous Deductions.*

Publication 587, *Business Use of Your Home.*

Publication 508, *Educational Expenses.*

Part I.—You can deduct some business expenses even if you do not itemize your deductions on Schedule A (Form 1040). Examples are expenses for travel (except commuting to and from work), meals, or lodging. List these expenses in Part I and use them in figuring your adjusted gross income on Form 1040, line 31.

Line 2.—You can deduct meals and lodging costs if you were on a business trip away from your main place of work. Do not deduct the cost of meals you ate on one-day trips, when you did not need sleep or rest.

Line 3.—If you use your own car in your work, you can deduct the cost of the business use. Enter the cost here after figuring it in Parts IV, V, and VI. Base the cost on your actual expenses (such as gas, oil, repairs, depreciation) or on a mileage rate.

The mileage rate is 18½ cents a mile up to 15,000 miles. After that, or for all business mileage on a fully depreciated car, the rate is 10 cents a mile. (For depreciation, see **Publication 463.**)

Figure your mileage rate amount and add it to the business part of what you spent on the car for parking fees, tolls, interest, and State and local taxes (except gasoline tax).

Line 4.—If you were an outside salesperson with other business expenses, list them on line 4. Examples are selling expenses or expenses for stationery and stamps. An outside salesperson does all selling outside the employer's place of business. A driver-salesperson whose main duties are service and delivery, such as delivering bread or milk, is not an outside salesperson. (For outside salesperson, see **Publication 463.**)

Line 5.—Show other business expenses on line 5 if your employer repaid you for them. If you were repaid for part of them, show here the amount you were repaid. Show the rest in Part II.

Part II.—You can deduct other business expenses only if (a) your employer did not repay you, and (b) you itemize your deductions on Schedule A (Form 1040). Report these expenses here and under Miscellaneous Deductions on Schedule A (Form 1040). Examples are union or professional dues and expenses for tools and uniforms. (For details, see **Publication 529.**)

You can deduct expenses for business use of the part of your home that you exclusively and consistently use for your work. If you are not self-employed, your working at home must be for your employer's convenience. (For business use of home, see **Publication 587.**)

If you show education expenses in Part I or Part II, you must fill out Part III.

Part III.—You can deduct the cost of education that helps you keep or improve your skills for the job you have now. This includes education that your employer, the law, or regulations require you to get in order to keep your job or your salary. Do not deduct the cost of study that helps you meet the basic requirements for your job or helps you get a new job. (For education expenses, see **Publication 508.**)

Part V.—If you trade in a car you used in business for a new one you also used in business, fill out lines 1 through 15. If you paid cash for the new car or traded in a car not used in business, fill out only lines 10 through 15. Refigure the basis for depreciation each year in the future that your percentage of business use changes.

PART I.—Employee Business Expenses Deductible in Figuring Adjusted Gross Income on Form 1040, Line 31

1 Fares for airplane, boat, bus, taxicab, train, etc.		_325_
2 Meals and lodging		_200_
3 Car expenses (from Part IV, line 21)		
4 Outside salesperson's expenses (see Part I instructions above) ▶		
5 Other (see Part I instructions above) ▶ _COUNTRY CLUB dues_		_475_
6 Add lines 1 through 5		_1,000_
7 Employer's payments for these expenses if not included on Form W–2		
8 Deductible business expenses (subtract line 7 from line 6). Enter here and include on Form 1040, line 24 .		_1,000_
9 Income from excess business expense payments (subtract line 6 from line 7). Enter here and include on Form 1040, line 21		

PART II.—Employee Business Expenses that are Deductible Only if You Itemize Deductions on Schedule A (Form 1040)

1 Business expenses not included above (list expense and amount) ▶

2 Total. Deduct under Miscellaneous Deductions, Schedule A (Form 1040) . . . .

PART III.—Information About Education Expenses Shown in Part I or Part II

1 Name of educational institution or activity ▶

2 Address ▶

3 Did you need this education to meet the basic requirements for your job? . . . . ☐ Yes ☐ No

4 Will this study program qualify you for a new job? . . . . ☐ Yes ☐ No

5 If your answer to question 3 or 4 is No, explain (1) why you are getting the education and (2) what the relationship was between the courses you took and your job. (If you need more space, attach a statement) ▶

6 List your main subjects, or describe your educational activity ▶

| Form **4684**
 Department of the Treasury
 Internal Revenue Service | **Casualties and Thefts**
 ▶ See instructions on back.
 ▶ Attach to Form 1040. | **1979** |

Name(s) as shown on Form 1040   *Lewis M. Taxpayer*

Social Security Number   0 00 | 00 | 0000

Part I Casualty or Theft	Item or article	Item or article	Item or article	Item or article
1 Kind of property	GOLF CLUbS			
2 Cost or basis	900			
3 Insurance or other reimbursement	—			
4 Gain from casualty or theft. If line 3 is more than line 2, enter difference here and on line 15 or 20 below. Also, skip lines 5 through 14 . . . . *If line 2 is more than line 3, enter zero on line 4 and complete lines 5 through 14.*				
5 Fair market value of property before casualty or theft	900			
6 Fair market value of property after casualty or theft	—			
7 Subtract line 6 from line 5	900			
8 Enter smaller of line 2 or line 7	900			
Note: *If the loss was to property used in a trade or business or for income-producing purposes and totally destroyed by a casualty or lost from theft, enter on line 8, in each column, the amount from line 2.*				
9 Subtract line 3 from line 8	900			

10 Casualty or theft loss. Add amounts on line 9	900
11 Enter part of line 9 that is from trade, business, or income producing property here and on line 15 or 20 below .	—
12 Subtract line 11 from line 10	900
13 Enter the amount from line 12 or $100, whichever is smaller	100
14 Subtract line 13 from line 12. Enter here and on line 15 or 20 below	800

Part II Summary of Gains and Losses

(A) Identify casualty or theft	(B) Losses from casualties or thefts		(C) Gains from casualties or thefts includible in income
	(i) Trade, business, rental or royalty property	(ii) Other property	
Casualty or Theft of Property Held One Year or Less			
15			
16 Totals. Add amounts on line 15 for each column		800	
17 Combine line 16, columns (B)(i) and (C). Enter here and on Form 4797, Part II, line 10, column g **(Note:** *if Form 4797 is not required for other transactions, enter amount on Form 1040, line 16—identify as "4684")* .			
18 Enter amount from line 16, column (B)(ii) here and on Schedule A (Form 1040), line 29—identify as "4684" .			800
Casualty or Theft of Property Held More Than One Year			
19 Any casualty or theft gains from Form 4797, Part III, line 25			
20			
21 Total losses. Add amounts on line 20, columns (B)(i) and (B)(ii) . .			////
22 Total gains. Add lines 19 and 20, column (C)			
23 Add line 21, columns (B)(i) and (B)(ii)			
24 If the loss on line 23 is more than the gain on line 22			
a. Combine line 21, column (B)(i) and line 22. Enter here and on Form 4797, Part II, line 10, column g **(Note:** *if Form 4797 is not required for other transactions, enter amount on Form 1040, line 16—identify as "4684")*			
b. Enter amount from line 21, column (B)(ii) here and on Schedule A (Form 1040), line 29—identify as "4684"			
25 If the loss on line 23 is equal to or smaller than the gain on line 22, enter the difference here and on Form 4797, Part I, line 4, column g—identify as "Gain from Form 4684, Part II, line 25"			

Form **4684** (197

Form **4684** Department of the Treasury Internal Revenue Service	**Casualties and Thefts** ▶ See instructions on back. ▶ Attach to Form 1040.	19**79**

Name(s) as shown on Form 1040

Lewis M. Taxpayer

Social Security Number   *000 00 0000*

Part I — Casualty or Theft

	Item or article	Item or article	Item or article	Item or article
1 Kind of property	*Shrubs & bushes*			
2 Cost or basis	*1100*			
3 Insurance or other reimbursement	—			
4 Gain from casualty or theft. If line 3 is more than line 2, enter difference here and on line 15 or 20 below. Also, skip lines 5 through 14 . . . . *If line 2 is more than line 3, enter zero on line 4 and complete lines 5 through 14.*				
5 Fair market value of property before casualty or theft	*1100*			
6 Fair market value of property after casualty or theft	—			
7 Subtract line 6 from line 5	*1100*			
8 Enter smaller of line 2 or line 7 . . . . **Note:** *If the loss was to property used in a trade or business or for income-producing purposes and totally destroyed by a casualty or lost from theft, enter on line 8, in each column, the amount from line 2.*	*1100*			
9 Subtract line 3 from line 8	*1100*			

10 Casualty or theft loss. Add amounts on line 9		*1100*
11 Enter part of line 9 that is from trade, business, or income producing property here and on line 15 or 20 below .		—
12 Subtract line 11 from line 10		*1100*
13 Enter the amount from line 12 or $100, whichever is smaller		*100*
14 Subtract line 13 from line 12. Enter here and on line 15 or 20 below		*1000*

Part II — Summary of Gains and Losses

(A) Identify casualty or theft	(B) Losses from casualties or thefts		(C) Gains from casualties or thefts includible in income
	(i) Trade, business, rental or royalty property	(ii) Other property	
Casualty or Theft of Property Held One Year or Less			
15			
16 Totals. Add amounts on line 15 for each column		*1000*	
17 Combine line 16, columns (B)(i) and (C). Enter here and on Form 4797, Part II, line 10, column g (**Note:** if Form 4797 is not required for other transactions, enter amount on Form 1040, line 16—identify as "4684") .			
18 Enter amount from line 16, column (B)(ii) here and on Schedule A (Form 1040), line 29—identify as "4684" .			*1000*
Casualty or Theft of Property Held More Than One Year			
19 Any casualty or theft gains from Form 4797, Part III, line 25			
20			
21 Total losses. Add amounts on line 20, columns (B)(i) and (B)(ii) . . .			
22 Total gains. Add lines 19 and 20, column (C)			
23 Add line 21, columns (B)(i) and (B)(ii)			
24 If the loss on line 23 is more than the gain on line 22			
a. Combine line 21, column (B)(i) and line 22. Enter here and on Form 4797, Part II, line 10, column g (**Note:** if Form 4797 is not required for other transactions, enter amount on Form 1040, line 16—identify as "4684")			
b. Enter amount from line 21, column (B)(ii) here and on Schedule A (Form 1040), line 29—identify as "4684"			
25 If the loss on line 23 is equal to or smaller than the gain on line 22, enter the difference here and on Form 4797, Part I, line 4, column g—identify as "Gain from Form 4684, Part II, line 25"			

Form **4684** (1979)

Form **5695**	**Energy Credits**	**1979**
Department of the Treasury Internal Revenue Service	▶ Attach to Form 1040. ▶ See Instructions on back.	29

Name(s) as shown on Form 1040	Your social security number
Lewis M. & Pat J. TAXPAYER	000 00 0000

Enter in the space below the address of your principal residence on which the credit is claimed if it is different from the address shown on Form 1040.

Part I   **Fill in your energy conservation costs (but do not include repair or maintenance costs).** If you have an unused energy credit carryover from the previous tax year and no energy savings costs this year, skip to Part III, line 20.

Was your principal residence substantially completed before April 20, 1977? . . . . ☒ Yes ☐ No
If you checked "No," do not fill in Part I.

1	Energy Conservation Items:		
a	Insulation	1a	250
b	Storm (or thermal) windows or doors	1b	1750
c	Caulking or weatherstripping	1c	
d	Other items (list here) _____		
	_____		
	_____		
	_____		
	_____		
	_____	1d	
2	Total (add lines 1a through 1d)	2	2000
3	Maximum amount	3	$2,000 00
4	Enter the total energy conservation costs for this residence from your 1978 Form 5695, line 2 . . .	4	—
5	Subtract line 4 from line 3	5	2000
6	Enter the amount on line 2 or line 5, whichever is less	6	2000
7	Enter 15% of line 6	7	300

Part II   **Fill in your renewable energy source costs (but do not include repair or maintenance costs).** If you have an unused energy credit carryover from the previous year and no energy savings costs this year, skip to Part III, line 20.

8	Renewable Energy Source Items:		
a	Solar	8a	
b	Geothermal	8b	
c	Wind	8c	
9	Total (add lines 8a through 8c)	9	
10	Maximum amount	10	$10,000 00
11	Enter the total renewable energy source costs for this residence from your 1978 Form 5695, line 5 . .	11	
12	Subtract line 11 from line 10	12	
13	Enter amount on line 9 or line 12, whichever is less	13	
14	Enter 20% of line 13	14	
15	Subtract amount on line 11 from $2,000. If zero or less, enter zero	15	
16	Enter amount on line 13 or line 15, whichever is less	16	
17	Enter 10% of line 16	17	
18	Add lines 14 and 17	18	

Part III   **Fill in this part to figure the limitation**

19	Add line 7 and line 18. If less than $10, enter zero	19	300
20	Enter your unused energy credit carryover from the previous tax year	20	
21	Add lines 19 and 20	21	300
22	Enter the amount of tax shown on Form 1040, line 37	22	716
23	Add lines 38 through 44 from Form 1040 and enter the total	23	40
24	Subtract line 23 from line 22. If zero or less, enter zero	24	676
25	Residential energy credit. Enter the amount on line 21 or line 24, whichever is less. Also, enter this amount on Form 1040, line 45	25	300

Form **5695** (1979)

the return yourself: "Probably no back-up for much of this. Lot of padding. Probably also has donations to charities that are not legitimate tax-deductible organizations."

Looking at exactly the same numbers on your return as produced by Marvin, Harry will say: "Maybe a little high. But if it's up that high, Marvin probably has seen receipts, for the big stuff at least." And, he'll make a note on his worksheet to check during the audit, but not to expect to pick up much on that item.

Harry will still review your return just as thoroughly if Marvin has prepared it, but he'll start out accepting a lot.

He will assume, for example, that Marvin has asked you all the basic questions on matters of interest, capital gains, all areas of income, and that he has computed everything correctly. With deductions, he expects that Marvin has seen most of the receipts and canceled checks, and whatever disputes there might be will be of a fairly sophisticated nature.

With that rental property where you're claiming a loss, he's going to double-check the way Marvin calculated depreciation of the house. Did he figure it over a lifetime of twenty years or thirty?

But, if you've done the return yourself, he will expect that you not only depreciated the house over an unreasonably short period of years, but that you also included the land on which the house stands in your depreciation figures. According to the IRS, land doesn't depreciate, only structures on it. So he'll fully expect to get something back from you there.

For that business trip you've deducted, he'll expect that Marvin allowed you to throw in a side trip and a few other items, but that the real purpose was indeed for business, and you've got the canceled plane ticket, paid hotel bill, and the rest.

Without Marvin, Harry will look at the same numbers, and assume that you and your wife wanted a vacation, and that you cleverly took time out from your holiday and had two meetings and one lunch with potential business customers during the week. He expects to correct that balance at your expense during the audit.

He will be more skeptical about all your deductions if you have done the return yourself, and expect lots of all kinds of errors. His attitude is, trying to learn the law on the night of April 14 is not going to work. You might even be a basically honest human being, just trying to save yourself some money doing it yourself. Doesn't matter to Harry.

What he sees is you, late that night, surrounded by four different paperback tax manuals. He knows, and I agree, that most people can get all the processing information they need from IRS Publication 17, "Your Federal Income Tax." The Lasser book, the Block book and the rest really don't give you much more, and the IRS book is yours for nothing.

The real point to Harry, of course, is that whatever you use, you're going to make mistakes. You're going to think that you are entitled to deduct the $250 you gave to your local Home-owner Civic Association because it is a non-profit organization. It is non-profit, but it is not on the Service's list of approved charitable organizations. You won't know enough to call the IRS.

Harry will expect that kind of thing and complete misreadings of the law from you, and he will look for them.

He wouldn't expect the same from Marvin the professional. From him, other problems: he expects sophisticated interpretations, some dancing through the grayer areas of the law, arguments where Marvin knows the courts are still deciding between an IRS interpretation and that of one of his colleagues.

Whether there is a Marvin involved or not, Harry is supposed to do what the Manual tells him to do, partly because the National Office thinks that's the best way to conduct an audit, and partly because they'd like to see all taxpayers treated equally, the way Congress has told them.

In fact, Harry conducts the audit pretty much as he pleases, staying within the spirit of the Manual but adapting it to what he feels is necessary. As we know, he is out there on the field of battle. The guys who write the Manual are back at headquarters.

For example, here is the Manual on Contributions:

321.1(10) *(9–27–76)*   4233
Contributions

(1) Verify amounts claimed and determine that the deduction has been taken in the proper year.

(2) Determine whether the payments were made to qualified organizations.

(3) Ascertain that percentage limitations have not been exceeded.

(4) Determine if contributions claimed are nondeductible personal expenses and ascertain if donor received benefits or consideration in return.

(5) In a case where property is contributed, verify the fair market value of the property at the time of gift and determine whether the donor retains any control over the property.

As you can see, the Manual has not suggested to Harry whether he should allow you to take that extra contribution you claim you made to Dartmouth, but which check you've misplaced. Nor does it say anything about those contributions dropped into the church collection plate, the ones nobody ever gets a receipt for. (That's up to his judgment and discretion.)

And it certainly doesn't say anything about his Contributions Table, the sliding scale of what he and other Agents in his office have decided is reasonable for your district, and your income. That scale Harry uses, but there's not a word in the Manual.

Obviously, something else the Manual doesn't tell Harry is how to use that charity table as an audit weapon. It doesn't tell him to pretend that he is distressed when you can't come up with that other canceled check to Dartmouth. It doesn't tell him that maybe he should bargain a bit with Marvin, maybe disallow a hundred dollars there, if he sees he's going to have to let you off scot-free with nearly everything else.

On the contrary, Harry has been told he may *never* bargain. That order brings nothing but a grin from Harry, because he knows that if he didn't bargain, he wouldn't be able to close a single case. Not one. As we shall see, once he gets into the room with Marvin, the National Office is far away indeed.

One of the special forms Marvin attached to your return was a Form 2441, to claim a "child care credit." Harry mutters, "You're kidding." Now checking, he finds that you have indeed taken a credit of $40, the percentage allowed (20 percent of $200) for sending your son to summer camp. Harry shakes his head. He knows the law entitles you to claim the credit when both parents are working, and he knows how you would both whine if he questioned it. He has heard it so many times: how it would be impossible to work if the kid were home on the loose all summer. Still it goes against his grain that people making your kind of money take a credit of $40. He makes a note to at least force you to produce your receipt for the camp, and to ask the age of the child. He must be under fifteen for this credit.

The Manual also suggests that he do a couple of other things:

321.1(15) *(9–27–76)*   4233
Child Care Expenses
(1) Verify amounts claimed and determine that the deduction is claimed in the proper year.
(2) Determine the reasonableness of payments, the relationship of the payee, and whether multiple duties were performed.
(3) Determine whether payments made are deductible under the technical provisions of the law.

Under energy credits, he sees that you've taken $300, which is the maximum allowed. "Probably have receipts," he thinks. "Better see if they've taken this credit in any other year." He knows you are entitled to $300, but that is a one-time lump sum figure. "Principal residence?" he notes on his sheet. The deduction is allowed only if the energy-saving devices are installed in your principal residence. Lots of people spend the money on their second homes, and Harry takes their deduction away from them, even as they protest that he is penalizing them for trying to be responsible citizens and save energy. He never argues. He merely reads them the tax code, and gets on with the audit.

Your energy credit rings a bell, and he glances again at your high interest deduction from mortgage payments. He has no way of knowing for sure from the return, but he figures there's a good chance you might be paying a high interest rate on that mortgage, which might well mean you've got a new house. And a new house doesn't get any energy credit, no matter how stupid the law is. "House built before 4/20/77?" he writes, and hopes he won't have to go through his defense of that law with you, as he has with so many people. He wishes the damn National Office would do something to let people know how this law really works.

He sees you've also taken an interest deduction of $720, paid to your bank for a car loan. "Must be a helluva car," he says. "Maybe two cars?" He checks and sees you have two dependents, so maybe you're carrying a loan for one of the kids. "Whose loan?" he scribbles. If you have been sloppy here, Harry will make you pay. If you are like so many other indulgent fathers he has encountered, you are making the payments even though she signed for the loan. In that case, you are not entitled to the interest deductions. Good intentions have nothing to do with the tax law, or Harry. Looking at your return, he thinks he might just take the $300 he figures you have deducted for interest on your daughter's loan. But he also wonders if you were smart enough to consult with Marvin before you and your daughter bought the car. We shall see.

Another car thought: Maybe it's the wife's car. She's got some kind of business, with a $1445 deduction for car expenses. "Double interest deduction?" he writes, wondering if you're trying to take that one twice.

One thing he's sure of: "On $12,000 taxable income, this guy sure ain't buying no Mercedes, not on me he ain't."

For the car and all the other interest deductions you have itemized, the Manual directs Harry to examine the following:

321.1(11) *(9–27–76)*   4233
Interest

(1) Verify amounts claimed and determine that the deduction has been taken in the proper year.

(2) Determine whether the payments are for interest or for other items, such as discounts, finance charges or principal.

(3) Ascertain whether the interest payments are made on a valid, existing debt owed by taxpayer.

(4) Ascertain whether the debt was incurred to carry or purchase obligations, the income from which is tax-exempt, or was incurred to purchase a single premium life insurance, endowment or annuity contract after March 1, 1954.

(5) Determine if the proper amount of tax was withheld where recipient was a nonresident alien or other foreign entity.

We have already gotten a sense of how Harry looks at "Contributions" in general, and seen what the Manual directs. With your return, Harry smiles at your entry, "A Georgian tea set," he says. "For Chrissake."

At this point, Harry doesn't know how you came by that set, and he is more than a little curious. It's worth $3000, you claim. All he sees on the return is "Georgian Tea Set, donated to Brookline Restoration Society."

Actually, your grandmother died and left the set to you, along with the wish that it be given at some point to a worthwhile historical association. You really didn't need those pieces around to be polished, so you donated them to the Restoration Society in the Massachusetts town where she lived. And, on Marvin's advice, you had an appraiser determine their value: $3000. You have his evaluation and his $150 bill as evidence.

Harry nods, gives Marvin his due, and writes, "Possibly" next to the appraisal and the hefty deduction. He knows that he might "possibly" knock that down, appraiser or no appraiser. And he will, if he thinks he'll need that money from you, if the rest of your return is airtight. "Double-check on appraiser," he reminds himself. "Make sure legit, not part of shelter scam."

Harry suspects, though, that he may not have to bother. Marvin will fight over that, he knows. But there is this other deduction for "8 boxes" of goods donated to the Salvation Army. Harry puts that on his "must" list.

When Harry reaches "Casualty or Theft Loss(es)," he smiles again.

"$900 for golf clubs stolen from country club locker? Not even Jack Nicklaus spends that kind of money for golf clubs," Harry mutters. "And he also has a casualty loss of $1100 on storm damage to rosebushes and trees? Wait a minute . . ." He flips your return to page one and looks at your address. "These people live in a condo. What's he doing claiming rosebushes?" He shrugs, thinking again of Marvin, and decides that the deduction must have some basis in fact. He notes: "Second home?" He looks at the numbers again and says: "Well, I think we've got something of a gambler here, claiming all that in one mouthful. Smells like the old maintenance man deduction."

Harry knows very well that there are gardeners, maintenance men and their companies who provide the usual services of mowing the lawn of your country home, tending the roses, pruning the trees. None of which is deductible. But Harry also knows they offer yet another service. They give you a solemnly drafted document that says you had to pay them a special amount because you got hit by a terrible storm last year. That document is the proof of your casualty deduction. Harry knows that the value of the trees and shrubs the maintenance company says you lost in the storm is just about to the penny the amount you paid them last year to do their normal cutting, mowing, pruning.

One of these days, Harry tells himself, he really is going to go out and take apart the records of one of those damn maintenance companies. One of these days. He doesn't have the time right now. So he makes a note to ask you what you deducted last year for "Casualty Loss" on those same damn rosebushes. He wonders if you took this same deduction last year, maybe the year before that. Perhaps it's a perennial, just like some of those pretty flowers that were blown away. He considers pulling your returns for the last two years to see for himself, decides to keep that in mind, for now at least. "Certainly worth asking t/p for some back returns," he says.

Your returns for relevant "open years" are available to Harry. Normally, this means one or two years preceding the one he is auditing. If he has any special doubts, any questions with a history, he is expected to pull those returns and examine them. Of course that is extra time and work for Harry, so unless his suspicion is fairly deep, he'll stick with the year and return in question.

There might be unexpected developments in the audit session, however, which will cause Harry to regret that he hadn't checked an earlier return, and he will ask you to pull it out of your records for him. You are not required to show him that, and Harry knows it. But most taxpayers are so intimidated by Harry they pull the return out, or rush home during the lunch break and find it. If there's a Marvin involved, Harry expects him to object. Marvin might have a copy in his office, or he will have some other record. He's got to keep one or the other for at least three years, according to the law. Sometimes, Harry knows, Marvin wants to placate him, especially when an audit is going badly for Marvin's client, so Marvin produces a copy. Always worth a try, Harry figures. The last thing he wants to do is interrupt an audit to go call up a return from the computer himself. That not only shows Harry didn't do all his homework, it means the audit must be kept hanging.

Further, at that stage, Harry is going to need a very good reason to obtain the thing. Thanks to Nixon and since Watergate, he can't get hold of any taxpayer info he wants, simply by asking. The good old days are gone. Now, he must have a solid reason for reaching back into the computer's precious banks.

With your Casualty and Theft Losses, he finishes his notes, which are shorthand for the Manual's paragraph 321.1(14):

321.1(14) *(3–28–79)*   4233
Casualty and Theft Losses
[Supplemented by MS CR 42G–395]

(1) Determine that a theft or a casualty has actually occurred and that the loss was the direct result of such occurrence.

(2) Determine that the amount claimed is equal to the difference in value before and after the loss (limited by cost or other basis), and that the taxpayer was the owner of the property.

(3) Ascertain whether insurance proceeds have been received or are anticipated.

(4) Ascertain that the loss is claimed in the proper year. Casualty losses are deductible in the year incurred and theft losses in the year discovered.

(5) Determine if gains from involuntary conversion are reported which would change the tax treatment of the casualty and theft losses.

(6) Analyze any losses claimed for assets located in a foreign country.

Harry spots a minor item he decides to check while he's at it. He sees that you paid Marvin $600. "All for tax advice?" he wonders. If some of Marvin's time was for advice not related to preparing the return, it might not be deductible.

He pauses at $500 for "business publications and subscriptions." "Let's break all that down," he says, and notes that he should pick up something there. "That is high, even for this kind of income."

"Both going to school?" Harry wonders, making a note to check where, what, when, and especially, why. Harry has erased countless deductions from folks who were trying to improve their minds or shift jobs, none of which is his business because the tax law says it isn't.

321.1(16) (9–27–76)   4233
Educational Expenses

(1) Verify amounts claimed and determine that the deduction is claimed in the proper year.

(2) Determine if the expenses were primarily incurred for the purpose of maintaining or improving skills or meeting express requirements for retention of status.

(3) Ascertain whether any reimbursement has been made.

Around about this time, Harry looks back at all his notes. "These people certainly have an awful lot of 'miscellaneous deductions.' " He begins to wonder if Marvin is playing the "normal" game with him, taking a lot of deductions within what he estimates will be the "normal" range for people of your income, figuring that they might slip by the computer. And if they don't, well, he'll certainly be able to get some of them past Harry. Some is better than none.

You've deducted for the safe-deposit box. "Check receipt," Harry writes, and looks again at your return. "No dividend income? Very little interest income?" he says, slowly. He will ask you what is in that box. There might indeed be undeclared income, and it might be neatly stacked away in that box. A common suspicion of his.

He picks up your Schedule D, "Capital Gains and Losses." This page bothers him. He sees you claim a long-term capital gain of $2000, and a short-term capital loss of $4500.

321.1(22) *(9-27-76)*   4233
Capital Gains and Losses

(1) Consider and verify as necessary the various factors involved in arriving at the gains or losses reported (e.g. holding period, basis, adjusted basis, selling price, expense of sale, etc.).

(2) Determine whether income from the sale of assets should be taxed as ordinary income rather than as capital gains in cases such as:

    (a) sales of depreciable property to related taxpayers;

    (b) collapsible corporations;

    (c) dealings in a manner which would constitute a trade or business;

    (d) redemptions of stock by a closely held corporation;

    (e) dealings with related individuals (substance vs. form).

(3) Determine the propriety of capital loss carryovers to the year under audit. Also check limitations on capital losses.

(4) Ascertain whether capital losses are reflected as ordinary losses in such cases as:

    (a) nonbusiness bad debts;

    (b) payments on certain notes by a guarantor;

> (c) certain casualty and theft losses which
> may be required to be offset against capital
> gains.
>   (5) Be alert to the wash sale provisions of the
> code and regulations.
>   (6) Ascertain whether sales which reflected
> no gain or loss are bona fide. Sales to related
> individuals below fair market value could result
> in gift tax liability to the taxpayer. Sales, trans-
> fers to and exchanges with controlled foreign
> entities for adjusted basis but below fair market
> value could result in recognized gain.
>   (7) Verify sales of property reported on the
> installment basis and determine if all require-
> ments pertaining thereto have been complied
> with.

The long-term gain was 100 shares of BP Manufacturing that you bought at 50 and sold at 70. What concerns Harry most is the dates of those transactions. You held the stock, apparently, for one year and two days. Holding it for more than one year entitles you to a long-term gain which means that only 40 percent of your profit on that can be taxed. If you had sold the stock a few days sooner, it would have been normal income, what the IRS calls "ordinary income," and 100 percent of your profit would be taxable.

Harry figures that Marvin has seen the broker's confirmation slips and done the calculations correctly on the long-term capital gain. But he wants to double-check those slips and the dates for the purchase and sale. There's a bit of money involved here, and he has handled plenty of returns where the dates were off by just a day or two. "But I called the broker and told him to sell but not before a certain date had passed" is the sad refrain he's heard again and again. To which he replies: "Sorry, it isn't when you called him. It's when he sold the thing. If he slipped up, nothing I can do about that." So he will check you out very carefully here.

But that one is nothing compared to what he'll do with the short-term loss. What Harry sees on your return and almost doesn't believe is a "Personal loan" with a bankruptcy being claimed as a short-term loss in the amount of $4500. He bristles. "Who's he trying to kid? Probably lent the money to his daughter, and she scribbled a note, 'I am unable to repay this.' And he expects me to buy that? Consider the loan worthless, and give him $4500? No way. This is a joke."

Actually, what you did was to lend the money to your hopeless brother-in-law Roger so he could use it and some other money he could put together, shame people into lending him, to start yet another business. You loaned it to him on his promise and your oath that this was positively the last time. Yes, certainly, you told him, everyone did need magnetic can openers, and how could he miss. The slob did, before a year was up. Bankrupt.

You have all the documents Marvin warned you to get. And you have one thing to thank Roger for: he did give you a nonbusiness bad-debt deduction. You are entitled to claim the $4500 as a short-term capital loss.

Harry's only twinge of doubt is Marvin. Would he really try to get away with the father-daughter loan charade? Of course, if he did, I might just have myself a candidate for the Problem Preparer's Program, which is always good for points with Bradley. At the very least, I'll slap him with a nice negligence penalty.

Harry is certain he's got something good here. The capital gain is a matter of record. But it's going to be very, very difficult for you to prove the worthlessness of that loan. And it's only deductible, of course, when it is worthless. Zero. To prove that is not merely a matter of record, Harry knows. On that one, he's going to get a very full and lucid explanation from you, or you get—zero.

He's going to ask you for five particular pieces of information: the nature of the debt; the creditor's name and the business or family relationship; the date the debt became due; what effort has been made to collect; the reason you think the debt is worthless.

Next Harry sees on Form 2106 that you have deducted $525 for "travel, meals and lodging," money you claim you spent in connection with your regular business, but for which your com-

pany did not reimburse you. He glances again at the Schedule
C you filed for your consulting work and just as he expects,
finds heavy T and E deductions there ($1515). "Double dip-
ping?" he wonders. Have you been reimbursed by your employer, but been taking the deductions anyway? Or claiming
those expenses as if they were spent in connection with the
consulting work? He will make you prove all of that, and pay
special attention to your receipts. He figures to do well in both
places.

There's a related deduction he considers on Form 2106, Employee Business Expenses. "Country club dues: $475." He notes
on his pad: "50%?" Most people who take that one cannot
prove it is used more than half the time for business purposes.
Less than half, and they lose the whole deduction.

He already knows what you will tell him. "My company
expects every vice-president to entertain clients this way, but
they don't expect to reimburse me. What can I do? Believe me,
if I didn't need it for the job, I wouldn't join the stupid place.
Truth is, I don't even like golf that much." He's heard it countless times before. Always the same story, which doesn't affect
him. Proof does.

Some people don't have the proof and give Harry an especially hard time. What he usually does then is simply disallow
what you can't prove. What he can also do, and has done, is
actually go out to those country clubs and ask people about the
difficult taxpayer. He questions other members and employees
on how you use the club, how often you appear to bring business clients out there. He asks fellow members if you try to
develop business with them, use the club to make contacts.
Sometimes that yields the information Harry wants in order to
disallow your deduction. Other times, it simply embarrasses
you terribly, having every member and employee of your club
know that you're in trouble with the IRS, and that alone is good
enough reason so far as Harry is concerned for going out there.

Appropriately, paragraph 321.14 in Harry's Manual is especially long and detailed:

321.14 *(9-27-76)*   4233
Travel and Entertainment

(1) *General*

The amounts spent for travel and entertainment items are deductible if they are ordinary and necessary business expenses. The records should be in sufficient detail to establish the following:

(a) the relationship of the expenditure to the business;

(b) the payee and place of expenditure;

(c) the amount of the expenditure;

(d) the identity of the persons involved, including parties entertained, if any.

(2) *Techniques*

(a) Ascertain if the questions on the return pertaining to expense account information have been completed. If unanswered, inquiry should be made.

(b) Discuss with the taxpayer his/her employer's reimbursement policy to determine the correctness of the answers to the questions and to establish whether the taxpayer may have received additional compensation through the use of company-owned facilities, paid vacations, etc.

(c) If the taxpayer has claimed a deduction, procure an analysis of all expenses, both reimbursed and unreimbursed. Such expenses should be broken down into the broad categories of transportation, meals and lodging.

(d) Examine selected items within each of the broad categories.

1 Expenses for cash and through use of credit cards should be closely scrutinized.

2 If a diary is kept, ascertain the manner and method used in maintaining it. Test a sufficient number of entries to determine the reliability and credibility of the diary.

(e) Where the total of the travel and entertainment expenses appears to be disproportionate to the income and business activities, it may be advisable to reconcile the amount of the deduction by preparing an analysis of cash availability. The total of all funds received from salaries, commissions, drawings on account, investments and savings, less estimated amounts spent for personal living expenses, and actual savings and investments, will reflect

the maximum amount that could have been
spent for travel and entertainment expenses.

(f) Determine that the expenses are properly claimed for adjusted gross income and for
taxable income purposes, respectively.

(g) If the records with respect to these ex-
penditures are inadequate, consideration
should be given to the issuance of appropriate
letter.

(h) Consider whether the facts of the case
warrant fraud referral, or the application of the
civil fraud or negligence penalty.

"He lost money renting a house? We'll see about that," Harry
says, shaking his head, glancing at Schedule E. "Vacation property?" he writes on his pad. "T/p use it himself? How many
days? How usage determined? How repairs divided, capital and
other? Depreciation? How computed?"

Harry scans the numbers on the rental house, and when he
hits "$375 for repairs" it triggers something in his mind.
"Could have replaced the stove for that amount." He scribbles,
"Replace or repair?" If you have replaced something, then it is
a capital expenditure, and you have to depreciate it over a
period of years, not deduct it in one lump, as you have.

Even with Marvin, Harry knows this is an area rich with
differences of interpretation. Paragraph 322.13 tells him:

322.13 *(9-27-76)*   4233
Rental and Royalty Income

(1) Scrutinize transactions with related taxpayers, and controlled foreign entities. Look for
such features as: shifting income, renting for an
inadequate consideration to owner, etc.

(2) Determine if an accrual basis taxpayer
has property accrued income of this type at
year end. This is especially true with respect to
income which is not fixed (based on sales,
profits, productions, etc.).

(3) Determine whether there may have been
income from sources which have no corre-
sponding asset recorded. This is especially true
with regard to royalty income.

(4) Be alert to ostensible rental contracts
which may be conditional sales.

(5) Be alert to prepaid rent or lease deposit
items which may constitute income.

He sees your large refund on federal income taxes. "State?" he asks. "Declared?"

If you have a refund from the state, you have to declare it as income if it is for a year when you itemized your deductions. If you receive a refund from the federal government, you do not have to declare it. Another instance of the prevailing logic.

Harry doesn't see any state refund declared, and he'll ask about it. Even with Marvin, that one could slip by. Without Marvin, Harry would be sure to catch you there, convert that nice refund to taxable income, and readjust your whole return for you.

He picks up your wife's Schedule C again. He has already marked her T and E for examination. Now he wonders about her deduction for the use of her car. "Verify. Traffic fines?" Many people claim those, if they are collected in the course of business, but they are not allowable.

"He's claimed office in the home," Harry says, "she has not. Double-check she does not use his office at home." If she does, you will lose your entire claim because the law says the office space may be used by you and you only.

Eying her profit for the year, he is reminded to probe, as he does with everyone on commissioned earnings, to be sure she hasn't "run away from income," that she hasn't used any tricks to avoid taking any income that was due her, delaying it for the next year.

Harry taps all your forms together into a pile and sits back. He stares at the pile, and does not like it. It's too pat. It's got substantial income, including lots of self-employed income with all those deductions, he intends to attack. There's lots of room for adjustment on this one, he decides.

By the time he's through, Harry will have covered everything the computer started out with, plus all the "dangerous" deductions we discussed in Chapter 5; plus everything else his instincts lead him to.

He's also been doing something else that's important for you to know. He has been constantly filtering and weighing questions of "substance vs. form."

He knows very well that something on your return might have every appearance of correctness, yet, on inspection, it might not meet the "substance" of the law, which is to say it violates the law as Harry and the IRS interpret the *intent* of the law.

As we saw, during his training Harry was very carefully taught to follow exactly what he is told the law is. Later, in the field, he begins to see that there is a foggy area, "substance vs. form."

He begins to encounter returns, individual as well as business, that have only the appearance of legality. T/ps set up sham transactions for the single purpose of saving taxes. He finds fake liquidations, spinoffs, stock manipulations.

Not long ago, he had a man who owned 100 shares of stock worth $5000 when he bought them. He got a friend to buy the stock from him for $3000, which gave the man a $2000 loss.

Nothing illegal there. But the man then bought the stock back from the friend, soon after thirty days from the time of the original sale.

The law says that if you own an asset and sell it at a loss, you may not deduct that loss if you repurchase the asset within 30 days of the sale.

In this case, the man had followed the letter of the law, buying the stock back after thirty days. Still, Harry was suspicious. He went to the man's friend, who admitted that he had signed an agreement to sell the stock back to the man after thirty days.

Clearly, even though the letter of the law was observed, the intent was to get around it. Harry was happy to inform the clever t/p that his $2000 deduction would be disallowed.

Harry has spent about an hour and a half or two hours examining your return. It's possible, by the time he finishes, that he has scratched lots of notes to himself on several specific items, yet he is still left with a large hole in his portrait of you. Your numbers do not fit together.

Puzzled and dissatisfied, he walks down the hall to Bernice. Bernice was the original office auditor who trained Harry when he joined up. She has fifteen years with the IRS, is the most senior auditor on the staff.

"What do you make of this one, Bernice?" Harry asks, handing her your return. "$45,000 in earnings, hardly anything in interest, not a penny in dividends. Lots of deductions. I can't quite figure out what they do with their money. Couldn't spend only on tax-deductible items. There just isn't enough dough for their life style."

"Alimony?" Bernice asks, flipping through the return.

"First place I looked. No alimony. Nothing special like that."

"How about child care? Is she receiving child care?"

"Nothing shows," Harry replies. "Odd. I don't even find an excessively high mortgage deduction, not for where they live."

"Well," Bernice says, "maybe one of them's the beneficiary of a trust. Check on that."

"Right."

"Or maybe not so clean. Maybe there's a second, unreported brokerage account. If you get into the audit and have any reason to suspect that, we can check with the post office carrier on it. Also, check both their client lists for their commission work, that free-lance stuff. Make sure they're reporting all their income. Looks to me like there's a good shot at underreporting here." Bernice flips a page. "I see he even lists a safe-deposit box."

"That's what I'm wondering," Harry says.

"Well, we can always find out what's in it," Bernice replies flatly. "No problem at all."

"Right."

"This guy isn't an owner of his company, is he?" Bernice asks.

"Employee. Vice-president."

Bernice shrugs. "The big stuff comes from the ones who own the company. Can skim off the top, keep two sets of books, make cash deals. Biggest cases I ever had were that sort of thing, medium-size businesses, where one or two partners have complete control. That's when you end up with these accounts in the Bahamas."

Harry shakes his head. "This guy doesn't qualify."

"Well," Bernice says, handing back your return, "all you can do is ask. You get suspicious, you may have to pull in a Special Agent."

Pre-Audit Strategy

INTERNAL REVENUE SERVICE   DEPARTMENT OF THE TREASURY

District Director, Richmond District   Form Number:

Date   Tax Year(s):

Day and Date of Appointment:

Time:

Place of Appointment:

My Telephone Number:

Your Federal tax return for the above year(s) has been assigned to me for examination. Because I need additional information to verify certain items reported on your return, I would like to meet with you at the time and place shown above.

If you filed a joint return, either you or your spouse may keep the appointment or you may have an attorney, a certified public accountant, an individual enrolled to practice before the Internal Revenue Service, or a qualified unenrolled individual represent or accompany you. If you are not present, however, your representative must have written authorization to represent you. Form 2848-D, Authorization and Declaration, may be used for this purpose and if your representative does not have copies of this form, they may be obtained from one of our offices. Also, any other individual, even though not qualified to

represent you, may accompany you as a witness and assist in
establishing the facts in your case.

About the records needed to examine your return—

To help me make the examination as brief as possible, please
have the following information available if applicable to your
return:

Workpapers used in preparing your return;
All books and records concerning your income, expenses,
and deductions;
Bank statements and canceled checks;
Duplicate deposit slips;
Savings account passbooks;
Information on other invested funds;
Records of all loans and repayments;
Purchase invoices covering acquisitions of capital items;
Records covering purchases or sales of real estate or other
property;
Information on any nontaxable income;
Your copy of your Federal tax return for ————

The law requires taxpayers to substantiate all items affecting
their tax liabilities when requested to do so. If you do not keep
this appointment or do not arrange another, we will have to
proceed on the basis of available return information.

About the examination and your appeal rights—

We realize some taxpayers may be concerned about an examination of their tax returns. We hope we can relieve any concern
you may have by briefly explaining why we examine, what our
procedures are, and what your appeal rights are if you do not
agree with the results.

We examine returns to verify the correctness of income,
exemptions, credits, and deductions. We find that the vast majority of taxpayers are honest and have nothing to fear from an
examination of their tax returns. An examination of such a
taxpayer's return does not suggest a suspicion of dishonesty or
criminal liability. In many cases, no change is made to the tax
liability reported or the taxpayer receives a refund. However, if

taxpayers do not substantiate items when requested, we have to act on available return information that may be incomplete. That is why your cooperation is so important.

I will go over your return and records and then explain any proposals to change your tax liability. I want you to understand fully any recommended increase or decrease in your tax, so please don't hesitate to ask questions about anything not clear to you.

If changes are recommended and you agree with them, I will ask you to sign an agreement form. By signing you will indicate your agreement to the amount shown on the form as additional tax you owe, or as a refund due you, and simplify closing your case.

Most people agree with our proposals, and we believe this is because they find our examiners to be fair. But you don't have to agree. If you choose, we can easily arrange for you to have your case given further consideration. You need only tell me you want to discuss the issue informally with my supervisor, and we will do our best to arrange a meeting immediately. If this discussion does not result in agreement, you may take your case to a conferee for further consideration.

In addition to these district office appeal rights, you may request the Service's Appellate Division, which is separate from the district office, to consider your case. I will be glad to explain this procedure and also how to appeal outside the Service to the courts.

I will also be happy to furnish you a copy of our Publication 556, Audit of Returns, Appeal Rights and Claims for Refund, which explains in detail our procedures covering examination of tax returns and appeal rights. You can get a copy of this publication by writing us for it or by asking for it when we meet.

About repetitive examinations—

We try to avoid unnecessary repetitive examinations of the same items on returns filed by individuals, but this occasionally happens. Therefore, if this is an examination of your individual return and if the issues raised in the course of this examination are the same as those examined in either of the 2 previous years and the examination resulted in no change to your tax liability, please notify me. The examination of your return will then be suspended pending a review of our files to determine whether it should proceed.

About your appointment—

Your appointment is the next step. If the date, time or place of the appointment is inconvenient for you, please contact me to make more suitable arrangements.

Sincerely yours,

Examiner

ENCLOSURE:
PUBLICATION 876, PRIVACY ACT NOTICE

"They're going to send me to jail," you say to Marvin over the phone.

"You won't go to jail," Marvin replies. "Pull all of your records together and come in. We'd better review everything."

"I don't even know if I have all my records. They want to audit me for 1979. For Chrissake, that's two years ago, Marvin."

"You've got the records," Marvin says, slowly spacing out each word. "Go look in the filing case you bought. That second-hand thing I had you get to keep all your records in? The thing we deducted last year?"

"Oh, yeah. That."

"Come in Thursday at ten. We'll work everything out."

Marvin's assurance is comforting, but you are still terribly disturbed. What could you do for a living, you wonder, in Brazil? Well, you really won't have to find out unless you have been lying to Marvin all along. Even then, as we'll see, you can avoid catastrophe. Your pre-audit session is essential to your defense and mental health.

First, though, a piece of early strategy advice: Schedule the audit for Marvin's office.

Do not let Harry come to your home. If that happens, you are giving him much more than you should. As he drives down your street, he will evaluate your neighborhood and match that with the income you reported. Are you earning enough to afford your home? He will quickly check everything, from the new paint job on the house to the number of cars in the driveway, and the number of bikes as well, if you are claiming children as dependents.

Inside, the same process. Harry's experienced eye appraises all it sees, from the value of a painting on the wall to a refurbished kitchen to the amount of space you actually take for that home office.

Many District Directors prefer to have their Harrys go to your office for the audit, where Harry can make a firsthand appraisal of how things are going for you. So when you are arranging the time and place with Harry, be firm. Tell him that holding the audit any place but Marvin's office doesn't make sense. All your records are there. Harry probably won't give you an argument. Records are what he needs at this stage of things. If he feels, later, that he or an associate had better take a look at your home, they can and will.

One exception to this advice: If your audit is a relatively simple matter, just a few items they want to check, you might be asked to come into the IRS office. In that case, as I told you, you are not dealing with our Harry, but with a less experienced, lower-ranking office auditor.

Review everything with Marvin. He will probably advise you to let matters stand and do the audit at the IRS office. In fact, Marvin might tell you that the audit will be so simple you really don't need him and his expensive services at the audit session.

If you are called in for an "office audit," you may still request that it be done in Marvin's office. But in that case you are going to be assigned to a tougher auditor.

If the prospect of facing Harry simply overwhelms you, two options are available.

You may postpone the day. Postponements are not supposed to be for the faint of heart, though I have seen it used for that purpose. Delay is supposed to be for more substantial reasons. If you had planned a trip, or you need more time to pull all your records together, set another date. But do not think you can delay things indefinitely. If you postpone once, then break that date and set up another, be sure you keep it. You have reached Harry's tolerance level. Remember, he wants your case off his desk. If you keep him waiting, he'll be that much more determined to make the wait worthwhile when he finally does do the audit. Still, you are not required to accept the first date Harry gives you.

The second option you have is to send Marvin to meet Harry alone. You are not required to go to the audit yourself, so long as Marvin has your power of attorney.

At first glance, this might seem like the solution to all your problems, but I don't recommend it, except in special circumstances.

When our friends Mr. Loophole or Ms. Superstar get called in for an audit, they don't go, I am sure, because they can't afford to lose the time—an audit can go on for days. But they can afford several Marvins. The same holds true for most very big earners. Your favorite movie star has a business manager, a super-Marvin, who takes 5 percent of everything the star earns, and handles all his money matters. Pays all the bills, keeps all the records, makes all the investments, and when it's audit time, handles the audit so that the star doesn't lose a minute before the camera or on the tennis court.

Your situation is different. If you send Marvin alone, chances are he will charge you more. In fact, the extra amount you pay him might be greater than the settlement you reach with Harry.

Further, bear in mind that Marvin is still working for two people, for you and for himself. If you put him alone in a room with Harry, you might be leading him into temptation. He might be easier with Harry than he would be if you were there observing.

This is a subtle matter. I am not saying that Marvin is going to sell you out. If you really distrust him that much, get yourself a new Marvin. But I have handled audit sessions with clients present and without, and I can tell you that there is a continual subconscious pull when I am alone that isn't present otherwise. Recognizing it, I am on the watch for it. Other tax preparers have told me they think they fight even harder for clients when they are alone, perhaps overcompensating for the possibility of softness. Neither way is good.

Harry himself would rather have you present. He wants to fit your face to his portrait. Also, if he has you in the room, he might be able to elicit information from you that he didn't find on your return. But you can guard against that, as we'll see shortly.

Another good reason Harry wants you there is that your presence can speed things up. If he is alone with Marvin and the question of a travel deduction comes up, Harry might ask Marvin if your wife went along on the trip. Marvin isn't sure, but since it was a convention, he thinks she probably did. You usually take her to conventions. Marvin says, "Let me check that out." Those are words Harry hates to hear. They mean delay. They irritate him, something you do not want to happen. He might decide to let you have the travel deduction, but really cut you up on your casualty loss claim where Marvin has brought together all your documentation, which is suspect to start with.

I really feel that being there yourself is important. If you turn the whole thing over to Marvin and run and hide, you are giving up control of a major aspect of your financial life. And besides, as you will see, the whole process need not be that painful.

Let's assume, then, that you and Marvin are going to see this through together. And by "you," I mean you alone, or with your spouse. It is not necessary for both of you to give the time and nervous energy to Marvin for the pre-audit strategy session, or to Harry for the audit.

I have seen many cases where couples go through everything together, many others where one of them takes it alone. Makes absolutely no difference, just so long as one of you is totally familiar with all the financial matters of the other.

Traditionally it has been men who earn the family's income, but that condition is, of course, changing. More than half the

married women in America work today. Increasingly, I find
women wanting to be involved in all the tax matters that affect
their families. Fine. But bear one thing in mind: it doesn't make
much difference to Harry if he faces you and/or your spouse in
the audit. If there are two of you, he might try to get one of you to
answer a question, then get the other to corroborate. Or contra-
dict, a common ploy. One of you might have a genuine lapse of
memory. And then unexpected and unwelcome events occur.

Whatever you decide, planning your strategy for the audit is
just as important to you as it was to Harry. Never go into an
audit without a strategy, or you're asking to be slaughtered.

Central to all your planning should be this piece of information: The IRS is after people with substantial amounts of unreported income. That is the big crime in their eyes—
unreported income.

Bear in mind that this is different from padding a deduction,
or trying to take one where you aren't entitled to. In such
instances, Harry will say, "Sorry about that item. No." He'll do
the arithmetic over again, and send you a bill. In most cases,
remember, the IRS would rather have your money than send
you to jail.

Same for mishandling tax funds. At the IRS, I heard of
countless cases of businessmen, usually small ones, who used
the money from payroll taxes to pay off creditors and keep their
business going. They were gambling that they'd have the payroll tax money eventually. Those people got fined. Only the
most flagrant abusers ended up in jail.

Meanwhile, Marvin constitutes a human fail-safe system. He
knows the difference between a "matter of interpretation," or
"overlooking a few dollars," and "fraud, civil or criminal."
And he is not going to allow you to commit fraud.

Fraud is bad for you, Marvin knows, and very bad for him.
If he knowingly helps you commit fraud, he is liable for a fine
of $5000, or three years in prison, or both, as well as the costs
of the prosecution.

He also knows that if he is an unwitting accomplice to your
fraud, if you slip great lies right past him, he will still be fined,

and though not sent to jail, he can be further punished by the IRS. He might end up in the Problem Preparer's Program.

Beyond such dangers, the whole nature of planned theft is repugnant to Marvin's entire personality and character.

Of course, if you have been lying and keeping things from him, then he cannot protect you from yourself. In that case, when you go in to see Marvin for your pre-audit strategy session, if the amounts you have been hiding from him are substantial, you had better confess. You had better tell him then that in fact you have more than a Series E Savings Bond in that safe-deposit box. You had better tell him that you have more than one stockbroker.

Marvin will stare at you when you relate the news, but he will digest it. He has heard such things before. He will tell you, of course, that he will have to share the information with Harry at the very beginning of the audit session. "This is something you overlooked," he will tell you. "That's what you will tell him. Overlooked."

Then he will figure out approximately what it's going to cost you in new taxes and penalties. Which is still a lot better than doing time in a federal prison.

There are, however, some things Marvin does not want to hear. If, for example, what you have forgotten to tell him about is a fee from your free-lance work, or a stock sale worth $1000 or $1500 to you, he'd rather not know.

Marvin is on to a few things.

You may recall that back in Chapter 3 I told you of holes in the IRS system. One of them concerned those reports called 1099s. Some of those information slips for dividends, interest, miscellaneous items the IRS receives are pieces of paper and 85 percent of those they are incapable of processing. I heard the Commissioner himself say that unreported income in the range of $2000–$3000 is beyond them. The odds are extremely high that it will remain unreported and undetected.

Is Harry going to know about your unreported $1500? Probably not.

All of which Marvin might be aware of himself. But if you tell him, he has no choice.

When you go into Marvin's office and give him the letter from Harry, it will tell Marvin the boundaries of the skirmish to come. On that form letter Harry has marked the items he wants to examine and for which he asks you to bring all the relevant material you have.

When Marvin looks at that, he just might have a surprise for you. He might advise you of one of your little-known rights.

"Damn it," Marvin says, "we don't have to put up with this. They're auditing you for the same damn things they audited you for last year, and the year before that. High medical expenses and high travel and entertainment. And both years, you proved every penny to them and they didn't disallow a thing. Leave this to me. I'm going to tell them to stop."

In fact, if you have been audited year after year for the same things, and you have proved your case each year, you can call the IRS and tell them to stop. And, amazingly, they just might.

But since you've never been audited before, let's assume otherwise. Because the letter from Harry lists many questionable areas, Marvin has his work nicely laid out for him. You should know that Harry is hardly prohibited by law from asking you about anything else. But in practice he will stick to the specified items, unless something significant and unexpected presents itself.

Here Harry is playing according to the unwritten rules. He has cited specific matters, asked you to bring in your papers to support your case on those matters. If he asks you for something else during the audit, he knows that Marvin is going to say, "Excuse me, Mr. Harry, but you didn't ask for that. We can go to Visa for verification of the interest we paid to them last year . . . if you want." Which means, as both Marvin and Harry know, if you want to keep this case hanging for six weeks until we hear from Visa.

One of the first things Marvin will do is to evaluate the strengths and weaknesses of your entire return and tell you what you have to bargain with. He will tell you what things were not taken that might now be thrown at the auditor.

For example, that trip to Chicago. Yes, you had a business meeting, but you spent a day and a half visiting your sister. So Marvin won that tug-of war at preparation time, and didn't allow you to take the trip on the return. He said it was just too risky, could trigger an audit. Harry still might not allow a nickel of it, but bringing it up in the audit will show him how careful and circumspect you have been.

Or the four dinner parties that you originally told Marvin he should include under "home entertainment." Another one you lost, when Marvin shook his head and muttered, "Too tough to prove." Now, something to be raised in the audit.

You are beginning to reconsider Marvin's conservative ways. You are beginning to reconsider Marvin. In fact, from this point on, if he does his job, Marvin should be given combat pay.

One major difference between the approaches of Marvin and Harry is a dollar range. Harry doesn't build his attack in order to retrieve a certain number of dollars. He's not operating under dollar quotas, but time pressures. He expects that the money will come, if he handles the audit correctly. But he can't be sure what the total will be, because he doesn't know how much you have really cheated. You might have heavy and suspect deductions of all sorts, but be able to show him adequate documentation for everything.

Marvin, on the other hand, knows more than Harry, in that he knows exactly how much you've cheated. What Marvin now has to do is look over the soft areas and decide how much you might be able to keep, how much you might lose. In the end, your accountant wants to come up with a dollar range. He wants to be able to say to you, "Well, you started out with $45,000 in income, we ended up getting a refund of $3800. At the worst, we might have to give them back $1500, at the best, only $300. Can you live within that range? If $1500 is too much, at what point do we stop and fight? At what point do we settle?"

Establishing a dollar range will enable Marvin to plan. He will go into the audit knowing where you are weak, and how much he can give up to Harry on charities, while holding firm on casualty losses.

If you are actually entitled to every dollar you claimed, Mar-

vin should fight to keep your return unscratched. For the sake
of reality, let us assume otherwise. Marvin is then going to play
a game with Harry. He is going to want to let Harry win some
rounds, take some dollars from you. But he is going to want to
limit those dollars, and in agreeing with you on what that limit
should be he knows where and when to give, where and when
to be firm.

Marvin and Harry will play poker and Marvin is going to
play for you, with your money. You have to tell him what his
bankroll is, how much you expect to end up with. Whether he
folds, sticks, or raises is up to him.

Setting that dollar figure is also very important to your san-
ity. If Marvin reviews everything with you and says that the
most it will cost you is $500, you should be able to sleep well
indeed. You should no longer be plagued by visions of Harry's
backing a van up to your door. The horrendous unknown is
replaced by a bill for $500.

Planning his strategy, Marvin will check the work sheets he
used when he was preparing your returns. And now he will ask
some questions he might have let pass before.

"I saw your receipt for the safe-deposit box rental," he says,
glancing at some chicken scratches on his pad. "What's in
there? Your Series E Savings Bonds and the other stocks? Like
BP Manufacturing?"

"Yeah," you reply, now really trying to remember.

"You haven't got any cash in there, have you? Because if you
have, *if we overlooked* some cash income, you better tell me
right away."

"No, no cash. Where would I get cash?"

"Just be sure," Marvin warns. "They can get in and take a
look if they really want to."

"Break into my safe-deposit box? Why, that's outrageous,"
you say, your voice rising. "What kind of country are we living
in?"

Marvin holds up a hand. "Please don't raise your voice. And
please don't lecture the auditor about the Bill of Rights. Lots
of people hide money in safe-deposit boxes. Do you?"

"No."

Marvin nods and looks back to the return, talking to himself as he goes along.

"Okay, child care credit," he says. "Bring in your receipt for that, and also a brochure from the camp. It'll have the dates of the camp session." He looks at your puzzled face. "If you don't have one, call the camp and get one. And by the way, remember to point out your son was fourteen years old when he was at camp, didn't turn fifteen until the following year.

"Energy, energy," he says, and pauses. "I'll handle this one. We're a little weak here."

"How can we be?" you say. "I've got all the receipts from the lumber yard, from Sears. Everything's covered. Storm windows, insulation, everything."

Marvin nods. "I know. I know. Trouble is, it's all for your country house, which is not your principal residence, and that's where the installations are supposed to be made."

"Marvin, why didn't you tell me?"

"I did. I warned you. But you insisted that couldn't be the law. It's okay. It's worth a gamble," he says. "Look, bring the canceled checks. If asked, be sure to make the point that you are trying to restore the country place so you can move into it, make it your principal residence. If you're not asked, just say nothing. He may only be after the receipts."

"That's good. Think he'll buy that?"

"Who knows? Try it, but be prepared to lose this one. And if we lose it, we lose it all. No bargaining here. So if he disallows, it's going to cost you $300 in tax credits."

"Jesus."

"Take it easy. You'll survive."

He goes back to his papers. "Car loan, no problem. There you followed my advice for once, took out the loan yourself. Just bring in all the bank papers.

"Charity . . . charity," he mutters. "Few hundred of that, no receipts. Might have to give him something there." He looks up. "He's going to go after that Georgian tea set. Be sure to have the appraiser's receipt, and those pictures I told you to take of the set. You have those?"

"Yeah," you reply. "How can we be in trouble? We had an independent appraiser."

"Not a lot of trouble, but appraising is subjective, to a certain degree. So he might not want to give us the full amount. But if he doesn't, I'd make him give us something in return. We're pretty strong there, much more than we will be with those boxes you gave to the Salvation Army. But let me handle that."

"Marvin, how much will he knock off?"

"Don't be such a pessimist," he replies. "Maybe $300."

"Another $300?"

"Look, I told you this before," he says, a bit wearily. "It's not $300 that you have to write out a check for. It's $300 worth of deductions that will be *disallowed*. When that's computed against your whole tax picture, in your bracket, it might mean back taxes of, say, $50. So don't get alarmed."

"And the credit we lost?"

"*If* we lose the energy credit, that's a little different. A credit we take off the tax bill, after the whole thing is computed. So those are like real dollars. In your case, *if* we lose that one, it will mean $300 more in taxes that you'll have to pay. That is true. But even if it happens, it's not the end of the world. Remember, we start out with that $3800 refund."

Marvin now spends some time with your Casualty Losses. After checking all his worksheets, he says: "On the rosebushes, trees, and stuff, just give me that report from the maintenance company. He may not believe it, but the report is enough to fight over, and I'd appeal this one, if necessary. But we won't have to," he says. "Now on the theft, those golf clubs, your wallet, remind me what happened there."

You tell him that they were lifted from your locker at the club, while you were out having a dip in the pool.

"How old were they, the clubs?"

"Practically brand-new. Bought them at the beginning of the season, they were stolen in mid-August."

"And the rest was cash and those $50 liability charges on the credit cards?"

"Right."

He looks back to his notes. "I asked you if you had contacted your insurance company, and you said, 'Yes, but they wouldn't pay.' "

He looks right at you. "Have you collected anything?"

Your eyes fall away. "I got a check for $300."

"You should have told me."

"Okay, so I should have told you. What happens now?"

"What happens now is that you're going to lose that $300 in deductions. No question he'll ask about that. As for the rest? Credit card slips we got and can prove. Cash in wallet, you reported to cops, and not enough for him to get excited about anyway. But the price of the clubs? You paid $500, he might say something less because they're used." He holds up a hand before you can protest. "It won't be too bad. Might have to give a little, not a lot."

The next item, "tax preparer's fee," he dismisses with a wave of his hand. "I got the bill right here."

But with "business publications and subscriptions," he sighs. "I told you it was high." He consults his worksheets, shrugs. "We've got some general magazines in there. I think we even took *The New York Times.*" He shakes his head. "Don't know how in the world I gave you that one. Well, we're shaky. Maybe $150. We'll see."

"Continuing education?" he mutters. "No problem there. You've got the marketing course, your wife the one in finance. All related to your present jobs. Just bring in the tuition bills, canceled checks." He pauses. "He's going to ask you if you were reimbursed by your employer. You told me neither of you were."

"Absolutely not," you insist.

"You don't have to raise your voice," Marvin says, looking back to his papers. "Capital gains? Nothing to worry about. He'll be checking the dates. Just be sure you have the broker's confirmation slips. You still have those, don't you?"

"Sure."

"Fine. They're important," Marvin replies. "Don't lose them, whatever you do . . . Oh, while we're on this, you don't have any other brokerage accounts? Any we might have *over-looked?*"

Since you don't trust yourself to speak, you shake your head, pulling the corners of your mouth down for emphasis. Marvin nods in return.

"Did you ever get the copy of that bankruptcy filing by your brother-in-law I told you to get? You don't have that, we're going to lose the $4500 loss on that loan, sure as I'm sitting here."

"Marvin, trust me a little, will you." You pull the thing snappily out of your briefcase. "Right here."

"Good work." He cannot hide the note of surprise in his voice.

Marvin studies your rental property carefully. "We'll show him our computation," he finally tells you. "He'll probably come up with a different depreciation. The IRS has their tables for that, but we can bicker. Who's to say what the useful life of your house is? Tables, tables," Marvin mutters, shaking his head. "Tables are not gospel. They love those things more than money. I've been through this one hundreds of times. Last case was an optometrist. The IRS had their precious tables. His equipment depreciates over six years, they claimed. Well, I showed them that my client—an awfully good eye doctor, by the way, if you need one—I showed them that he had such high volume, high usage of the equipment that he actually wore it out in two years. And they accepted it," he adds with a slight smile. "What's the useful life of that old house of yours? How old you tell me? Turn of the century?"

"1935, Marvin."

"That old, huh?" he says. He never understood why you bought the thing in the first place. "Oh, and for the $585 for repairs, give me the sheets from the management company. If they did their job right, no problem there either.

"Country club dues," he continues. "There, those diaries I had you keep should save your life. You and your wife, my records show, used the club eighty-seven times, and we can prove that more than 50 percent of the time was business-related. IRS knows that most taxpayers don't keep such records, and they lop off those deductions every time. But my motto is, when you're entitled, you're entitled."

Turning now to your Schedule C, your consulting work, he stirs a bit. "Here's where they're going to try and hit us, but dammit, we're going to give them a good fight. This office in the home, for example. I know he has to land on that. But I was careful there. A picture actually might not hurt. Bring in a picture of the office. I get tired of some of these damn IRS people. Take it for granted they can nail you with things like that."

Then Marvin stops and shakes his head. "Here's the big problem. Your Travel and Entertainment deductions. Those trips. Be sure you've got your diaries in order here, all the American Express chits, airline tickets. Everything documented. And well organized. It's important to be well organized. Shows him we've been careful and know what we're doing. And I don't want to waste his time."

He reviews all your consulting income carefully. He wants to be sure he's familiar with each account, so he can quickly and accurately reproduce the income figures for all your major clients. "You've reported all the income from those clients who have furnished 1099s. I know that."

He glances at your wife's Schedule C. "Can she come to the audit, if necessary?" he asks.

"Sure, I suppose so."

"Might not be necessary," he mutters. "They're going to question us hard about that convention in Vegas you both took together. But we can back that one up. She went for her business. You went for your consulting work. But just remember, if he says, 'Gee, these bills seem awfully high,' remind him how expensive everything has gotten in Vegas. He knows, but I want him to think that you care about high costs," Marvin says. " 'You should see what some people spend at those places, ridiculous.' Say something like that. They like it if they think you're frugal."

He glances again at his worksheets. "Yeah, that's what I

thought. That was the convention, you remember, after it you flew to L.A. to visit your in-laws for a couple of days. I was very careful to take only the round-trip air fare to Vegas and only those hotel, food, and other expenses at the convention. If he brings up the question of side trips there, be honest. But only answer the questions he asks. If he doesn't bring it up, don't volunteer anything. Remember, he can't afford to go to Vegas, or fly around the country visiting."

He finishes up with your wife's Schedule C. "We've got all the receipts here. Might give us a fight over the mileage I deducted for the business use of her car. Probably argue, but I'll take care of that one. We have her appointment calendar. You also have a full-time family car and that should be good enough."

Now Marvin has finished his review and rehearsal. He busies himself with his pencil and adding machine, surveying the whole return once again, in the light of his complete revised estimate.

"Well," he tells you, staring at the machine's tape, shaking his head slightly, "I would say that if we have any luck at all, we should end up having to pay no more than $700–$750."

He has been deliberately cautious, as usual, always estimating on the down side. But you gasp anyway.

"Remember now, we started out with $45,000 in income, plus a long-term capital gain, rents, and interest, and we knocked that down to $12,000. That's thousands of dollars. Your tax bill was only $486. That is not, in my opinion, so terrible. But it's your money."

"Supposing we don't have any luck at all?"

"Well," he replies, returning to that magic tape, "with no luck at all, then . . . maybe $2000."

"You're joking."

"Nope. But I can't imagine such a thing."

"Well, what do you really imagine?"

"Don't hold me to this. But I can't imagine anything worse than $750."

Suddenly, compared to $2000, that doesn't seem so bad. "And maybe better?"

"All I can do is try."

With that, you and Marvin review one last time what your acceptable margins are, what bankroll you will give him for the poker game with Harry. You agree on a maximum of $1000 that you will accept as reasonable, or at least, livable. Beyond that, you and Marvin agree, something is drastically out of line. And you might want to appeal the auditor's findings, whether to an IRS Appeals Officer, the Tax Court or the U. S. District Court. Somehow, that seems unlikely. (You say to yourself $1250, but don't tell Marvin.)

You leave Marvin's office with something very important accomplished. Perhaps even more important than having worked out your whole strategy for Harry, you have worked out a number for yourself. You have replaced the unknown terror with a number you can live with. As I said, that knowledge alone should begin to calm you down and put you in shape for the audit itself.

10 | 23 Pieces of Advice

for the Audit Session

To put you at further ease, let me arm you with some specific pieces of advice collected over the years. Things to do and not to do, to say and not to say in the great confrontation.

1. How to dress for the audit. Dress the way you normally do for business. Remember, Harry has a picture of you in his mind. You do not want to disturb that picture in a way that will pique his curiosity.

So don't try to disguise yourself. If you are a business consultant and stroll in wearing an old, frayed suit thinking Harry will see how bad things have gotten, all you will do is make him suspicious.

On the other hand, if you are pulling down $150,000 a year in the record business, show up in the same jeans you wear to the studio. Harry also expects that.

Needless to say, it is equally unwise to flaunt wealth at Harry. Go light on the jewelry, fancy watches, custom-made suits, expensive dresses.

The most elaborate example of dressing down that I've heard was a tale that was told around the IRS about Frank Costello.

It didn't come from a Costello audit, but the ploy was appropriate.

Supposedly, Costello was to appear in court, and the day before, his lawyer reviewed the case with him. At the end of their discussion, the lawyer added one special piece of advice: "Don't wear that suit to court tomorrow."

Costello, an extremely dapper man, was offended. "What's wrong with this suit?" he asked in his gravelly voice. "Cost me a lot of money. I got the best tailor in New York."

"That's the point, Frank," the lawyer said. "You are going to be appearing before a jury of people who make less than your tailor. Please wear another suit."

Costello shrugged. "I can wear another suit. But it'll be just as good."

"Do me a favor. On the way to court tomorrow, stop at Robert Hall's and pick a suit off the rack, put it on and wear it. Any suit that fits you."

"What's Robert Hall?" Costello asked, frowning.

The lawyer told him. "Men's clothing store. There's one right by Times Square. Go pick out a suit."

The next morning, the case was scheduled for 10:00 A.M. and at 9:45 Costello had not yet appeared. The lawyer waited, but when Costello still hadn't arrived just before 10, he grew anxious. He asked the judge for a slight delay, and began calling around. No Costello. Then about 10:15, Costello called him.

"It's me," he said.

"My God, Frank, are you all right? Where are you?"

"I'm in that store you sent me to."

"You're still in Robert Hall? Frank, please, just pick a suit, any suit, and get down here."

"I've been looking at their stuff."

"Yes?"

"I'd rather go to jail."

2. Be on time. In fact, be early, especially if you're scheduled first thing in the morning, or just after lunch. You can be certain Harry will be on schedule at those times of the day. Always bear in mind that Harry has time pressures. One of the most irritating things to any auditor is to be kept waiting by a taxpayer.

I have heard numerous stories from auditors about taxpayers who not only keep them waiting, but then compound their gaffe, when they finally arrive, by telling the auditor that they are very busy and certainly hope this whole thing can be wrapped up quickly because they have an important meeting at noon. Auditors are human. In those situations they will lash back. You will have a very long and very costly audit.

3. You do not have to accept the auditor assigned to you. Few people are aware of this important right.

Let's say Harry comes in and he's in a foul mood. He is short-tempered and abusive. He rushes you, is curt, accusatory, cuts Marvin off in midsentence.

You do not have to suffer him. You can tell him that he is being abusive and unfair and that you are going to request a new audit with a different auditor.

And don't be afraid that Harry will get back at you; that he'll find out who is taking over the case and have him rip you apart.

The IRS is very sensitive to taxpayer complaints about audits, especially if they come through congressmen. They have trained Harry to comport himself with evenness and firmness, to be detached and formal but always respectful. If he isn't and you report him as you should, he is in trouble. Not you.

4. Don't take into the audit more than you are asked for. As we saw, Harry's letter establishes the boundaries of the audit. Stick to that. If he decides in the course of the audit to broaden the original scope, let him try. Let him say, "I'd like to talk about medical deductions," and let Marvin apply the delay ploy: "Excuse me, Mr. Harry, but you didn't ask for that. We can get it . . . if you want."

Harry might just forget his questions about "medical" in the name of closing the case.

Ditto, copies of previous IRS returns. If Harry wants them, let him get them.

You gain nothing by being overly cooperative.

I got a call for help recently from an actor in New York with a dreadful, but typical, story. He and his wife had been called for an audit, but all the IRS wanted to check was their child care credit. Though the couple didn't know this at the time, they were part of that special TCMP I mentioned, designed to make sure that t/ps who were claiming this credit were actually entitled to it. All the auditor asked them for was documentation for that one credit.

The actor's wife took time off from work, since he was ill, and went to the audit alone, bringing with her not only their child care material but just about every other piece of financial information she could find.

The agent first reviewed the child care stuff, declared everything in order, and then inquired about the rest of her treasure chest. Mrs. Actor handed everything over to him with a smile. The auditor accepted her gifts with a smile, began reviewing them, and before they knew it, Mr. and Mrs. Actor were the subjects of a full-blown audit stretching over two years of returns.

5. Try to act natural.   Natural, under the circumstances.

If you've developed your audit strategy with Marvin and have a pretty clear idea where things will work out and what it will cost you, you should be able to relax a bit.

But if you can't, if you are naturally and visibly nervous, it's a good idea to tell Harry, "I'm nervous. This is my first audit, Mr. Harry, and I must admit, it's a bit awesome."

Expressed that way you are telling Harry that (a) you are not trembling because you know in your heart you are guilty; (b) you are in awe of this process, his process.

6. Attitude is nearly everything.   Harry wants you to take this audit seriously. He expects you to be concerned. Your money is at stake. If you are not, if you are too nonchalant about the whole thing, Harry might well resent you and your attitude.

It's a little like being back in grammar school, where you got a grade for "Attitude." If Harry feels you are taking him and the audit with proper seriousness, and that you are a reasonably honest taxpayer, he will frequently allow you the benefit of a doubt.

This is especially true if you have most of your documentation available and organized. Then if you hit a deduction or two that you can't back up with a piece of paper, he'll be much more inclined to accept your word and Marvin's argument.

7. Let Marvin do the talking.   Marvin has not only done your return, he's reviewed it with you in preparation for the audit. If there is anything Harry has to know, Marvin should have that information.

You might be starting an unusual kind of business. And in order for Harry to understand why you have such high start-up costs, he has to understand some of the basics of your business. Don't you explain it to him. You have already explained it to Marvin. Let him explain it to Harry.

As we know, Harry has various reasons for preferring that Marvin is with you, and not the least of them is that now it's one pro talking to another. The less you say the better.

Harry also wants Marvin there because he knows that you will believe him. If they wrestle through a complicated point, Harry wants Marvin to tell you, "Okay, let's give him that." You'll accept it from Marvin because you trust him and you're paying him. If Harry were alone with you, he still wouldn't be able to convince you, even after wasting lots of time explaining.

8. Whenever you are asked a technical question, or something you and Marvin haven't yet considered, refer it to Marvin.
There are times when you, not Marvin, must reply to certain questions. But don't feel as though you must try to answer a technical question from Harry, or leap into the unknown. Don't be concerned that he will consider you uncooperative, or by referring to Marvin, Harry will get unduly suspicious. Harry has asked the difficult question of you because he wants to trip you up.

So let Marvin protect you. Simply reply, "I don't know . . . Marvin?" Then let the pros work it out. Once again, by talking, you can only say something that will hurt you.

9. Don't be flip with Harry.   There are, of course, those non-technical questions Harry will put to you, to which you have to respond. I had a client who had moved from Texas to Washington, D.C., for a new job. Since the company did not reimburse him for the move, we took it as a deduction.

We got audited, and when we reached that item the agent asked him: "Did you get the job offer before you flew up here, or after?"

It was not a question for me to answer, even though the moving allowance hung on the reply. If I had tried, I'm sure I would have been told: "I didn't ask you. I asked him." And he would have been right.

My client recognized the meaning of the question, paused a moment, then smiled. "Which answer is the best answer?" he said, warmly.

The agent bristled. "The truthful answer is the *only* one I want," he said, and from that point on what had been a reasonably painless and friendly session became a mean grilling.

If you must answer one of Harry's questions, be direct, brief, and very businesslike.

10. Never volunteer information.   An extension of the previous point. If there is something simple and obvious to clear up—that you had three business trips, not two—then clear it up and again become the silent observer.

If there is any information you think will help your case, tell Marvin in your pre-audit strategy session. Let him decide whether it will really help. And if so, how to use it.

11. Don't be chatty.   Being chatty is one of the most dangerous things you can do in an audit. You are bound to say something that will hang you.

You might be talking out of nervousness. Or you might feel the need to make Harry like you. Both understandable, but fatal errors.

You get no points from Harry for being nice. Do not be unpleasant, but do not try to win Harry over. Harry is not interested in you as a wonderful human being. If you persist, he might listen, but Harry listens in a special way. Everything you tell him is tax data.

If you start talking about how proud you are of your daughter (hoping he has a daughter too), how she'd done so well at college and has now married a wonderful guy, Harry does not put down his pencil, smile, and pull out a picture of his own daughter. What Harry does is ask you when she got married. And when you tell him, he looks at your return and says, "But you claimed her as an exemption. Did you furnish over half her support? Does she now file a joint return with her husband? May I have her married name, please, and her social security number, if you've got it?"

There are also audits, Agents tell me, when taxpayers get chatty, and seriously waste their time.

One Agent told me about running such an audit on the Friday he was scheduled to go off on vacation with his family. At the outset, he wasn't concerned. The return didn't seem that complex, and he thought there'd be enough time to go through the audit, get back to his office, and write up his report before going off.

But he couldn't shut the taxpayer up. "The guy went on and on," he told me, "and not about his taxes. About anything and everything. He wanted to talk about inflation. About baseball. The cost of hospital care. The man was incredible. At one point, I thought he was deliberately trying to distract me. Some of them do that, you know. But this jerk, I finally decided, simply couldn't stop talking.

"No matter how many times I said to him, nicely, 'Let's try to stick to your return, and get this over with,' it did no good. Finally, about 2:30, I was getting a headache, and damn worried that I wasn't going to finish this before vacation. And you know how they hate you to leave a case open while you're away.

"So I told the man: 'We have two choices. Either you shut up and we finish this audit, or I'll hold it open for another two weeks and when I come back I'll check every single item on your return.'

"Even that didn't work. I said the hell with it. Naturally, I took some flack for leaving it hanging. But two weeks later I came back and tore that damn thing apart."

12. Do not let Harry draw you out.   Agents are clever at catching you when you least expect it. When there is a break in the routine for example. Marvin goes to the bathroom. Or you all stretch for a minute, freshen the coffee. Harry might ask you what seems an innocent question, something aside from the business of the audit. But there *is* nothing aside from that business. When he observes that it is a hot day, he might be leading you into a discussion of how to escape the heat, which in your case could mean using your country house. Harry has his eyes on the deductions you have taken for that house.

A woman Agent from New Jersey told me how simple it could all be. Whenever she sensed something wasn't right during an audit she put her pencil down, pushed her chair away from the desk, and pretended to be tired.

"My head's spinning from all these numbers," she'd say, reaching for her coffee. "Let's take a break and clear out the cobwebs."

That completely disarmed taxpayers. They knew it wasn't the same as the referee ringing the bell at the end of a round, but still they dropped their guard. Then she'd begin talking generally about the stock market, how it went down again yesterday, and before long the t/p is mentioning the name of a broker who is not the broker of record on his confirmation slips.

13. Don't rush the auditor, or allow him to rush you.   Be sure Harry knows that you will give him as much time as he needs.

Some people try to hurry the audit, thinking that if they can push it along they can slip things past Harry. That won't work. Harry will sense it, and be extra slow and careful.

Similarly, be sure you don't let Harry rush you. He can force you into costly statements and mistakes.

14. Don't plead that everyone else does it. That argument is meaningless to Harry.

If you have a deduction that is questionable, but a situation where you did spend the money because that is how things are done in your business—certain kinds of traditionally accepted payments, for example—explain it all to Marvin, and then let him weave it around the law and into the argument.

When you tell Harry that "everyone else does it," you simply irritate him. The worst story I ever heard on this came from an agent who was being pestered by a t/p. "My neighbor does it . . . my brother-in-law does it . . ." It was increasingly bothersome. Finally, having told the t/p repeatedly that someone else's mistake was no defense, the agent stopped the audit and took down the names and addresses of every one of those friends and relatives who did it. Then, he had all of their returns pulled and audited too.

15. Don't try the paper-dumping ploy. There are taxpayers and tax advisors who think they are going to bury and confuse Harry under mountains of supposed documentation. They actually bring cartons of canceled checks and bills and chits and laundry lists into the audit and give them to Harry. "Here is our evidence," they say. "Help yourself."

They imagine that the mass will either overwhelm him, or convince him that everything is documented ten times over.

What they succeed in doing is infuriating Harry. Whenever an auditor is presented with that situation, you can be certain that he will accept the challenge. He will play that game with you. He can play almost any one you want. I have heard scores of auditors talk about such paper dumpings. They all do the same thing. They ask the taxpayer about nearly every single thing on the return, and examine every single scrap of paper.

An auditor from Indiana told me that he once got a paper dumper when he was especially loaded with cases. He went immediately to his supervisor, told him what had happened and showed him the return in question.

The supervisor could see it was a most promising return.

"I'm going to reassign all your cases," he said. "Have a good time."

16. Don't walk in without records. It might seem unlikely but some people do not keep records, still take substantial deductions, and then face the auditor empty-handed.

George M. Cohan, the composer, was one of these people. He entertained lavishly, but never kept any records. Finally, when the IRS disallowed his deductions, he fought them and won a court ruling. The Tax Court said he was able to show that he had entertained, and since he didn't have the records to back up the amounts he deducted, the court made a reasonable estimate.

Officially, the IRS has said for years that they wouldn't follow that court ruling, but they do.

When I was there, I heard about a rather infamous Cohan rule t/p. The fellow was a salesman for a New York dress manufacturer. He traveled constantly, and he was very successful. Every year he would declare more than $100,000 in salary and commissions, take heavy deductions for all his business-related expenses, and every year he would be audited.

The man never kept any records. He went into each audit with nothing—not a single diary, paid hotel bill, or restaurant stub.

When the auditor asked him how he arrived at $6000 for travel, $7500 for hotels, $14,000 for entertainment, and so on, the salesman answered the same way.

"I make a lot of money. It costs me a lot to make it."

"I see you make a lot."

"I don't hide anything from you."

"But still, you have to be able to document your expenses."

"Don't you think a traveling salesman has to travel?"

"Of course."

"And when he travels, don't you think he has to sleep somewhere?"

"Yes, but . . ."

"And don't you think a salesman who places the kind of

orders I place is expected to pick up all the checks?"

"Perhaps."

"Okay, then, we agree. In principle, we agree. It's just a matter of particulars. If you think $14,000 is too much for entertainment, what do you think is fair? $12,000 . . . $10,000?"

And so it went. They negotiated each item.

This is not an advisable strategy. Wherever there is no documentation, Harry could disallow everything. Once again, "attitude" is everything.

In fact, the IRS has issued rulings that require taxpayers to keep records. You might get away with it the first time, but after that, expect a negligence penalty of 5 percent of your tax liability.

17. Don't use the audit as a political forum. As I noted earlier, it is not wise to berate Harry with your views. He couldn't care less if you think we're spending too much for arms, and too little for solar energy development, or vice versa. He will, however, deeply resent having his time wasted, and that's all you'll be doing.

18. Don't try for sympathy. Two problems here.

First, it's a further waste of Harry's time. He will make his decisions on the basis of the information and evidence he has, what you and Marvin explain to him. Harry can relate to survival. He can understand a small businessman who is struggling to stay out of bankruptcy. But he needs evidence. Sad stories are not evidence.

Second, if you start with the sad stories, you are violating Rule #11: you are being chatty.

Do not mistake Harry for your deductible psychotherapist. If you tell Harry that your wife has thrown you out of the house, changed all the locks, is suing for divorce, and won't let you in to get your tax records, do not expect him to say, "Gee, that's tough. Feel like talking about it?"

To Harry, all that is your problem, not his. It is your responsibility to provide the records and information he requires. He takes your responsibility very seriously. Your wife won't let you get your records? Then, he might decide to go on the information at hand. And we know where that can lead.

19. Don't allow Harry to go on a fishing expedition.   You and Marvin both have work papers. All your secrets and much of your strategy are scratched on them.

If Harry says, "Let me see how you came up with those figures," do not voluntarily give him the papers. He is unlikely to demand them.

Similarly, you might want to show him a single stub in your checkbook to verify a claim. You have lost the check itself. Fine. But don't hand the checkbook over to him. May as well toss yourself into a pool with a shark.

20. Don't try to take Harry to lunch.   The National Office has a policy: you may not buy Harry lunch. He may accept coffee or a *soft* drink from you, while the audit is going on. But no lunch.

Still, Harry has to eat. When it comes lunchtime, he will reveal his human side and admit that he is getting hungry.

If Marvin wants to go to lunch with Harry, fine. They'll go to some modest place that Marvin knows Harry can afford. But don't you join them. Excuse yourself. Say you have a previous lunch appointment. Or you promised your wife or husband that you'd pick up the watch from the repair shop, the car from the garage, whatever is most likely for you to be doing.

The danger, of course, in your going to lunch is that you will talk. It's a perfect setting for Harry to learn more about you.

21. Do not arrive with a stereotype of Harry in mind.   Harry might be Harriet. The IRS is an equal opportunity employer, and in recent years has actively recruited women, blacks, various minorities. When I was there, and even before, the Service, like the accounting profession, was pretty much all male and white. That is changing, and you could be disarmed and careless if you expect a pale and paunchy rumpled fellow with dandruff and glasses, and in walks a tall and stunning black woman.

22. Do not try to bribe Harry.   Bribes, or attempted bribes, are taken extremely seriously at the IRS.

If Harry receives the slightest whiff of a bribe, he is likely to take one of two steps.

He probably will give you a reprieve and say, "You know, I really don't like the way this conversation is going at all. I mean, someone might misunderstand you and think that you were actually offering an agent of the Internal Revenue Service a bribe. You wouldn't want anyone to make that mistake, I assure you."

Or he might do what I've heard of a number of agents doing, lead you on. He might just play the game with you, and let you offer him the bribe. If he takes you to court on that charge, he'll have to prove it, of course. But he will only go to court if he is sure he can. If he does, you could get five years and $10,000.

23. Do not underestimate Harry.

Let me pull all these points together for you. They make a good checklist to review the morning of your great confrontation with Harry.

1. Dress the way you normally do for business.
2. Be on time.
3. You do not have to accept the auditor assigned to you.
4. Don't take into the audit more than you are asked for.
5. Try to act natural.
6. Attitude is nearly everything.
7. In general, let Marvin do all the talking.
8. Whenever you are asked a technical question, or something you and Marvin haven't yet considered, refer it to Marvin.
9. Don't be flip with Harry.
10. Never volunteer information.

11. Don't be chatty.
12. Do not let Harry draw you out.
13. Don't rush the auditor, or allow him to rush you.
14. Don't plead that everyone else does it.
15. Don't try the paper-dumping ploy.
16. Don't walk in without records.
17. Don't use the audit as a political forum.
18. Don't try for sympathy.
19. Don't allow Harry to go on a fishing expedition.
20. Don't try to take Harry to lunch.
21. Do not arrive with a stereotype of Harry in mind.
22. Do not try to bribe Harry.
23. Do not underestimate Harry.

11 | The Great
Confrontation

If you have never been audited, I have some good news for you. In most instances, it is not nearly so bad as you imagine.

But it can be exhausting because of the inherent tension of the thing, and because you do have to be constantly alert, even with Marvin there at your side. Or Harry will trip you up. He's always looking for a chance to do that.

And it can stretch out. I'd allow a whole day for the kind of audit we have been sketching, a nonbusiness individual return with a large number of deductions. Marvin, from his own experience, should be able to give you a pretty good estimate.

On the morning of your audit, you arrive at Marvin's office half an hour early, and arrange all your records so you can impress Harry with your thoroughness. When he asks for interest receipts, you want to be able to say, "Here you are," and reach directly for the right pile.

Harry arrives at 9:30, as scheduled. It is quite possible, by the way, that Harry and Marvin will know each other from previous audits. If that is the case, Marvin will have had a happy advantage when he was planning strategy with you. He will be able to anticipate some of the areas Harry is sure to be tough on, how much Harry is likely to give you a break, and where. He will also be able to advise you about Harry's personal style.

More likely, they have not met, so when Harry comes in Marvin will offer him a cup of coffee and ask about two or three of Harry's colleagues he has dealt with over the years.

Harry will be cordial if not friendly, sip his coffee, and arrange his papers. There will be no way you can tell by looking at him that he is quite skeptical about your return. There will be no way you can tell anything about his feelings.

For Harry, this is just another audit, one of twenty on his desk. For you, it is a living nightmare. And he knows that. He intends, in fact, to take full advantage of your nervousness.

In planning his pre-audit strategy, Harry carefully plotted the course of the audit. He will proceed according to his agenda, and you will too.

Usually, at the start, he will ask you to verify the data at the top of your return. He will ask you if you are married, how many children you have, how old they are. Some of this information he has before him, some, such as the age of your children, he doesn't. He is both verifying and probing with these apparently obvious questions. With the age of the kids, he wants to see if they have filed their own returns, even though you're claiming them as dependents.

The questions and Harry himself seem obvious. But Harry is never obvious. Keep that in mind.

He will also verify that you did not prepare the return, that it was done by Marvin, and that he sent you a signed copy. If not, Marvin could be slapped with a $100 fine.

If there was a refund due, he'll ask if it went to you. If it went to Marvin, he could be hit for another $500. This is an IRS restriction, intended to stop preparers who say, "Okay, you're going to get a refund of $300. Of course, you know government bureaucrats. Who can tell when they'll send it to you? But if you really want the money now for that vacation, I'll make you a loan." Which puts them in the quick personal financing business, with its usual high interest charges.

Marvin has primed you for the most important of the early

questions from Harry. "Do you have any income that you forgot to declare?"

He asks it of you, and it is you, not Marvin, who must answer. If you decided not to tell Marvin or Harry about that $1400 in the "overlooked" commission, be sure your voice is steady when you answer.

"No."

"No other income? You're certain?"

"Right."

"None from stocks, beside what you've declared here?"

You shake your head.

"You own any other stock?"

"Yes," you reply, having gone through this in the pre-audit strategy session with Marvin. "But nondividend stock."

"What about savings accounts?" Harry asks, knowing that you show almost no interest income.

Now there is that "overlooked" item you did tell Marvin about, for some reason. "Not savings account. But we did overlook one item of interest. We caught it reviewing everything for this audit." You smile, flushing with honesty. "Overlooked this interest from my wife's old checking account. They pay interest now."

Harry reads the bank slip, nods. "Okay. $60. That it?"

He stuns you with his calmness. You nod slowly.

"You or your wife receive any alimony?" Harry asks, now covering Bernice's little list.

"Alimony?"

"That's right. People do get divorced these days, as you might have heard, and some people pay alimony, while others receive it." His tone is insulting, his manner bullying, as he intends. He wants to put you on the defensive from the beginning, and keep you there. "My question is really quite simple. Do you, or your wife, receive any alimony?"

"Why, no," you reply, still somewhat puzzled by the question.

"We would have declared that as income," Marvin tells him, "if there had been any."

"Child care?" Harry asks, ignoring Marvin.

You shake your head. "No, no child care either."

"Either of you a trust beneficiary?"

You look at Marvin.

"He doesn't understand that term," Marvin says. "I can tell you neither one receives income from a trust. If they did, I assure you we would have declared it as well."

Harry's eyes never leave your face, all the while Marvin answers. "How many brokerage accounts do you have?"

"One." Your throat feels suddenly constricted. "Just the one I show there."

Harry then does a lot of writing and looks up at you again. "Okay, let me ask you a few questions about some of these deductions. You do have quite a few of them."

"All well documented," Marvin says with a pleasant smile. "And, oh, by the way, we have a couple more miscellaneous deductions I'd like to talk to you about at the end of the audit, ones we didn't take before but I'd like to take now."

Harry stares at Marvin. "Even more?"

"As I said, Mr. Harry, all well documented."

"I'll be the judge of that now, won't I," he replies. "What's this energy credit for?"

Marvin asks you for the receipts from the lumber yard and Sears, which you go right to. Harry watches you as you hand them to Marvin who hands them to him.

"You don't have to be afraid," he says to you. "You won't catch anything. I'm not a leper. You can hand things directly to me."

Marvin forces a chuckle. "I think you'll find it's a little faster this way. We've got things organized and I don't want to waste your time giving you the wrong papers."

Marvin is launching a double defense. He wants Harry to be dealing with him, not you. And he doesn't want you, by mistake, handing Harry some papers that Harry should not see.

Harry reads Marvin, and recognizes a pro. He takes the receipts, canceled checks, turns the checks over. "Is this the only time you've ever claimed the energy credit?"

"Absolutely," Marvin says quickly. "This is our total credit."

"Let me see your return for 1980, the year after this one," he says to you, intending to see how much he can push you and Marvin around. "I want to verify that you didn't take the energy credit again, if you don't mind."

"1980 return . . ." you say, with some panic. You know you didn't bring it with you. You aren't even certain you know exactly where it is.

"He doesn't have it with him," Marvin says slowly, a slightly caustic tone in his voice.

"Okay, were you his paid tax preparer that year?"

"Yes, I was. And I don't have it available, either."

"Then you're in some trouble, Mr. Marvin. You know you're supposed to keep copies of client returns on file for three years."

"Or keep records on those returns," Marvin replies evenly. "And that's what I've got here. And those records show no energy credit for that year."

"You don't have a copy of the return?" Harry asks him.

"No, Mr. Harry, I don't," Marvin answers. "I'm certainly not going to lie to you about a thing like that, especially when I know how easy it is for you to get a copy from your computer, if you want it." Marvin smiles and shrugs, pretending that he'd be a foolish player, placing himself in a clear checkmate situation if he lied to Harry on that one, all the time knowing of course exactly what he's really doing—that it is not so convenient for Harry to retrieve the return—and also knowing that Harry knows.

Which is the way the game is played. Harry does know, and figures if he doesn't get you here, he will somewhere else. "Okay," he says. "Maybe I will have to pull that 1980 return. We shall see." He glances again at the 1979 return. "This energy-saving stuff, the storm windows, insulation, it went into your principal residence?"

"It's going to be," Marvin answers for you.

Harry looks up quickly. "Going to be?"

"They're making these improvements, getting the house in shape so they can move into it."

Harry looks at page one of your return. "In other words, these energy improvements were not installed at 4318 Belvedere?"

"No, but . . ."

"That's a condo?"

"Yes."

"What's this other home?"

"Presently a weekend and summer home. But as I said, they're fixing it up so they can move there."

"Sorry. I can't allow that $300 credit."

"But how can you raise kids in the city today?" you protest. "It's a jungle."

"The law," Harry replies in answer to your urban crisis, "is that you are entitled to energy credits only in your principal residence. This is not your principal residence, period."

"Give us a break," Marvin says plaintively. "What about half?"

Harry stares at him. "There's no such thing as half a principal residence."

Marvin sighs and tosses a hand in the air. The process has hardly begun and you are already depressed. This guy Harry is batting two for two and you can envision him going through your entire return, disallowing every single item.

Though he doesn't show it, Marvin is not feeling so badly at all. True, he has given Harry your undeclared interest income and the energy credit, but he expected to give him both anyway. And, since they both came at the very beginning of the audit, perhaps Harry will already feel less pressure to slice up all the other soft items that lie ahead.

Indeed, Marvin is buoyed by Harry's choice and handling of the next two items; it seems as though Harry wants to slow down a bit, give a little as well as take.

Harry dismisses the child care credit and the deduction for Marvin's tax advice as fast as you can pass the camp brochure and the other papers through Marvin. In fact you are slightly disappointed that he doesn't even open the camp brochure, since you had taken all that trouble to call the owner of the camp and get the damn thing.

Then you sense another shift, as though Harry is visibly changing gears. He is studying his notes for what seems like ages. Suddenly, still looking down at them, he asks you: "What church do you attend?"

There is something about Harry in combination with church that tells you not to lie on this one. "I'm afraid I'm not much of a churchgoer, Mr. Harry. My wife attends pretty regularly though, St. Matthew's Episcopal on Grant Ave." You have told the truth and you shall be rewarded.

Harry has his mind on those cash contributions made at the door, which are listed as deductions on your joint return. If you had pretended and mentioned a church, he might have asked you if by any chance you knew the Roberts family, who also go to that church. And if you said, "Yes," Harry would mutter something about what nice people they are. He would, however, be thinking something else. He has made up that nice Roberts family, and caught you in one of the agent's standard ploys. For lying to Harry about church, you will be punished by having all of your undocumented contributions lopped off.

"You certainly are a charitable taxpayer," Harry says. "Want to tell me about that Georgian tea set?"

"We got the appraisal right here," Marvin says, waving his fingers at you to hand him the thing. You know from your strategy session to let him handle this. You pass over the appraisal and the photographs you took then, at Marvin's insistence.

"Wait a minute," Harry says. "Before I even see that stuff, I've never heard of this . . ."—he lifts your return off the desk for a closer view—". . .this Brookline Restoration Society. Is it an acceptable charity? I'll have to check it out."

You breathe in so quickly a revealing hiss comes from your mouth.

"Oh, it's on the approved list, Mr. Harry. I assure you," Marvin says. "I checked it out myself. But if you have doubts, use my phone. Call your office." He extends an open hand toward the telephone.

"That's fine. I'll check it out when I get back," he replies. Marvin knows he will not, but you now are wondering if your $3000 deduction, and in fact your whole audit, will remain hanging until Harry gets around to checking that list.

Harry takes the documents on the tea set from Marvin, looks them over, studies the photos, then shrugs. "I have to tell you, $3000 is an awful lot of money for that set."

"We had a member of the professional association of appraisers," Marvin says. "Paid him $150. You've got the bill right there, Mr. Harry. This is not some number we've pulled out of thin air."

"I still think it's high. I could get another appraiser, Mr. Marvin, and you know very well he might come up with a $2000 appraisal."

"Not for this set," Marvin insists. "Look at those pictures."

"Let's go on," Harry says, knowing that he could come back to that set and take some of the deduction away from you, if he needs to. But probably he won't have to. Not with that $800 Salvation Army deduction coming up. "One question," he says to you. "Where'd you get that tea set?"

"Where'd I get it?"

"Yes. Where'd it come from?"

"From my grandmother," you answer honestly. "She died last year. Left it to me, but she wanted it to be given to some appropriate historical society. Which is what we did. Brookline Restoration Society is quite a wonderful group."

You thought you answered brilliantly, so you are confused when you see Marvin glaring at you, and Harry writing all those notes again.

"When did she die?" he asks. "The exact date, please." And you know that you were not so brilliant. You have given him some information he really did not have to be given. After you tell him the date, he says: "And these items to the Salvation Army, they were from her estate?"

"Yes, they were," Marvin interjects, "some beautiful things."

You sink back in your chair, again deflated, and watch. In moments, the two of them sound like a couple of merchants in a Turkish bazaar. Harry is arguing that on the basis of the documentation he has there, he doesn't have to allow any value for this broken-down furniture, while Marvin is informing him that your grandmother was a woman of exquisite taste. The Georgian tea set is only one small example.

"All right, Mr. Marvin," Harry finally says. "This list of furniture and old clothes, I'll allow that they're worth something, but they're not worth $800. You don't have adequate documentation for that. You know the law says it's your responsibility to prove its value. I really don't have to allow any of it."

Your heart sinks. Jesus Christ, you think, there goes $800.

"Well, Mr. Harry, I've had an awful lot of audits with less documentation than what you have there, and never been totally disallowed. I mean, I think it's worth the full $800. But I admit, it would be hard for us at this point to prove more than $500."

Harry nods. "For now, let's consider that a reasonable figure." He scribbles on his pad.

Knowing that your grandmother died, Harry next moves obliquely to an item about which he is habitually curious.

"Tell me," he asks, exploring this new avenue you've inadvertently handed him, "has your grandmother's estate been settled yet?" He knows that whatever she left you is not taxable, but he still wants to know more about what you do with your money.

"Yes," you reply. "She was hardly a wealthy woman. But I received $15,000 and the house is up for sale."

"What did you do with that money?" Harry asks. To a degree, it could solve his early puzzle. It could explain how you live the way you do on $12,000 taxable income.

"It's not taxable," Marvin reminds him, nicely affecting surprise that Harry even asked.

Harry nods. "What have you done with that?" he asks again.

Though you may not be aware of it, you do not have to tell

Harry. He's not entitled to that information. Yet you do sense that the way you handle this is important. Instinctively, you know you want to deflect Harry, but not bruise him.

You might tell him part truth, and part something else. "Some of it we just spent. I mean, the cost of everything is ridiculous today . . . I've invested a little. I've given some to my children. Some to Dartmouth. They're having a special campaign and this was kind of found money for me . . ."

Or you may turn again to Marvin, who tells him: "Mr. Harry, I'm sorry to even say this, but I really do believe you are overextending the bounds of this audit. And anyway, the distribution of the cash funds wasn't until January of this year, so it has absolutely nothing to do with this return."

"How much did you put into that safe-deposit box?" Harry persists on asking you, calm as ever.

"None," you reply.

"What's in there?"

"Investment property. Series E Savings Bonds, deed to the rental property, and that BP Manufacturing stock we sold."

"And?"

"And what, Mr. Harry?"

"And what else?"

"That's it," you tell him, hoping your voice is just as flat as his.

Harry nods. "Okay," he says.

The car loan for your daughter is a breeze. He barely glances at your signature on the bank loan.

The casualty losses take time, but you are silent. Marvin tells him immediately of your delayed insurance payment on the golf clubs, and then they review all of the related backup material. You expect him to diminish the value of those stolen clubs, so when he starts to talk about their being used, you are silenced by Marvin's raised palm. Harry ends up giving you the rosebushes with nothing more than a frightening stare, and taking $200 off the value of the clubs. Plus, of course, the $300 the insurance company paid you.

The rosebushes trigger a number of questions from him about

how much property you actually own. "Condominium? Country place for second home? *And* rental property?"

"All modest, as you can see for yourself," Marvin assures him. He does not want Harry to start imagining that you have mountains of cash income you are tucking away in real estate.

"Tell me how you lost money on that rental property," he asks you.

Again, Marvin to the rescue. "Give me the papers on that, please," and you do so.

This is the kind of dish both Marvin and Harry relish. After first establishing that you do not use the property more than fourteen days a year for yourself, that it really is a "rental property," they then have a long discussion about "useful life," "salvage value," "computation methods," and "depreciation."

And then Harry shakes his head. "Mr. Marvin, I'm very sorry, but what all this really comes down to is that that building has a useful life of thirty years, not twenty, as you computed."

"Mr. Harry, I have to tell you that I am aware of the tables you people have, and they're good ones. Usually. Not for this building, however. For this building, you're wrong. Actually I think that twenty years for a thing that old is generous. It's in sad shape. Mortar crumbling. Look at the repair bills for one year. Frankly, it's amazing to me they can get anybody to rent it. But you don't have to take my word for it. Send someone out to look at it."

Harry shakes his head again. "That won't be necessary. I've got a clear enough picture," he says. "Now, you know I'm not permitted to bargain with you, Mr. Marvin, but don't you think twenty-five years might be more reasonable than what you have?"

Marvin sighs. He hesitates. He is playing his role fully. "Well, maybe so, maybe so. Okay, do the computation."

For your education deductions, Harry inspects your checks and canceled bills, asks you a bit about the courses and why they were necessary for your work and that of your wife. You answer only what's asked, sensing that he is fishing for something. He is. He is trying to obtain a clearer focus on just what you both do and how you work. That will make it easier for him to question you in a minute about the much more substantial deductions you have for Travel and Entertainment.

"Were you reimbursed for these courses by your employers?" he asks.

"No, sir," you tell him, much less emphatically than you had told Marvin in your practice session.

"Were you reimbursed for any of these Travel and Entertainment expenses? In fact, doesn't your employer give you an expense account?"

"Give me the diary for the country club and the backup for those other business expenses," Marvin says.

"For my consulting work too?"

"No, just the stuff your company didn't reimburse you for."

You hand him the diary and a small batch of restaurant stubs, credit card slips bound by a rubber band.

Marvin flips through them, passes them across to Harry. "Here is all the documentation for Form 2106," Marvin tells him.

Harry goes through the diary, then starts looking closely at the receipts. He checks to see if the handwriting is all the same on those stubs you have torn off the bottom of restaurant bills. And whether the same pen was used on all of them.

He asks questions along the way. "Who is Curruthers? . . . What's your business connection? . . . What was this trip to Boston for?" All in that unwavering voice, barely glancing up from the papers. He is probing to be sure you are familiar with your own supposed expenses, and, among other things, he is also trying to see if you are doubling them. In other words, did your company actually reimburse you for these expenses, and do you have a second receipt that you are now using for your own deduction? Harry knows very well that you could have attached the Diners Club slip to your company expense account and pocketed the stub from the bottom of the restaurant check for yourself. The very stub he is now holding.

"*Are* you reimbursed by your company for your expenses in connection with business?" Harry asks again.

"Yes," you reply, looking at Marvin.

"These are additional," Marvin says, and picks up the defense.

They might indeed be additional. Here you traveled first class to Dallas because you wanted to have a chance to talk with Curruthers. You ran into him at the airport and he was flying first class. Your company has a firm rule: No one travels first class within the continental United States. You paid the difference.

Here, you have several high restaurant bills because you felt it was good business to take those particular clients to those particular restaurants, even though they are above the unwritten ceiling set by your boss.

Marvin does all the explaining. Harry asks if you have any carbons of your company expense accounts. He wants to compare exact charges, dates, and amounts for a few of these items. You do not have such carbons. Harry is not surprised. He says, "Okay, let's go on," and puts the deductions aside for the moment. You have plenty of documentation and Marvin's arguments have been well taken. Harry is thinking he might allow you the full $1000 you claimed.

Harry looks at his watch. "It's noon," he says. "Why don't we break for lunch. I need my strength before we get into your Schedule C." He practically smiles, Marvin chortles falsely, and you barely nod. He has exactly the sense of humor you expected.

You mutter something about errands you've got to get done, and resist your planned friendliness ploy. You were half-thinking of inviting Harry to lunch, knowing he couldn't accept. But now you do not want to play games with this man. He might say, sorry, he can't accept your invitation, but we can all pay our own way. Then you'd have to actually eat with him. Marvin suggests a small, inexpensive place around the corner with good burgers, where they can go; it's agreed that everyone will meet back in the office at one.

You eat a salad. Something tells you to eat light, and not to have a drink.

After lunch, Harry opens as promised with Schedule C. You

dive into the large envelope jammed full of all your other diaries and notebooks, American Express and Diners Club chits, each pile bound together, and hand the mess to Marvin. He sorts the stuff out, passes it along.

To Harry, this is a three-star dessert. He checks all the receipts for one month, punches them out on his calculator, adds them up, and decides your total at least makes sense. He compares the largest restaurant chits to numbers he has written on his worksheet, numbers taken from those other expenses where your employer supposedly didn't reimburse you. He spends time on one batch, noting dates, amounts, names, then looks up.

"Let's talk about travel," he says. "I see a big T and E here. Explain that, will you?"

Marvin leans forward, locates the documentation for the Vegas trip. "That," he says pointing, "is for the air tickets, hotel bill, related expenses to Las Vegas."

"I can see that," Harry says, "but what did you go to Vegas for?" He asks you, and you must listen carefully to the way Harry frames his questions.

"It was for a convention associated with my consulting work," you tell him.

"How long was the trip?" Harry asks.

"Five days."

"How many days was the convention?" he asks. Notice he has not phrased the question: "Was it all on business?"

Marvin is alert to this kind of trap. "Now, Mr. Harry, really, I think you should know better than that. We've taken five days because it was *all* for business. One day to fly out. Then two days for the official conference meetings. And then the closing lunch on the fourth day. They saw some customers for dinner that night, and stayed the fifth day to meet with some other customers who were still there, and, frankly, to get a little rest. A conference like that is nonstop and he was exhausted."

"That's quite a hotel bill," Harry says. "Want to tell me about it?"

"Las Vegas, Mr. Harry, is not Bangor, Maine," Marvin reminds him, and goes on to inform Harry about the high-living habits of many of your customers, especially when they go to one of these gatherings.

"This wasn't claimed as unreimbursed employee business expense, was it, Mr. Marvin?"

"No, no, no."

Harry nods, starts to make some notes, and without looking up, he says: "I was in Las Vegas once. Lost $100 before I knew it. Barely got through one free drink and it was gone." He chuckles, still writing notes. "You have any luck?"

This time you are up for Harry. Somehow you know that gambling winnings are income, and supposed to be declared. "I'm not much for casinos, for gambling at all. Fun to watch some of the characters in there. And the free shows are terrific. One night after dinner we went and saw Dom DeLuise. Really funny guy."

Harry hears you, quite clearly, looks up from his figuring and says to Marvin: "I'm not going to allow that deduction for the last day's expenses. Unless you have some documentation of real business need, it won't hold. He could have come home and rested."

Marvin shrugs. This is one of the weak points he discussed with you in your strategy session. "What can I say?" he tells Harry. "I think he's entitled to that final day."

"No. Not sufficient justification."

"Okay." This is one Marvin had planned to give up. It will mean a loss of about $125 from your Travel and Entertainment deductions.

"Now, another thing about this Vegas convention," Harry continues. "Apparently, your wife went with you, and she has also deducted the expenses of that trip. Could you explain that one to me?"

Marvin does. The convention was related to her regular business, as well as to your consulting business. You are beginning to advise people in her company, something she helped to arrange for you by getting her boss over for dinner one night.

Harry asks for all of your wife's diaries and receipts related to the convention, and piles through them. He deducts $40 from her last day, the day of rest. He compares some of her receipts with yours. Then, examining her canceled plane ticket, he says: "You people make a side trip? After you got your strength back?"

"We went to Los Angeles," you reply.

"You will find," Marvin tells him, practically singing, "that the only thing deducted were the costs of the flight to Vegas, and the hotel and other expenses at the convention. Not a penny there for Los Angeles."

Harry almost smiles. He checks out Marvin's claim, punching numbers through his pocket calculator and finally nods. "Okay," he says. He barely questions Marvin about your other big convention trip, the one to Hilton Head where you took your wife, but where Marvin had carefully not deducted her expenses, since it really was a pleasure, not a business, trip for her. Though he only nods throughout Marvin's happy exposition of this, you think his nod is just a touch warmer.

There are several other Schedule C items Harry looks at very closely, but his mood really does seem to have mellowed. He allows the office in the home for you. He had questions about Marvin's formula for your wife's car deduction, made certain that she hadn't included any parking tickets in her deduction, which you thought was really picky. But he let it all stand, and seemed satisfied that she had not "run away" from any income this year.

You are starting to get a little punchy by the time Harry turns to "Capital Gains and Losses." Harry expected this and took it into consideration when planning his pre-audit strategy. He'd like you to be a bit weary for this item. He's already gotten you to open up once, with information about your grandmother's death. If you've had a couple of martinis at lunch, you might be even more talkative.

"I'd like to verify these transactions," he says. "Not a fortune involved here, but enough. Let's start with the capital gain."

"Let me have the brokerage slips," Marvin says to you.

You hand him that pile and he sorts it out. "Here," he says, handing a sheet to Harry, "is the purchase confirmation from

the broker on 100 shares of BP Manufacturing at 50. And, here
. . . here . . ." his voice trails off. He looks at you. "I've got only
one slip here. Where's the sales confirmation slip for this?"

"I gave it to you."

"No. You only gave me the purchase slip," he says, a bit
sharply. "Look in your papers there."

You stare at the mounds and start fishing through. Canceled
checks to the phone company. All those receipts from the post
office. Electric bills. Where the hell is that piece of paper?
"Jesus," you say softly, growing cold. "I know the thing is here
somewhere."

Marvin and Harry watch you, silently.

You look into your briefcase. Nothing. You are lightheaded.

Finally Marvin says, "What'd you do, misplace it?"

"I'm afraid so," you reply, not acting. "Marvin, I know I had
the thing. You saw it."

"I did see it, Mr. Harry," Marvin tells him. "Check that stuff
over there," he tells you. "Maybe it's in with those other papers."

You grab at everything. Come up with nothing.

"Mr. Harry, I saw it. Made a note of it here on my work
sheets. Gain of $20 a share, total of $2000."

"It's not the amount," Harry says. "It's the date."

"I know, I know. But he's apparently lost it."

"Taxpayer has to prove his claims."

"And we will," Marvin tells him, firmly and calmly. "We
will. We'll do whatever you want us to do. He's got a legitimate
long-term capital gain here. If you want, we'll get it reproduced
from the broker."

Marvin is playing somewhat on Harry's time pressures, but
in this instance, he is quite prepared to request Harry to keep
the whole audit open until he gets the slip. He does not intend
to let you lose this honest and substantial claim. There's a great,
great difference between long-term and short-term gain.

Indeed there is something in Marvin's manner and voice, and
your genuine panic, that register with Harry. Also, by this time

he has decided that Marvin is a solid, respectable professional, and you are relatively honest.

"All right," Harry says. "I'll take your word for it."

"Thank you," Marvin says. "I assure you, it's the truth."

Harry finally smiles. "You wouldn't try it if it weren't, would you?"

Marvin returns the smile.

You are very wet under the armpits.

Harry has saved his best for last. "About this personal loan," he says, "I'd like to know more, a lot more. First of all, I need proof of the loan."

Through Marvin, you show him the standard loan form you got from your bank, again at Marvin's pleading, which shows that you had indeed loaned your brother-in-law Roger $4500, to be repaid on demand within one year at an interest rate of 8 percent.

"Who is Roger Ash?"

"My hopeless brother-in-law."

Harry nods. "This isn't deductible. This note hasn't been canceled. You haven't proven that it's worthless. You haven't proven the year it became worthless. Nothing."

Now you hold up your hand to silence Marvin. "Just one minute. My brother-in-law came to me, and I had to lend him that money so he could start a new business. He was desperate. He's got a family to support, and I couldn't refuse him."

"Gifts aren't deductible," Harry says calmly.

"Excuse me, please. Excuse me," Marvin says, firmly. "First of all, this is a bona-fide loan. It is not any gift. So don't try to push my client around, Mr. Harry. Furthermore, we have the proof of Roger's bankruptcy. Here's a photostat of his bankruptcy petition."

Harry reads it through. "If this was a business loan, what kind of stock did you get in the company?"

"It was a *personal* loan," Marvin answers. "As you can see from that bankruptcy petition, my client's brother-in-law went into personal bankruptcy. And as you can also see from the date on their letter of agreement and that petition, the whole thing transpired within a year, and the deduction is taken in the correct year."

Harry reads through once again everything related to the loan, then gives all those documents back to Marvin. He looks through his own notes and papers. "Well," he says, "that does it for me. I'm done."

"Mr. Harry," Marvin says, "just before you do your computations, there are a couple of things here that we hadn't claimed, but I'd like you to consider."

You think Marvin has lost his mind. The thing is over, you are still alive, and Harry should not be stirred up in any way. But Marvin persists, pulling out those bills and checks for four parties you wanted to claim as "home entertainment," including the one where your wife's boss came to the house. And that trip to Chicago. You want to strangle him.

Actually, Marvin knows what he is doing. Though Agents have been known to grant overlooked items at these times, Marvin does not expect to get a nickel from any of it. He is really after those few deductions where Harry hasn't yet decided how much to allow you. Marvin is showing him all over again, as a kind of summation before judge and jury, just how conservative and circumspect you and he have been from the beginning.

Harry then busies himself with his notes and numbers and calculator. In rough form, he redoes your taxes. Whatever he decides to disallow is subtracted from your total of deductions. He cannot complete the entire computation while sitting there, but after a while he can and does give you one result.

"I am going to propose a deficiency of a disallowance of $1700 in claimed deductions and $300 in credits," he says, "plus additional income of $60 from that overlooked bank interest."

Marvin starts to calculate what that will mean in your tax bracket.

"I don't have the precise figures," Harry continues, "but I would estimate that that would mean for you a total adjustment of about $615 in back taxes, plus interest of some $75."

"Seems about right to me," Marvin says.

Harry pulls out a form. He fills in the estimates and asks if you agree. If you do, he'll fill out the rest of it and ask you to sign. It says that you accept his estimates and agree to pay. He wants you to sign it, needless to say, so he can have a bill sent to you and close the case.

He extends the paper to you.

He probably won't tell you what your alternatives are. Even though he is supposed to tell you that you do not have to accept his decisions, that you have several ways to appeal, Harry, like so many agents I have known, somehow always forgets that part of the process.

He will also forget to tell you that if you choose, you may pay the assessed tax in installments. However, Marvin is well aware of your appeal rights and the processes, and your option to spread out the payments. He will tell you, if you are faced with a tentative figure from Harry that is either unjustified or extremely high.

But here the amount is within the limits that you and Marvin agreed upon in your strategy session, so you sign. You hurriedly collect your papers, thank Marvin, even thank Harry, and leave.

It is only outside, when you are waiting for the elevator that you feel free to sigh. And then, you suddenly realize that Harry, the dreaded invincible Harry, has overlooked something. He did not ask you about those "business publications and subscriptions."

You glance quickly at the frosted glass door to Marvin's office, half expecting to see Harry burst through, gun drawn. Is that possible, you wonder? Did he really overlook something? Do I really have a whole year of *The New York Times* deductible? My good Lord.

As you fill with a new kind of personal pride and power, you resist the urge to escape by the stairwell. You are fourteen stories up, you remind yourself. You will wait for the elevator, dammit. You know your rights.

12 | How to Find
a Marvin

It continually amazes me that so many people who really do need a Marvin's help don't have it. They don't realize, I suppose, that their own personal financial affairs are like a small company, and, like a small company, require advice and guidance from someone trained to give it.

People always think they'll save hundreds of dollars by doing their own returns. Illusory money. Actually, they cheat themselves. In their ignorance, they can't take advantage of every deduction, credit, aspect of the tax law they are entitled to. Beyond that, there are new rulings issued every week, and continued court decisions that change regulations and the tax law. Any good tax advisor will easily save you what he charges.

In my view, the only people who don't need tax help are those who file short forms, the 1040As, and don't itemize deductions. I'm thinking of people on salary, with gross incomes under $15,000, who rent an apartment and are either single or newly married, with no children. They have no major expenses other than normal living expenses. Their taxes are withheld at the job, and when income tax time comes they can fill in the few lines themselves.

If they don't trust themselves to do even a 1040A, they can

turn to a commercial preparer of the H&R Block variety, and for a few dollars have the thing filled out in twenty minutes.

Indeed, people with financial affairs that simple can probably save themselves the small fee. All over the country, there are a growing number of public-interest law organizations and groups of accounting students at local colleges who will do simple returns for free, or next to nothing.

If you aren't in that category, and don't have help, reconsider your own situation.

If you know that your return this year is considerably more complicated than it was three years ago, you can see very clearly what's happening to your personal company.

Have you sold a house in the last year? Retired? Set up a new tax portfolio, so that now you're trading more, looking for more income from your investments? Or quite simply, forgetting inflation, are you now earning 25 percent more than you were three years ago, with good prospects in the coming years?

All solid reasons to have tax help.

Let's make a distinction in the kind of help you might want or need.

First, there is a tax preparer. Maybe, at this stage of things, all you need is a Marvin whom you visit once a year, lugging along all your real and imagined documentation. You have the one session we observed in Chapter 2; he does your return, and, presumably, if you are audited, Marvin is available to fight the IRS with you.

There is also a tax advisor. He or she could be the same Marvin, but now you are going to be calling this Marvin throughout the year with questions, especially the sort of questions we cover in the next chapter, the sort of things that could put you in an awful lot of tax trouble.

There's a good chance that you will have a second, maybe a third session with Marvin, if he's your advisor as well as your preparer. You might see him in October or November, to review the tax year up to that point, and plan some year-end activity to save you tax dollars. You might also pop in during the summer, a few months after you've done your return with

him, to make sure that your finances are evolving as you and
he expected them to, back in March. How often you see him
obviously will determine what you'll have to pay him.

Let's consider the kinds of help available, and the level you
might need.

Commercial Preparers.   These include H&R Block, Beneficial
Finance, Montgomery Ward, to name a few. I don't think very
highly of them.

Basically, all these services do is fill in the lines, taking the
information you give them and putting it where it belongs.

Such preparers are lightly trained and generally incapable of
giving you substantial advice. They rarely analyze a situation
to figure out how you can take advantage of the tax law, or offer
much tax advice for next year.

Also, they are terribly conservative. Remember, these businesses came into existence partly because the IRS cut back on
their own public counseling. To me, having one of the big
commercial places to do your return is like having the IRS do
it. I mentioned Marvin's worry that an audit can take up more
of his time than he can reasonably charge you. Imagine what
some undertrained commercial preparer in a supermarket operation thinks.

That's why the offer some of them make is so empty. They
promise to go with you, if you are audited. Well, to start with,
they cut the chances of an audit way down by their extreme
conservatism. If there is one, they will go with you, but only to
"explain." They don't fight like Marvin does. All they do is say,
"Here is the canceled check the taxpayer showed me . . . Here
is what I saw for that other item."

To be sure, these services don't charge much. For relatively
uncomplicated returns, they will charge between $40 and $80
to prepare your federal, state, and local returns. "Relatively
uncomplicated" means itemizing deductions plus a few other
forms, such as limited capital gains and losses, and income
averaging.

Independent Preparer. This is a person with a background in taxes who does tax returns, generally as a sideline.

Quality can vary greatly. Remember, there are no laws or IRS requirements to be a tax preparer. Anyone may hang up a shingle.

In smaller cities, the independents tend to be the comptroller of a local business or the officer of a local bank, picking up some extra dollars nights and weekends.

Many former IRS employees become independent preparers, but usually work at it during tax season only. They tend to know what they're doing, but my impression is that they do it as if they were still in the IRS. You get precious few breaks from them.

If you select an independent, try to get one who works in taxes all year round, rather than a "seasonal"—one who works just in the tax season. Because if you need "seasonals" for an audit, they aren't available.

People at this level are preparers, not advisors. In general, I consider them better equipped than most commercial preparers, and they do charge a bit more. For the same "relatively uncomplicated" return, figure anywhere from $75 to $150.

Accountant. At this level, you're beginning to take your money seriously.

There are accountants, and there are Certified Public Accountants. CPA's pass a tough exam that covers a variety of accounting and business subjects, including, of course, taxes. Their grasp of your affairs, therefore, should be better, and they will charge more than a colleague who is an accountant but has not yet passed the test.

However, regular accountants who handle taxes as part of their practices can give you very good value. They still have solid backgrounds in taxes, there are a lot of them to choose from, and they are full-time, year-round professionals.

They charge less than CPAs but more than independents, again depending on how much time you want from them. They are capable of offering real guidance, not merely doing your return.

I'd say they charge around $150 and up for the return. If you want to use them throughout the year, figure between $300 and $400 for basic advice and planning.

CPA, Tax CPA, or Tax Lawyer. These are the specialists. Most likely they will charge by the hour and the fees vary enormously. A fair range is $40 to $100 an hour. But it's not likely you'll need someone in a large firm, although your business might. As an "Individual," unless you're in the very highest of brackets, and regularly moving hundreds of thousands of dollars through your personal fortune, you don't really need the specialist.

Many CPAs and tax lawyers are connected with small offices, often as partners. Perhaps two, three, four in the firm. You can find extremely good advice and service here, for much less than a large firm would cost you. You aren't contributing to the overhead of that big firm. Figure something in the range of $400 to $1000 to have one of these Marvins do your return and consult with you throughout the year.

Enrolled Agent. I've found that most people have never heard of EAs, largely I suppose because they are a fairly new breed, and until recently, have not been able to advertise their services.

Enrolled Agents are people who have passed a special test on tax laws, given by the IRS. It is a truly thorough, difficult exam, and those who pass are not only qualified to prepare returns, they are permitted by the IRS to practice tax law before the IRS, just as a lawyer or a CPA may do.

So they can do your return, fight for you in the audit, and if there is an administrative appeal process on Harry's judgment from the audit, they can handle that as well. An EA is not licensed to represent you in a regular court of law, however.

They tend to deal in complex tax issues, often untried areas of the tax law. But their knowledge and practice keep them continually involved in all aspects of taxes, so they have the breadth to advise you on both business and personal affairs.

In the hierarchy of tax professionals, I would put EAs somewhere between noncertified accountants and the level of CPAs and tax lawyers. Their prices range around $400, for the return and counseling on a regular basis.

There are some 15,000 Enrolled Agents in America, and you can find one by checking your phone directory, or writing to National Association of Enrolled Agents, 16952 Ventura Boulevard, Encino, California 91316.

Once you've considered your own needs, and have some idea of the level of help you require, the best way to find a specific Marvin is to ask your friends. Simple as that. Ask the people you know. They are likely to be people whose income and needs are similar to yours.

If you have a lawyer, or a close relationship with a banker, possibly an insurance agent, check with them, too. They will have a fair idea of your own financial condition, and know several tax professionals from their own work; you will then begin to see what sort of advice and service different tax pros offer, and for how much.

Next, call a few. Interview them, either on the phone or in person. (Be sure they know why you're coming, that you're looking for someone to handle your affairs. This visit, in other words, is not a consultation, for which you expect a bill. Don't expect an appointment or a long phone conversation during tax season, from January to mid-April.)

Ask them these questions:

• How do you normally work with individuals? Once a year, to do the return? Do you recommend more meetings? Why? If I have a question, are you available for phone consultation?

• What do you charge, and for which services? How much for the return alone? How much for the return and a half-dozen phone conversations a year? Or another one or two consulting sessions a year?

• Do you specialize in some aspect of taxes? How much of your work is with individuals like me? How much with businesses? How much of your operation is doing tax returns? (You want someone who does more than just prepare returns.)

• How long have you been in the business? What sort of background do you have? Ex-IRS? Training?

• Do you work alone? Staff? Services available in the office? (You might start out with minimal needs, and soon require more sophisticated help. Is it available in this office, or would you then need to look elsewhere?)

• What's your philosophy, approach to taxes? Would you consider yourself very conservative? Prefer to take risks?

The last questions are quite important and have nothing to do with political science. You might want someone who is very conservative in an effort to cut down your anxiety about being audited. Fine, shop around until you find such a tax advisor.

One of the ways you can measure a tax pro's philosophy is to find out how often his clients get audited. If he tells you "never," he might be exaggerating, but you can reasonably assume you have a Marvin who will win every tug-of-war with you. If you are searching for the safest way, and don't care about paying taxes you really needn't be paying, look no further.

You will get a more reliable reading of Marvin's audit record from his clients. So check your friends on how they've done in the audit session. By the way, you will have to ask each Marvin whether his fee includes the audit. No set rule there.

If I were searching, I'd look for someone who in fact does get audited now and then. Then I'd have a sign that he is willing to take a few chances, which is what I want.

My own philosophy, as I've said, is to take everything you're entitled to and be prepared to defend it. Indeed, I look at the return as merely the first step in a negotiation. In effect, I and my client are saying, "Okay, Harry, here is our first offer. You don't like it, let's sit down and talk things over. You can then tell us what you do like, and we'll agree on a new number that we both can live with."

That doesn't mean I'm cavalier about the numbers I start with on the return. Nor am I playing the game of that traveling salesman I told you about in Chapter 10, who had no documentation and negotiated everything.

It means just what I said: I take everything I believe the law allows, and if the IRS chooses to inform me that I have misunderstood the law, I'm quite willing to argue, discuss, and reason with them.

13 | Preventive Care

It's one thing for Marvin to save your dollars and your mind during the tortuous audit process. But no Marvin, however smart and valiant, can help you if you do certain things with your money and tell him about it later.

I'm not thinking of esoteric, complex deals here, but a number of transactions that are quite central to all our lives. The buying and selling of your home, for example, or divorce, or buying and selling stocks. All of these can profoundly affect your tax situation either well or badly, depending on how you handle them.

You are, after all, a tax amateur. You can't be expected to know what the tax implications are on these and a number of other important matters. Point is, if you act without first consulting Marvin and getting his professional advice, you might move in innocence and commit tax suicide.

As a matter of fact, that's what the IRS expects you to do. They expect to hurt you on these items. So Harry will be quite surprised when he starts probing your year-end stock sales, and finds everything in order. Or when he asks about your deduction for support of an elderly parent, and finds you have a real, legitimate multiple-support agreement with your brother and sister.

So let me sketch thirteen possible developments in your life that can seriously affect your tax picture. Think about these and try to remember them. Whenever any such situation presents itself, an alarm should ring in your head, warning you to call and check with Marvin before you make a move.

1. Buying and/or selling your home.   For most people, a home is the largest financial investment they ever make. Yet few people can think of their homes in cold financial terms. As a result, they hurt themselves in a variety of ways.

• If you buy a home, be sure you set up a simple record system with Marvin to keep track of the increasing value of the place. If you buy for $85,000, and then over the next few years you finish the cellar, add a room, plant trees, shrubbery, and build a patio, you have increased the value of the house by the amount of your costs. Let's say, $35,000. Which means $120,000 of invested value, when you go to sell it. Imagine that you actually get $140,000 for it.

Now, if you've kept records along the way, as Marvin advised you to do, you will have a long-term capital gain of $20,000 on the house, the difference between what you've invested and what you sold it for. However, if you didn't talk to Marvin about all the improvements, and you have no record of them, then you are going to have a capital gain of $55,000, the difference between what you bought the home for originally and what you sold it for. Harry is not going to allow you to add $35,000 to the value of the home, unless you have carefully documented all the costs of improvements over the years.

• Buyers, and sometimes sellers too, often have to pay "points" to obtain the mortgage financing they want. There are different kinds of "points," many of which are deductible. Marvin will tell you those that are and those that are not.

• If you're selling a home, you'll have to watch out for the gains you realize. If you're not replacing your home with a more expensive one, you'll probably have to pay taxes on that profit. It might mean estimated tax payments for you. (If you do replace it with a more expensive home, the tax is deferred.)

• Marvin can also warn you about the eighteen-month rule, a very important IRS rule that most taxpayers have never heard of, and that includes real estate brokers. If you sell your personal residence twice within eighteen months, you must pay taxes on your gain, and it may not be deferred. The IRS grants an exception if you are selling because your employer transferred you. Otherwise, the great tax deferral is lost.

I was consulted about such a case, too late to do anything. Sadly, it meant the innocent couple had to pay taxes on a long-term capital gain of $75,000. As a long-term gain, that meant 40 percent of their profit, or $30,000, was taxable. In their bracket, that amounted to $12,600 in additional income taxes for that year. And the saddest part of it was that if they had waited nine days to settle, they would have satisfied the eighteen-month rule. There hadn't even been any particular reason to rush matters. They simply didn't know, and they hadn't contacted me or anyone who did.

• Installment selling is another area where you should get advice. Full of tax traps. I saved a client from falling into one recently.

He owned a piece of real estate, free and clear, which he had inherited from his father years ago. A buyer approached him, and he agreed to sell for $150,000. The buyer paid him $25,000 in cash, and gave him a series of installment notes for the balance, agreeing to pay $25,000 a year, plus 8.5 percent interest.

It was a good arrangement for both parties. The buyer could pay over several years. And my client, who didn't need all the income at once, could spread it out and ease the tax bite.

After the buyer had paid $75,000 and interest, he said he wanted to sell to another man. And the other man wanted to pay for the land in the same manner, $25,000 a year, plus interest. My client had no objections, especially when the new buyer was willing to pay at a higher interest rate of 11 percent. The cost of money, after all, had gone up.

Fortunately, my client was responsive to all my warnings, and before closing the deal, the bell went off in his head, and he called me.

I killed the deal, and saved him a bundle in taxes. The IRS has another rule, one that makes no sense but is fully enforceable, which says, if you substitute one installment note for another, they must carry the same interest rate. If the second note has a higher interest rate, they will tax you on the whole balance of the money due. In this case, they would have taxed my client on the whole balance of the $75,000 owed him for the land, even though my client still would be receiving the balance in installments.

Homes are not only warm and wonderful shelters surrounded by white picket fences. So far as the IRS is concerned, they are complex tax instruments. Treat them delicately, friends, by checking with Marvin first.

2. Divorce.   A sad, emotionally wrenching affair, so common in America these days. But beyond the tears and pain, there are taxes. Divorce, separation, alimony, child care, custody proceedings all have a large impact on your taxes. You must have a Marvin to explain them to you, and to be sure your affairs are worked out as advantageously as possible. Don't expect your lawyer to know all the tax aspects of your divorce.

Remember, so far as the IRS is concerned, everything must be stated in the divorce decree, decree of separate maintenance, or separation agreement. So be sure you have Marvin involved.

An especially difficult situation can arise if you are contemplating divorce, but you don't yet have a formal agreement of separation. The tax law simply does not take that situation into account, as common as it is.

Sticky, and the IRS hates it. That's when people won't sign joint returns, or they take to forging. "Why the hell should I tell her exactly how much I really earned last year? It's only going to cost me more in alimony," says the outraged t/p, as he slowly scratches his wife's signature.

If you find yourself in that limbo status, you'll have to lean on Marvin. He can call your soon-to-be-ex's lawyer, and work things out, so the return can be filed according to the law, and no one will be cheated if there's a refund check due.

3. Marriage. Your tax picture will change if you go from "single" to "married." Most likely you'll then be filing a joint return, which usually has helpful tax advantages, depending on whether you are both producing income, at the same level, one much higher than the other, or whatever. There are a number of variables, which Marvin will explain to you. Please don't base your decision to marry or not on how it will affect your taxes. I have known people who have. And it is not much of a reason for doing it, or not doing it. But if you decide to marry, call Marvin so he can review with you what the tax change will be. Avoid tax surprises in your life.

Once married, if one of you stops working to have a baby, be sure to let Marvin know. You'll have a completely different tax structure then.

Similarly, when the baby arrives, and the mother returns to work, tell Marvin. Another big change in your joint taxes.

4. Investments. Don't call Marvin and ask him what he thinks of energy stocks these days.

• But do get from him a clear understanding, if you haven't from this book, of long-term capital gains and losses, and short-term capital gains and losses. Also, have him take some time and explain minimum tax to you, and how it could affect any investment you make. With those pieces of information in mind, you can handle your own investments without calling him every time you are thinking about selling some stock, or a piece of land, that will result in a gain or loss of $1000–$2000.

• However, if you are about to take an unusually large profit, tell Marvin. If you sell some gold, which you had bought without any idea of how the gold market works, but still find yourself with a $40,000 profit, let Marvin know. He might advise you, "Now's a good time to take a loss on that dog of a stock you've been carrying, that Alaskan airline with the little planes. Take the loss and get out, and we can apply those losses against the gold profit."

Or he might guide you into another investment instrument in such a way as to save you that heavy tax bite.

He can weave the knowledge of a large gain into your whole tax structure. But only if you tell him in time. Don't do what a client of mine did. She came to see me in March to do her return, and only then told me she had been playing around in option trading. She had lost a bundle, and at that point there wasn't a thing I could do for her. There was no way I could use those losses to offset some gains. No way I could plan her taxes, retroactively.

• If you have an offer for a tax shelter investment with promises of big tax write-offs, be sure and have Marvin look the thing over. He can explain the real benefits and risks to you, and believe him rather than the investment expert who's going to collect a commission if you choose to go in.

• Whenever you're thinking about selling investment property of a substantial amount, talk it over with Marvin. Many such deals involve depreciation and depletion. They are complex, and if you're not careful you could find yourself with unexpected and unwelcome paper gains.

Also, there are lots of expenses connected with buying and selling investment property, many of which are deductible, as Marvin can explain.

5. *Estate planning.*   This involves more than a will, or planning what's left after you die. It is also planning for your own retirement, and broadly considering the financial impact of your death on your spouse, children, elderly parents, everyone who is dependent on you in some way.

To plan an estate well, you need advice from your banker, investment broker, insurance agent, lawyer, and Marvin your tax professional. With all of them advising, you can shape a comprehensive plan. Usually, each of them has a different objective, and usually Marvin is the only one with nothing to sell you. He makes no commission on his advice, which is why I'd listen to him most.

• Estate planning is not only for rich folk. It's for everyone. Suppose you are earning $20,000. Not much, but still, there's the life insurance policy from your company worth $40,000, and another $25,000 policy you are carrying yourself. That's a total of $65,000, and if you get hit by a car and killed, that's double indemnity, or $130,000 going to your young wife. If you haven't taken the basic steps in planning, you've left no will. In that case, she may receive only half the money. She could remarry, and your child could lose everything. That and more because of laws you don't know about, all easily avoided.

• If you are earning, or beginning to earn, substantial amounts, you really are foolish not to do some estate planning. There are enormous and immediate tax advantages waiting for you.

One of the currently popular plans to reduce the amount of your estate, and thus the ultimate taxes on the estate, is to give your money away. The theory is, if you give it away, obviously, your estate will not have to pay taxes on that amount, up to set limits. The law allows you to give away up to $3000 a year to anyone you want without any gift tax consequences. You and your spouse may give away up to $6000 per year to each recipient. No gift taxes. Nothing, unless you happen to die within three years. If this happens, the law presumes that you gave the money away in order to reduce your estate before it was too late, and the IRS adds the amount of the gift back onto the estate.

But you'll want to examine this one very closely with Marvin. Remember, once you give the money away, it is gone. If you and your spouse start putting money into your child's education trust, it is certainly true that you'll be reducing your estate, and providing the kid with a nice cushion for college and for starting out in life. It is also true that in four or five years, when you have the investment opportunity of a lifetime, and you need a quick $25,000 cash, you cannot take the money from the kid's trust. The bank won't give in to you. It is there until that child reaches the age specified in the trust.

• You and Marvin will certainly want to take a look at your will, if it was drawn before the 1976 Tax Reform Act. For the first time in over thirty years, there was a massive overhaul of the federal estate tax laws.

One provision that I have had to explain to several clients is the so-called marital deduction. The law now allows you to leave your surviving spouse half of your estate, or $250,000, whichever is greater. Check your will to see what specific language is in it.

• Also, check with Marvin regarding the Orphans' Exclusion. If you and your spouse die in a common accident, according to the 1976 law, your estate may exclude $5000 per orphan for each year they are under age. If you leave a six-year-old, a two-year-old, and a newborn, that's thousands and thousands of estate tax-exempt money. And all you have to do to qualify is have it written into your will.

6. Family loans.   I touched on this before, but it's worth mentioning again. Anytime you want to help a member of your family, call Marvin so you can do it the right way. Anytime you are asked to help with a nephew's college tuition, or with a down payment on a house, or you're thinking about buying your daughter, who is going off to college, a car, or helping to finance your sister's new business, go over it with Marvin.

There are loan arrangements that work and others that don't satisfy IRS requirements. Marvin should know the ones that are best for you. Perhaps he'll suggest that a loan for that tuition is not the best thing, a straight gift would be wiser. Or to lend it in the form of a demand, noninterest-bearing note. Or to take stock in your sister's firm, but be certain that the stock is small business stock, qualified under Section 1244 of the Tax

Code. Or to buy that car in your own name, and let your daughter use it. All different techniques, all legal, all having different tax consequences.

• If you have your own company, remember that you and your company are tax relatives, so far as the IRS is concerned. You have a number of special opportunities to cut your own tax bill by interdealings with your company, but you'd better have lots of guidance from Marvin, or the IRS will stomp you.

There are right ways and wrong ways to get tax-free money out of your firm. You might be able to sell corporate stock to your son and daughter-in-law's partnership. Or, employ other legal vehicles. If Marvin guides you.

7. Hedge agreements.   These are tricky affairs, completely legal, according to the Tax Court. The IRS hates them, but reluctantly goes along with the Court.

Basically, what they do is protect you and your company, hedge your bets in a way, in case the IRS comes in, audits the company, and says that your salary is excessive.

Do they have that right? Yes, they can say that $45,000 is too high a salary for the work you do, for the amount of time you put into the company, for the size of the operation, compared with other similar companies in the field, etc., etc. Instead, they can say that a $25,000 salary is normal, and that the other $20,000 you have been paid is really a dividend.

That means the firm has a problem, and so do you. A dividend is not deductible by the firm, so it has more corporate tax to pay. And while you have less salary to be taxed, you now have $20,000 dividend income to be taxed. Salary carries a maximum tax of 50 percent, while dividends may be taxed at a rate as high as 70 percent.

However, if you and the firm anticipate such a problem, then you, with Marvin's help, could sign a hedge agreement. It says that in case the IRS does come in and disallows salary, you'll pay the excess back to the company. Thus the company is protected, and while you have less salary, there are other ways the company can make it up to you. And there are tax advantages to you in such a hedge agreement, if Marvin sets it up correctly.

8. Fringe benefits.   Fringes are part of the fabric of employment in America. Health benefits, the company car, business conventions, all-expense-paid travel and entertainment, financial planning, scholarship plans, life insurance, credit unions, prepaid legal plans, and so on.

The things to watch out for in terms of your taxes are the slightly richer benefits, like employee stock options, rights and warrants, and bonus and incentive plans. With those, Marvin should advise what's best for your tax structure: when to shift a bonus from one tax year to another; how to take advantage of your free-lance work, the self-employment fringes from consulting work.

Marvin can also keep you from stepping on an IRS booby trap. They look very closely at fringes, always trying to call some benefits taxable income. We've already seen what they do with the company automobile. Interest-free loans are another.

So if you get the good news that you will now be eligible for some of those special rewards, share it with Marvin.

9. Retirement plans.   Tax-qualified corporate pension plans, profit-sharing plans, nontax-qualified plans, IRAs, Keoghs. Confusing, important matters.

Tell Marvin what you now have from your employer, what you are thinking about in addition, discuss it all with him in relation to planning your estate. And then, as any new possibilities come across your desk, let him consider them with you.

There's a lot of impenetrable legalese in all retirement plans, and there are also a lot of involved tax meanings hidden there. Get Marvin to unravel and interpret.

10. Moving.   Let Marvin know, if you're going to move.

He'll tell you what you need to know about deductions in connection with your move, the receipts you'll require, etc.

If you're moving some distance, he might be able to suggest

a new Marvin in that area. If so, he should have a set of your tax records copied so you can take them with you.

11. Small corporation.   If you're in a position to own your own business, you have a chance to realize a large number of tax benefits. Indeed, if you are thinking about setting up your own company, discuss all the possibilities early with Marvin so he can guide you from the beginning.

Properly handled, you can then provide your own fringe-benefit program, for example, setting up a full health and medical plan with the corporation paying the premium and deducting it as a business expense. If you are not incorporated, merely self-employed, you pay the premiums for your Blue Cross or whatever.

Then it's just a medical expense for you, and even though deductible, you pay for it with after-tax dollars.

If you are in effect your own corporation, you can avail yourself of benefits from retirement plans far superior to anything available to you as a mere "individual."

There are even a certain number of personal expenses that you can convert into legitimate business expenses, if you've got a corporation.

But it all must be done knowingly by Marvin. For example, he will show you how your corporate minute book can be the most valuable book you ever write.

It is in here that all the business agreed upon by the Board of Directors at their meetings is written. Your small corporation might have as its officers and shareholders a few relatives, your lawyer, maybe Marvin. A close group, to be sure, but all perfectly legitimate. And if the corporation takes everyone out to a pleasant lunch every six months for a corporate meeting, it's all perfectly deductible, so long as the business of the company is discussed.

And what is discussed and decided better be written down in your minute book. It could save you thousands of dollars somewhere along the way. For example, assume the company is new, and the officers agree that your salary will be $30,000 a year to start, with increases each year of 10 percent, plus cost-of-living allowances. These days that could easily amount to a total increment of $5000. All those important numbers must be written in the book.

Let's say the company is slow starting, as so many are, and the first year, all it can pay you is $12,000. The next year is even worse: $6000. In the third year, everything fits together, business soars, and the corporation pays you $100,000.

When Harry comes along, he's going to say, "Sorry, that salary is excessive, extremely excessive. Do you realize you're going from $6000 to $100,000 in a year? I mean, I'm sure you did good work during that year, but let's not be ridiculous."

Whereupon, you reach for the corporate minute book, open to the appropriate page, hand it to Marvin.

"It's all right here, Mr. Harry," Marvin says. "Right in the minutes. He's got over $50,000 in back salary coming to him."

12. Major personal and/or business changes.   As a catchall, let me repeat: if there is any major change in your family during the year—a marriage, child, trust, death, divorce, you want to change your will—call Marvin.

Or, if there's a major change in your business life—you get fired, promoted, bring in a major new client to your own business, or to your free-lance consulting work, make up your mind on when you want to retire, increase your pension plan contributions, want to set up a new pension plan, file for bankruptcy, or one of your clients files for bankruptcy—check it out with Marvin in a call or during a short appointment: What does all this mean to me? What will it mean next April 15? What can I do about it?

13. Looking out for Numero Uno.   That's what this whole book is about, taking better care of your financial body and soul.

"What does all this mean to me, Marvin? . . . What will it mean next April 15, Marvin? . . . What can I do about it, Marvin?"

If you call Marvin whenever any of the events or possibilities we've been considering in this chapter presents itself, you'll be doing a lot "about it."

If you also check in with Marvin at least once a year in addition to the March–April wrestling match, you'll be doing a lot more "about it."

Before you know it, you might even hear a different tone in Marvin's voice. Instead of always sounding as if he's speaking to a small, difficult child, he'll actually begin to sound as if he's speaking to an intelligent adult who is paying him money for advice.

If you want to complete the conversion, start to call Marvin when *you* come on a possible tax maneuver that *you* think might just help your own situation. Remember, Marvin has 30–40 clients, and every time he comes upon an interesting item in *The Wall Street Journal* or *Barron's,* don't expect him to drop everything and call you.

But if you assume greater control of your own tax affairs, and without becoming a tax freak like Marvin or me, you begin to read a bit more about the stuff, think and talk a bit more about it, then you're going to find yourself coming up with a number of possible tax breaks. If you call Marvin at that point to check them out, he'll be somewhat amazed at first, but you will succeed doubly: you will get Marvin to think more about your situation; and you will undoubtedly improve it. I've never seen this fail.

And, of course, if you come that far, actively looking out for your own taxes, then you will be truly triumphant. Because then you will never again be terrified of the great, lurking, invisible, unknown monster called the IRS.

Just to review: with any of the following, listen to the alarm in your head, and call Marvin for preventive care:

    1. Buying and/or selling your home.
    2. Divorce.
    3. Marriage.
    4. Investments.

5. Estate planning.
6. Family loans.
7. Hedge agreements.
8. Fringe benefits.
9. Retirement plans.
10. Moving.
11. Small corporation.
12. Major personal and/or business changes.
13. Numero Uno.

About the Authors

PAUL N. STRASSELS was a tax law specialist with the IRS for five years, working in the National Office in Washington, D.C. He left the Service in 1975. He is now a columnist for several national tax and financial newsletters. Along with publishing his own newsletter, *The Washington Money Letter*, he continues to lecture on tax and financial matters. He lives in northern Virginia with his wife, Deborah, and their two children, Jennifer and Peter.

ROBERT WOOL, former political editor of *The New York Times Magazine,* editor-in-chief of *The Washington Post* Sunday magazine, and founding editor-in-chief of *Show* magazine, is the author of two novels and has written for several magazines. He is head of Robert Wool Books, the New York book-packaging company that produced this book. He lives in New York with his wife, Bridget Potter, and their daughter, Vanessa.